DATE DUE

Demco, Inc. 38-293

Baltic Musics/Baltic Musicologies

This volume is the first to bring together music scholars working on Baltic topics from throughout Europe, North America, and the Middle East for the purpose of exploring the impact of Nazi and Soviet occupation (1940-91) and the restoration of republican independence upon the production of musicological knowledge in and about the Baltic States of Lithuania, Latvia, and Estonia. Its collected essays sketch, for the first time, post-Soviet histories of the sociological dimensions of music study in the region, and examine methodological and ethical problems raised by music scholarship. They shed new light on such topics as the advent of Lithuanian musical modernism, the ecumenicity of Christian musics in Estonia, and the effects of Soviet nationalities policy upon the Latvian musicological discourse. Together, they confront those aspects of Baltic music study that still bear the marks of the Nazi and Soviet experience, and they suggest ways in which the turbulent cultural and political histories of the region might be negotiated by scholars presently active in the field.

This book was published as a special issue of the *Journal of Baltic Studies*.

Kevin C. Karnes is Assistant Professor of Music History at Emory University (USA). He is the author of *Music, Criticism, and the Challenge of History* (Oxford University Press, 2008), and co-editor of the revised and expanded edition of *Brahms and His World* (Princeton University Press, 2009).

Joachim Braun is Professor (Emeritus) of Music at Bar-Ilan University (Israel). He is the author of *On Jewish Music* (Peter Lang, 2006), *Music in Ancient Israel/Palestine* (Walter B. Eerdmans, 2002), and *Studies: Music in Latvia* (Musica Baltica, 2002).

Baltic Musics/Baltic Musicologies

The Landscape Since 1991

Edited by Kevin C. Karnes and
Joachim Braun

Routledge
Taylor & Francis Group
LONDON AND NEW YORK

First published 2009 by Routledge
2 Park Square, Milton Park, Abingdon, Oxon, OX14 4RN

Simultaneously published in the USA and Canada
by Routledge
270 Madison Avenue, New York, NY 10016

Routledge is an imprint of the Taylor & Francis Group, an informa business

© 2009 Edited by The Association for the Advancement of Baltic Studies

Typeset in Garamond by Value Chain, India
Printed and bound in Great Britain by MPG Books Ltd, Bodmin, Cornwall

British Library Cataloguing in Publication Data
A catalogue record for this book is available from the British Library

ISBN10: 0-415-47232-6
ISBN13: 978-0-415-47232-6

Contents

Notes on Contributors

Martin Boiko (Latvian spelling: Mārtiņš Boiko) was born in 1960 in Jūrmala, Latvia. He graduated in flute and music theory from the Emīls Dārziņš Music High School in Riga in 1979 and from the Latvian Academy of Music with an honors diploma in 1984 (thesis title: The Concept of Musical Rationality in the Musical Sociology of Max Weber). He received a PhD from the Institute of Musicology, University of Hamburg in 1995 (dissertation title: The Lithuanian sutartinės. A Study of Baltic Folk Music). In 1999 he received a scholarship from the Alexander von Humboldt Foundation that enabled study and research from 1999 to 2002 with Professor Max-Peter Baumann at the University of Bamberg. Since 2004 Boiko has been Professor of Musicology at the Latvian Academy of Music and Head of the Department of Communication at the Riga Stradiņš University.

Joachim Braun is Professor Emeritus of Musicology at Bar-Ilan University, Israel. He is author and editor of eight books, including Die Musikkultur Altisraels/Palästinas (Freiburg Universitätsverlag, 1999; English version: Music in Ancient Israel/Palestine, W. B. Eerdmans, 2002); Music in Latvia: Studies (Musica Baltica, 2002); On Jewish Music (Peter Lang, 2006); Verfemte Musik (Peter Lang, 1995; 2d ed., 1997); and Studies in Socio-Musical Sciences (Bar-Ilan University Press, 1998). He has contributed numerous articles to leading professional encyclopedias and periodicals, including The New Grove Dictionary of Music and Musicians, Die Musik in Geschichte und Gegenwart, and The Oxford Encyclopedia of Archaeology in the Near East. He has also lectured worldwide. At the center of his interests are sociological and semantic aspects of music, organology and the iconography of music, and Jewish/Israeli and Baltic musical cultures. His Music in Ancient Israel/Palestine has been hailed as a work of considerable accomplishment, impressive in its depth, range and detail, and destined to remain the leading study in its field for years to come (A. Davies, *Review of Biblical Literature*, December 2003). In 2003 he was named by the Latvian government to the Three Star Order for his contributions to Latvian musicology.

Gražina Daunoravičienė (Doctor Habil. of Art studies) received her degree from the Lithuanian Academy of Music and Theatre, where she is currently Professor of Music. She has held numerous academic scholarships and grants, including awards from the Ministry of Culture and Education of Saxon Lands and a DAAD grant, which enabled her to conduct research at the Moscow Tchaikovsky conservatoire and the Salzburg Mozarteum. She has also been invited to undertake work at Oxford University. She has edited two monographs on *Lithuanian Music* (2005, 2007), and is a founder and editor of the academic journal Lithuanian Musicology. She is presently editing a five-volume study, *The Language of Music*. She is a member of the Lithuanian Science Council and the Committee of Humanities and Social Sciences.

Jeffers Engelhardt is an Assistant Professor of the Anthropology of Music at Amherst College, USA. His research deals with music and religion (particularly Orthodox Christianity), music, human rights and cultural rights (particularly in East Africa), and the musics of post-socialist Eurasia and the Finno-Ugric world. He received his PhD in 2005 from the University of Chicago and is currently at work on a book-length ethnography of musical practices and religious renewal in the Orthodox Church of Estonia. He has published articles and reviews in *Ethnomusicology, Journal of the Royal Anthropological Institute, Yearbook for Traditional Music,* and a number of edited volumes.

Vita Gruodytė received a doctorate in musicology from the Lithuanian Academy of Music (2000) and since 2002 has been working as a translator and music teacher in France. She is the author of numerous articles concerning diverse musical traditions and contemporary music in particular. She contributes frequently to the Lithuanian journal *Kultūros barai* (*Domains of Culture*) and participates regularly in conferences and seminars in France and abroad. At present, she is preparing a book on Lithuanian music of the twentieth century.

Kevin C. Karnes is Assistant Professor of Music History at Emory University. He is the author of *Music, Criticism, and the Challenge of History: Shaping Modern Musical Thought in Late Nineteenth-Century Vienna* (Oxford and New York, Oxford University Press, 2008) and co-editor, with Walter Frisch, of the revised and expanded edition of *Brahms and His World* (Princeton, Princeton University Press, 2009). He is presently working on studies of the Latvian rock-opera *Lāčplēsis* and aspects of post-Wagnerian Wagnerism.

Urve Lippus (b. 1950) has been Professor and Head of the Department of Musicology at the Estonian Academy of Music and Theatre since 1995. She obtained a PhD from the University of Helsinki and a Candidate of Arts from the Moscow Conservatoire. She graduated from the Tallinn Conservatory (now the Estonian Academy of Music and Theatre) in 1975 and has lectured there since 1976. She was awarded a Mellon Fellowship for research at the University of Pennsylvania in 1992/1993. Her fields of research include Estonian folk music and music history and performance studies based on historical recordings. She is Editor of the series Publications in Estonian Music History.

INTRODUCTION

Twenty-six years ago, the *Journal of Baltic Studies* published a special issue on Baltic musicology – a volume whose editor, Joachim Braun, described as 'an historical event in Western Baltic musical culture, in Western Baltic scholarship, and in post-World-War-II Baltic musicology in general'. Indeed, as Braun correctly observed, that volume constituted 'formal documentation of the birth of Western Baltic musicology' (Braun 1983, p. 3). To be sure, the 1983 special issue was a milestone in all of the ways that Braun enumerated. Yet its editor's careful characterization of its contents was significant, for the volume did not provide a comprehensive snapshot of the state of Baltic music study but a picture of *Western* Baltic musicology. Its participants were drawn from the United States, Israel, and West Germany. The articles it contained made little reference to music scholarship produced in the Baltic republics themselves. And, where such references were made, they tended to disparage the research methods employed by Soviet Baltic scholars. A sign of the birth of Western Baltic musicology as a self-consciously existent field of academic discourse, the volume was also testimony to the divided nature of the musicological community of the Cold War period.

In planning and assembling the present volume, the editors have endeavored to cast a critical look at the state of Baltic music study as it stands two decades after the advent of *glasnost'* and *perestroika*. Today, one may no longer speak of a 'Western Baltic musicology' in the sense that Braun intended a quarter-century ago. Yet, as in many other fields of intellectual inquiry, the dissolution of Soviet authority in 1989–1991 did not lead to the quick and seamless integration of Lithuanian, Latvian, and Estonian musicology with the broader European academic community for which scholars on both sides of the Iron Curtain had hoped. Within the Baltic republics, the collapse of the Soviet academic system and the accompanying reorientation of the scholarly discourse have posed considerable methodological (not to mention financial) problems for musicologists, many of whom have endeavored, as quickly as possible, to appropriate and assimilate Western modes of historical and critical inquiry. In turn, the recent opening of Baltic libraries and archives has provided scholars in the West with unprecedented access to a wealth of materials, but cultural, bibliographical and linguistic differences have often proven difficult to negotiate. Our goal in compiling the present volume has been to bring together musicologists working on Baltic topics from throughout Europe, North America, and the Middle East for the purpose of exploring problems posed to present-day research by the legacies of Soviet and fascist German rule, and by the recent restoration of republican independence. This volume constitutes the first large-scale, collaborative attempt to examine the effects of political and social transition upon the production of musicological knowledge in and about the Baltic states, in ways that, we hope, will prove productive and beneficial for future work undertaken by scholars residing throughout the world.

Each of the seven authors represented in this collection was asked to reflect upon the present state of Baltic musicology, either by considering explicitly a specific historiographical problem or by examining a topic in Baltic music history that raises a particularly challenging set of historiographical questions. The contributions by Martin Boiko, Vita Gruodytė, and Urve Lippus take a direct approach to Baltic music historiography, sketching, for the first time, post-Soviet histories of the sociological dimensions of music study in Latvia, Lithuania and Estonia, respectively. Gražina Daunoravičienė and Jeffers Engelhardt responded to our invitation by exploring the historiographical dimensions of recent scholarship (including some of their own) examining specific musical phenomena or problems: respectively, the challenge of defining Lithuanian musical modernism, and the ecumenicity of Christian musics in Estonia. Finally, Joachim Braun and Kevin Karnes cast a critical glance toward the present-day Latvian and trans-Baltic musicological scenes, isolating threads in the contemporary discourse that still bear the marks of the Soviet experience, and suggesting some ways in which the scars of the past might be negotiated by scholars currently active in the field.

Reference

Braun, J. (1983) 'Special Issue: Baltic Musicology', *Journal of Baltic Studies*, 14, 1, pp. 3–81.

Kevin C. Karnes, *Emory University, USA*
Joachim Braun, *Bar-Ilan University, Israel*

RECONSIDERING MUSICOLOGY IN THE BALTIC STATES OF LITHUANIA, LATVIA, AND ESTONIA: 1990–2007

Joachim Braun

For this brief consideration of the present state of Baltic musicology, I have chosen to focus upon two problems, both of which are equally loaded and, in fact, interrelated. The first: how has Baltic musicology reflected upon the history of the dramatic events of the twentieth century – namely, World War II and the ensuing occupations? And second: has Baltic musicology found ways and means of disclosing the semantics of the music created during the critical periods of region's two great catastrophes, the fascist and communist dictatorships? In other words, how has musicological scholarship examined the responses of music and musicians to the totalitarian systems of the twentieth century?

For this investigation, I determined to begin by looking at the obvious *carte de visite* for Baltic musicology: the relevant entries in our three best and most recent encyclopedias, *Die Musik in Geschichte und Gegenwart* (MGG, Finscher 1994–96); the *Garland Encyclopedia of World Music* (Rice *et al.* 2000); and the second edition of the *New Grove Dictionary of Music and Musicians* (NG, Sadie 2001). All of these encyclopedias were published since the Baltic states regained their independence in 1991. (The relevant articles and their authors are listed in Table 1.)

My first question can be partially answered on the basis of a simple quantitative analysis – by observing the length of the text related to the relevant period of Soviet and fascist occupation in each encyclopedia entry. The result will undoubtedly show the extent of the importance that the editor (or the author) has attached to this subject. The results, shown in Table 2, illustrate the situation quite powerfully.

As we can see, coverage of the period of fascist German occupation is completely absent from four entries out of nine, and it is scarcely mentioned in the remaining five. From the Estonian entry in *MGG*, we learn that 'during World War Two and the German occupation (1941–44) there was a reduction in the number of choirs, though symphony concerts and opera performances continued' (*MGG*, ii, p. 215). Some additional information is provided in *NG* on the Estonian Radio Orchestra, which reportedly achieved 'particularly high standards during World War II under Olav Roots . . .' (*NG*, viii, p. 341). In Latvia, the negative impact of World War II is reduced simply to the 'Zerspaltung der Gesellschaft – Flucht nach Westen, Deportation nach Osten' ('splintering of society-flight to the West, deportation to the East') (*MGG*, viii, p. 1108). As for Lithuania, the only clearly reported result of the German occupation was the closure of the Kaunas Conservatory (*MGG*, v, p. 1379).

Is this really all there is to say about the tragic events of fascist German occupation during the Second World War? The physical and mental suffering of musicians,

TABLE 1 Coverage of the Baltic states in *MGG*, *Garland*, and *NG*: entries and authors

---

Reference literature
Die Musik in Geschichte und Gegenwart (*MGG*), ed. L. Finscher (Kassel, Bärenreiter, 1994–96).
The Garland Encyclopedia of World Music, Vol. 8, *Europe* (*Garland*), ed. T. Rice *et al.* (New York and London, Garland, 2000).
The New Grove Dictionary of Music and Musicians, 2d ed. (*NG*), ed. S. Sadie (London, Macmillan, 2001).

Coverage of Lithuania
MGG: J. Antanavičius, 'Litauen', v, cols 1374–81.
Garland: C. Goertyen, 'Lithuania', pp. 509–15.
NG: J. Antanavičius and J. Čiurlionyte, 'Lithuania', xiv, pp. 887–92.
NG: J. Antanavičius, 'Vilnius', xxvi, pp. 641–2.

Coverage of Latvia
MGG: J. Torgāns and M. Boiko, 'Lettland', v, cols 1101–10.
MGG: J. Torgāns, 'Riga', viii, cols 331–3.
GE: V. Muktupāvels, 'Latvia', pp. 499–508.
NG: J. Braun∗, A. Klotiņš and M. Boiko, 'Latvia', xiv, pp. 358–64.
NG: J. Braun∗ and A. Klotiņš, 'Riga', xxi, pp. 376–7.

Coverage of Estonia
MGG: I. Rüütel, E. Völker and L. Normet, 'Estland', iii, cols 172–83.
MGG: M. Pärtlas and K. Leichter, 'Tallinn', ix, cols 213–17.
Garland: J. Tall, 'Estonia', pp. 491–8.
NG: U. Lippus and I. Rüütel, 'Estonia', viii, pp. 340–7.
NG: U. Lippus, 'Tallinn', xxv, pp. 34–6.

∗My name appeared under the entries 'Latvia' and 'Riga' without my knowledge or consent, apparently because those entries partly reproduce the text originally published in the first (1980) edition of NG, which was authored in part by myself. The fact that an encyclopedia as prestigious as NG reprinted material over 20 years old in this instance – especially pertaining to a geographical region dramatically transformed during those same 20 years – is, to say the least, remarkable. This, however, must remain a topic for future discussion.

deportations to concentration camps, the expropriation of musical instruments and the domiciles of musical institutions – none of it is mentioned. Indeed, entire fields of musical activity were annihilated during the war years; for example, the violin classes created at the Latvian Conservatory by Professor Adolph Metz, a pupil of Auer, who was invited to the Conservatory by Jāzeps Vītols in 1922, were abruptly terminated with the killing of Metz in 1943 (Gaunt *et al.* 2004, pp. 425–6). There was rude and vulgar censorship imposed upon music reviewers; as Vizbulīte Bērziņa reports in her monograph on the ethnomusicologist and composer Jēkabs Graubiņš, music reviewers were 'not even allowed to call this country Latvia; forbidden was any reminder of the independence period' (Bērziņa 2006, p. 185; a study probably on par with the *chef-d'oeuvre* of Reinhard Kaiser 2004). And a great deal of music was banned by authorities; for example, the famous song *Lauztās priedes* by Emīls Dārziņš and many other songs by both Dārziņš and Vītols (Bērziņa 2006, pp. 180–97). But unfortunately, Baltic musicology has, by and large, not found it worthwhile to deal with the musical culture of this tragic period. This lack of attention to musical life during the years of fascist German occupation is, in my opinion, a striking lacuna in Baltic historical musicology of the 1990s and 2000s.

On the first Soviet year (1940–41) there is likewise hardly any information at all, except for an acknowledgement of the bare fact of Soviet occupation and the deportations that followed. Only a few words are dedicated to music *per se*. This was, however, a most tragic year, which rendered Baltic music lifeless for many years to come, and which shocked the local musical community through the sophisticated and brutal involvement of Soviet authorities in all aspects of musical life. The beginnings of inside conflicts between professional musicians (only now being reported in Bērziņa 2006) occurred during this time and ultimately led to the division of the

TABLE 2 Coverage of the Baltic states in *MGG*, *Garland*, and *NG*: amount of text devoted to Soviet and fascist German occupations

| | | | Length of text concerning relevant period (in lines and %) | |
| | | | Fascist German occupation (1941–1944) | Soviet occupation (1940–1941, 1945–1991) |
Entry	Source	Length of entry (in lines)	Lines (%)	Lines (%)
Lithuania	*MGG*	504	1 (0.2)	82 (16.1)
	Garland	486	0 (0.0)	40 (8.2)
	NG	614	1 (0.2)	66 (10.7)
Latvia	*MGG*	630	4 (0.6)	106 (17.8)
	Garland	601	0 (0.0)	28 (4.6)
	NG	810	0 (0.0)	49 (6.0)
Estonia	*MGG*	735	4 (0.5)	108 (14.6)
	Garland	702	0 (0.0)	22 (3.1)
	NG	936	2 (0.2)	27 (2.8)

musical community into groups of active collaborators, inert professionals, and more or less latent oppositionists. This was the beginning of later developments of the type described, for example, by Kevin C. Karnes in his work on Soviet Latvian music historiography (Karnes 2007). Moreover, during the years of Soviet occupation, some musical and musicological activities took place amidst the Baltic musical communities living in exile in the West. There is, however, no mention of this fact in our three encyclopedias.

We may now turn to our second question: namely, how have Baltic musicologists of the post-Soviet period dealt with the interpretation of music created under conditions of totalitarian censorship, and how have they sought to disclose the semantics of this music? Surprisingly enough, in those discussions of the period of Soviet occupation, which lasted nearly half a century, this subject is barely touched upon in our three encyclopedias. Here we would expect to find a relevant critical music historiography and a more or less analytical account of the ways in which intellectuals, in this case musicians and musicologists, responded creatively to the totalitarian ideological pressures and censorship under which they worked. Instead, what we have in our core reference works is an enumeration of composers active and institutions established during this period. This is quite clearly a reflection of the present state of Baltic musicology, where in fact we can hardly find – with only handful of exceptions – examples of the tragic predicament into which musicologists and musicians were placed during the years of Soviet rule. (Three of the rare exceptions are Bērziņa's work on Graubiņš [Bērziņš 2006], Urve's Lippus' splendid essay on Gustav Ernesaks [Lippus 2005], and Rūta Stanevičiūtė-Goštautienė's work on the musicologists V. Landsbergis and J. Ambrazas [Stanevičiūtė-Goštatienė 2007]). This is an extensive field of research, demanding an individual approach in every case, especially considering the various ways in which every musician or scholar was compelled to reckon with his or her conscience.

If some latent or open critical dissent has been noted in the musics of this time, then, in the cases of Latvia and Lithuania, it has been attributed to folk musics only. The Estonian entries in *MGG* and *NG* are the only ones to mention nonconformity in art music, but here too such nonconformity is mentioned only in the most vague and general way. On the whole, this presents, to my mind, a misleading picture of the state of the musical art during this period, and a substantial failure of recent Baltic musicology.

In this respect, considering what *MGG* and *NG* seem to regard as the exclusive domain of 'folk music', I would like to quote from one of my own forthcoming papers on European identity, which I recently delivered at the Malta conference on National Identity (Braun 2006):

> The very concept of dividing 'world music' into vernacular music (recently renamed Traditional Music) and art music (this form of elite audio art, now renamed Western Music), should be abandoned, or at least reconsidered. It is my opinion that European art music has penetrated the European imagination and imbued the people of the Western world to such extent that we have a right

to define European art music as a traditional music of Europeans, as a music of European identity.

I believe it is this division of the field of music into 'Traditional Music' and 'Western Music' that has resulted in the flawed methodology and consequently wrong evaluation of twentieth-century Baltic musical culture that we find so glaringly exhibited in our core encyclopedic reference works. This division ignores the eruption of professional music during the period of Soviet occupation, the latent non-conformism and dissent in that music, and the language of double meaning that, I would venture to say, saturated Baltic art music from the early 1960s onwards, perhaps more than any other European regional music. Marġeris Zariņš and Pauls Dambis, Arvo Pärt and Veljo Tormis, Osvaldas Balakauskas, Bronius Kutavičius, and many others exploited a kind of Aesopian musical language, be it in Baroque or Far Eastern stylizations, by using Latin titles or ancient folklore materials, or by employing modern compositional techniques.

An example of a latent language in Baltic music appeared as early as 1949. It was *Variations on a Theme by Jāzeps Vītols* for organ by Alfrēds Kalniņš (1979–1951), and I would even venture to argue that this was the first post-World War II attempt at a concealed work of art of protest and despair. The piece was first performed in 1951. It is enough to mention that the theme used by Kalniņš was one of the most beautiful and popular chorales written by Vītols; that the performance of a liturgical chorale in itself in the Soviet Union at that time has to be considered an act of non-conformism; that the variations culminate with a funeral march; and that neither local musicologists nor listeners nor the press took note of these facts. All these things allow us to assert that this composition was an artwork of dissent (Braun 1982). A different and more courageous form of latent protest began in the early 1960s with Marġeris Zariņš (1910–1993), who used generally permitted musical Baroque forms mixed with modern jazz (*Suite in the Baroque Style for 16 Instruments and Mezzo Soprano*, 1964), and who went on, in 1979, to explain his intentions overtly (Zariņš 1979). At the same time (the 1960s), other means of expressing nonconformity are employed in Estonia, when Edgar Arro (1911–1978) and Arvo Pärt (b. 1935) began giving their works Latin titles, which were widely considered strange and even dissident in Soviet culture but were nonetheless tolerated. Musical elements from East Asia also provided a vehicle for Baltic composers to express latent dissident sympathies through their works. The setting of Japanese Zen-Buddhist, polysemantic *haiku* became popular in vocal works of the 1960s (among the first were by Zariņš and the Estonian Kuldar Sink, 1942–1995). This influence derived from Daisetz Teitaro Suzuki's notion of 'remaining silent when feelings reach their highest pitch because no words are adequate' (Normet 1979), and reached its musical peak in Pärt's *Tabula Rasa* (1977) for two violins, chamber orchestra, and prepared piano.

The most important and influential style of this period was the 'New Folklore Wave', first discussed in the late 1960s by Michael Tarakanov (1968). Works associated with this 'wave' made extensive use of folkloric elements – a resource use that was officially accepted and even embraced by Communist Party politics and thus immune from official criticism. To be sure, musical works making use of such materials did not necessarily embody a character of resistance. But the most influential and significant works along these lines not only took full advantage of the essential ambiguity of folk texts but also turned to the most ancient layers of national mythology and history for its materials. This not only broadened the ideological meaning of works significantly but also allowed for a much broader use of modern, avant-garde means of musical expression that imitated ancient music. The first example of this movement in the post-war Soviet Union may be Dmitri Shostakovich's vocal cycle *From Jewish Folk Poetry* (1948; see Braun 1985). It was, however the great work by Krzysztof Penderecki (b. 1933) entitled *Threnody of the Victims of Hiroshima* (1960) for 52 string instruments that inspired many other composers living under Soviet occupation to voice their own dissent in their music. Penderecki himself was not clear about his intentions in this composition, which was originally titled *8'37"* and only later dedicated to the victims of Hiroshima. In his later comments on this and other works, the composer asserted (as formulated by Regina Chlopicka) that his music was a 'response of the independent artist towards a totalitarian system that was based on deceit and that questioned the system of religious and humanistic values established in Polish national tradition' (Chlopicka 2004). Penderecki described his own music mostly in somewhat ambiguous terms, claiming that art and music can transform the world. On his compositions of the 1980s such as the *St. Luke Passion*, *Paradise Lost*, *Polish Requiem*, *The Seven Gates of Jerusalem* and *Credo*, he wrote: 'This was not really political music that I was writing, but it was music that was appropriate to the time during which we were living in Poland' (Pendercki 1998, p. 85; cited in Chlopicka 2003, p. 288).

Whatever Penderecki meant with his remarks, it was his music and art that inspired many Baltic composers to aesthetic resistance. The first performance in Riga (1964) of Penderecki's *Threnody of the Victims of Hiroshima*, which clearly caused a sensation, was a starting point for a new approach to composition that combined modern means of musical expression with national, historical, and mythological themes. The first to respond to these ideas were the Latvian Pauls Dambis (b. 1936), with his lyrical and nostalgic *Sea Songs* (1971) on folk texts; Veljo Tormis (b. 1930), with the violent *Incantation of Iron* (1972); and Bronius Kutavičius (b. 1932), with his *Druzkian Variations* (1978). The most significant examples of such music, laden with semantic meaning, was probably Tormis' *Incantation of Iron* for chorus, tenor solo, baritone solo, and shaman drum, setting texts from the Estonian epic *Kalevipoeg* as completed by the contemporary Estonian poets August Annis, Paul-Erik Rummo and Jaan Kaplinski. This composition brought into Soviet concert halls the intemperate, untamed, ecstatic elemental force of pagan folk-rites fused with modern Estonian poetry, which projected the entire work into the reality of the present. The constant drone of the shaman drum and the tenor voice restricted to a third, both symbolizing the ancient national folk-ethos, juxtaposed with the hyper-modern clusters and incessant glissandi in the chorus, made clear the ideological nature of the work.

To be sure, it would be wrong to assert that the younger generation of Baltic composers and musicologists has been completely blind to this rich and meaningful voice of their teachers and mentors. Indeed, this subject has been taken up by some in the recent centennial tribute to the Soviet Latvian composer Jānis Ivanovs (1906–1983), a person of great intellect and philosophical thinking who wrote some ten works with Latin titles. Two leading personalities in Latvia's contemporary musical life, Juris Kalsons and Georgs Pelēcis, both of whom were students of Ivanovs, have recently suggested that Ivanovs' symphonies may be divided into several groups, one of which consists of 'protest' works (Pelēcis, cited in Znotiņš 2006, p. 7). Their teacher is quoted as follows: 'In the world there are great regularities which we can not grasp' (Karlsons, cited in Znotiņš 2006, p. 7).

To disclose the above mentioned methods of composition – to evince or at least to acknowledge the existence of such methods, to reveal the often hidden meanings of Baltic musics with reference to one or two examples – should, I believe, be expected from the defining reference literature of the late twentieth and early twenty-first centuries. A study of this phenomenon would surely help us to draw a new and more accurate picture of Baltic musical life from 1940 through the 1990s. The correction of this situation with respect to an area of such turbulent socio-political events as the Baltic is an urgent task of modern musicology.

References

Bērziņa, V. (2006) *Daudz baltu dieniņu. Jēkaba Graubiņa dzīvesstāsts* (Riga, Atēna).

Braun, J. (1982) 'Zur Hermeneutik der sowjetisch-baltischen Musik: ein Versuch der Deutung von Sinn und Stil', *Zeitschrift für Ostforschung*, 1, pp. 76–93.

Braun, J. (1985) 'On the Double Meaning of Jewish Elements in Dmitri Shostakovich's Music', *Musical Quarterly*, 71, 1, pp. 68–80.

Braun, J. (2006) 'Music as a Factor in the Shaping of European Identity', paper read at the 10th International Conference of the International Society for the Study of European Ideas, Malta.

Chlopicka, R. (2003) *Krzysztof Penderecki: Musica Sacra – Musica Profana* (Warsaw, Adam Mickiewisz Institute).

Chlopicka, R. (2004) 'Links between Penderecki's Music and the Polish National Tradition', in Loos, H. & Keym, N. (eds) (2004).

Finscher, L. (ed.) (1994–96) *Die Musik in Geschichte und Gegenwart* (Kassel, Bärenreiter).

Gaunt, D., Levine, P. A. & Palosuo (eds) (2004) *Collaboration and Resistance During the Holocaust: Belarus, Estonia, Latvia, Lithuania* (Bern, Peter Lang).

Kaiser, R. (2004) *Unerhörte Rettung. Die Such nach Edwin Geist* (Frankfurt am Main, Schöffling).

Karnes, K. C. (2007) 'Soviet Musicology and Contemporary Practice: A Latvian Icon Revisited', paper read at the 39th World Conference of the International Council for Traditional Music, Vienna.

Lippus, U. (2005), 'A Man and His Portraits: The Image of Gustav Ernesaks in (Soviet) Writings on Music', paper read at the conference 'Music's Intellectual History: Founders, Followers and Fads', Graduate Center of the City University of New York.

Loos, H. & Keym, N. (eds) (2004) *Nationale Musik im 20. Jahrhundert. Kompositorische und soziokulturelle Aspecte der Musikgeschichte zwischen Ost- und Westeuropa* (Leipzig, Gudrun Schröder Verlag).

Normet, L. (1979) 'Reflections of Orientalism in Modern Estonian Music', paper read at the Fifth Conference of Baltic Studies in Scandinavia, Stockholm.

Penderecki, K. (1998) *Labyrinth of Time: Five Addresses for the End of the Millennium* (Chapel Hill, Hinshaw).

Rice, T. *et al.* (eds) (2000) *The Garland Encyclopedia of World Music*, Vol. 8, *Europe* (New York and London, Garland).

Sadie, S. (ed.) (2001) *The New Grove Dictionary of Music and Musicians*, 2d ed. (London, Macmillan).

Silabriedis, O. (ed.) (2006) *Jānim Ivanovam – 100* (Riga, Mūzikas Saule).

Stanevičiūtė-Goštautienė, R. (2007) 'Narratives of Lithuanian National Music: Origins and Values', paper read at the 39th World Conference of the International Council for Traditional Music, Vienna.

Stanevičiūtė-Goštautienė, R. & Žiūraitytė, A. (eds) (2004) *Constructing Modernity and Reconstructing Nationality: Lithuanian Music in the 20th Century* (Vilnius, Kultūros barai).

Tarakanov, M. (1968) 'Neue Gestalten und neue Mittel in der Musik', *Beiträge zur Musikwissenschaft*, 1, 2, pp. 42–64.

Zariņš, M. (1979) 'Kurzemes Baroks: Dokumentāla fantāzija', *Māksla*, 4, p. 10.

Znotiņš, A. (2006) 'Nepazītais klasiķis', in Silabriedis, O. (ed.) (2006).

LATE- AND POST-SOVIET MUSIC SCHOLARSHIP AND THE TENACIOUS ECUMENICITY OF CHRISTIAN MUSICS IN ESTONIA

Jeffers Engelhardt

Religion, Music Making, and Music Scholarship in Estonia Since the Late 1980s

Since the late 1980s, religious renewal and revival, conversion, the restoration of religious spaces and institutions, missionary activity, new religious movements, and an influx of ideas, sounds and capital from abroad have profoundly reshaped the Estonian spiritual landscape. It is without paradox that many of these changes disclose broader historical continuities in Estonian religious life and practices. Contrary to many conventional Western narratives, these changes do not signal the 'return' of religion after the godless spiritual vacuum of the Soviet period (cf. Verdery 1999; Lankauskas 2002; Wanner 2003; Luehrmann 2005; Vallikivi 2005). Rather, these changes are the signs of new 'religious mobilizations' (Taylor 2006) that use ideas about the past and beliefs about the future to bring certain sacred, social and moral orders into being.

These religious changes involve music fundamentally and in a number of different ways. Whether it is in the Evangelical Lutheran worship service (*jumalateenistus*), the Orthodox liturgy (*liturgia*), the charismatic Protestant service of praise and testimony (*ülistus*), or the Catholic mass (*missa*), Christian musical practices in Estonia are changing in response to new practical needs, as the expression of new religious ideologies, and in order to renew their efficacy. In my fieldwork, I have witnessed this happening in a number of different ways: through the arrival of a digital synthesizer by way of sister congregations in Finland and Sweden to a small Pentecostal congregation led by a Roma pastor in the southern Estonian town of Võru; through the revision, publication, and imaginative local uses of hymnals and service books;[1] and through the changing sounds of Estonian Orthodox choirs as priests, choir leaders, and singers return from study and pilgrimage in Greece, Finland and the United States.

Change is also audible in the re-establishment and burgeoning of religious song festivals sponsored by the Estonian Evangelical Lutheran Church (EELC), the Orthodox Church of Estonia (OCE), and the Union of Free Evangelical and Baptist Churches of Estonia (UFEBCE), which create new ecumenical and transnational networks and establish a decidedly Christian perspective on the national choral tradition. This kind of public religious singing builds upon Republican-era models and the increasing regularity with which Christian musics such as Lutheran chorales, Urmas Sisask's 'Eesti missa' (1992), and Rudolf Tobias's 'Eks teie tea' (1909) have been performed at the All-Estonia Song Celebrations since the Singing Revolution of 1987–1991. As in the Republican era, churches have become one of the most important venues for concerts of choral music, Estonian traditional music (*pärimusmuusika*), jazz and improvised musics, symphonic and chamber music, and paraliturgical and evangelistic musics.

Religious change is registering in the Estonian music industry as well. One of the most notable developments in the Estonian traditional, jazz and improvised music scenes has been the widespread embrace of folk chorales and church hymnody as a melodic and textual resource in the work of Triskele (2000, 2001, 2002, 2003, 2005); Heinavanker (2007); Johanson and Vennad (1993, 2000); Vara (2003); Sofia Joons, Emma Härdelin, Meelika Hainsoo, Toivo Sõmer and Janne Strömstedt (*Strand . . . Rand* 2002); Helin-Mari Arder, Siim Aimla, Ain Agan and Mihkel Mälgand (*Mu süda, ärka üles* 2005); and Meelika Hainsoo, Mall Ney, Elo Kalda, Maarja Nuut, Olavi Kõrre and Toomas Valk (*Armastuse ja rõõmu laulud* 2007). Ensembles specializing in Christian musics like Vox Clamantis, Linnamuusikud, Orthodox Singers and Püha Miikaeli Poistekoor are mounting successful performing, recording and festival projects. And on a global scale, the renown of the Estonian Philharmonic Chamber Choir has been closely associated with the Christian traditions present in the music of the Estonian composers Arvo Pärt, Toivo Tulev, Galina Grigorjeva, Urmas Sisask and Cyrillus Kreek, especially through the Choir's many releases on ECM Records and Harmonia Mundi.

It comes as no surprise, then, that Estonian music scholarship is also registering these changes, most notably in musicologists' ever-increasing attention to the study of Christian musics. Significant work has been done on folk hymnody (Lippus 1988, 1993a, 1993b, 2003, 2006; Humal 1989; Kõmmus 2001), nineteenth-century Lutheran chorale books (Siitan 1992, 1994, 1995, 1998, 2000, 2001, 2003a, 2003b, 2003c, 2006), Protestant cantors in sixteenth- and seventeenth-century Tallinn (Heinmaa 1999, 2004), musical institutions and ideologies in the Republican-era Lutheran Church (Kõlar 2002, 2003b), Orthodox syncretism in Seto traditional singing (Sarv 2000; Kalkun 2001) and the creation of indigenous Estonian Orthodox hymnody (Sarapuu 2003). In conjunction with religious leaders, scholars of religion, and ecclesial historians, musicologists have also collaborated in reassessing issues of identity and the practical, aesthetic, and theological dimensions of Christian musics in Estonia through a number of conferences and publications (Salumäe *et al.* 2001; Kõlar 2003a). Finally, musicologists and folklorists have devoted more of their energies to the religious materials held in the Estonian Folklore Archives and the Estonian Theater and Music Museum (Kõmmus 2001, p. 75), and to teaching church music at the EELC Theological Institute and the Viljandi Cultural Academy of Tartu University.

This move within the musicological disciplines creates continuity with pre-Soviet Estonian musicology and historiography and is clear evidence of broader changes in the post-Soviet production of humanistic knowledge. At the same time, much of this work constructs Estonian identity as essentially Protestant Lutheran, renders fluid confessional categories as concrete institutional entities, naturalizes the alignment of musical style with particular beliefs, practices, and theologies, and is ambivalent in its secular approach to Christian musics. Here, I suggest that the tenacious ecumenicity of Christian musics in Estonia challenges the disciplinary practices and institutional ideologies that frame recent scholarship. In this context, ecumenicity refers to the interconfessional, catholic, more universally Christian scale of certain musics – thus to the opposite of denominationally exclusive Christian musics. Engaging this ecumenicity means engaging interactions between official theologies and lay practices, performances of ethnolinguistic and religious identities, expressions of sentiment and belief, and ways of contesting distinctions between sacred and secular. For historians and ethnographers, such engagement is vital in understanding the fullest spiritual and social significance of Christian musics in Estonia.

Cyrillus Kreek in Estonian Musical Life and Scholarship

The changes in Estonian musical life and scholarship I am interested in here are rooted in and integral to the spiritual renewal and nationalist elation of the Singing Revolution, the surge in conversions, baptisms, confirmations and church participation that Jaanus Plaat describes as the Estonian 'church boom' (*kirikubuum*) of the 1980s and 1990s (2001, pp. 239–381; 2003a, pp. 221–52), and the discursive and social transformations brought about by *glasnost'*, *perestroika*, and the re-establishment of an Estonian state. Much of this coalesced in events surrounding the 1989 centenary of Cyrillus Kreek (1889–1962), the composer, choral conductor, teacher, arranger and collector of folk hymnody and folk melodies whose biography, work, and reception emblematize the inherent ecumenicity of Christian musics in Estonia. Throughout his life, Kreek made hundreds of arrangements of Estonian and Swedish folk hymns and folk melodies, hundreds of canonic arrangements of Lutheran chorales from the collection of Johann Leberecht Ehregott Punschel (1778–1849), arrangements of Orthodox hymns, and several large-scale religious choral works, including his 'Requiem' (1927) and the seven *Psalms of David* (1914–1944). Kreek taught music theory at the Tallinn State Conservatory in 1940/41 and from 1944 until 1950 when, after being labeled a 'bourgeois nationalist', he was forced to leave his chair (Järg 2003, p. 26; Karjahärm & Luts 2005, p. 118; Karjahärm & Sirk 2007,

p. 715). Returning to his home in the coastal town of Haapsalu in 1950, Kreek worked until the end of his life as a freelance composer, music teacher and choral conductor (Lippus 2001). From the 1940s until the late 1980s, Kreek's religious works were not performed publicly for obvious political and ideological reasons.

In the early 1980s, however, a small number of Lutheran church choirs began singing Kreek's music in services (Kõlar 2003b, p. 54), giving voice to the increasing national-spiritual significance of his work and the decreasing personal and familial risks associated with active institutional religious involvement. Later in the 1980s, Kreek's religious music moved from churches into public spaces as well. In 1987, for instance, the Estonian Philharmonic Chamber Choir performed his 'Sacred Folk Melodies' (1916–1920) in public concerts for the first time since the 1920s, and the collection was published in 1989 (Järg 2003, p. 16). This was part of the thoroughgoing rehabilitation of Kreek that culminated with his centenary in 1989. Today, Kreek's music has pride of place in village and urban churches all over Estonia, at local, regional and national song festivals, and in the repertoire of a vast number of amateur and professional choirs. It has also become a valued resource for Estonian traditional, jazz and improvised musicians.

But Kreek is an ambiguous figure as well, in part because of the intriguing nature of his biography and in part because of the ecumenicity of his music. Cyrillus Kreek was born Karl Ustav Kreek in the western Estonian parish of Ridala in 1889. As is well known, this was a period of intense administrative and cultural Russification in tsarist Estland brought about by the reactionary policies of Alexander III (1845–1994), the desire to counter Baltic German hegemony in the Baltic provinces, the influence of Slavophilism and the Russian Orthodox Holy Synod and the politics of confession and conversion in the region (see Raun 1981, 2001, p. 80). These political, social, and religious dynamics had a decided impact on Kreek's formative years. When his father Gustav Kreek assumed a position as village schoolteacher at the Fällarna Orthodox school on the western Estonian island of Vormsi (Ormsö in Swedish) in 1896, the entire family was required to convert to Orthodoxy and take on Orthodox names in compliance with tsarist policy. A decade earlier, in 1886, 514 Estonian Swedes living on Vormsi had nominally converted to Orthodoxy in response to the official Russification (see Plaat 1999). Thus, Karl Ustav became Kirill (and later Cyrillus) and his father Gustav became Konstantin (his mother Maria remained Maria). Today, such stories are common in the many Estonian families of mixed Protestant and Orthodox background.

Beyond the seeming superficiality and political expediency of these conversions and name changes, however, one finds bases for the ecumenicity of Kreek's music and the meanings Estonians give it today. In addition to Kreek's prolonged later interest in folk hymnody and the musical forms of Western Christianity, his early exposure to the liturgical and musical traditions of Orthodoxy (Kõlar 2003b, p. 54) informed the more marginal aspects of his work drawn from Eastern Christianity – the seventh of his *Pslams of David* (Psalm 137, 1938/1944), which is based on a Russian Orthodox *znamennyi* melody, and his arrangements of translated Russian Orthodox liturgical chants, for example. Today, Orthodox Estonians use this part of Kreek's work to renew their liturgical musical practices and celebrate local Estonian Orthodox traditions. At the Cathedral of St. Simeon and the Prophetess Hanna in Tallinn, for instance, the choir sings Kreek's arrangement of a translated *znamennyi* hymn of praise for the Virgin Mary, the Birth-Giver of God, on the Feast of the Annunciation. They sing directly from photocopies of Kreek's manuscripts held in the Estonian Theater and Music Museum (a recording of this hymn sung by the choir of the Cathedral of St. Simeon and the Prophetess Hanna is available on Engelhardt 2004).

In drawing on Kreek's work in this way, Orthodox Estonians are undertaking a kind of applied musicology oriented towards the renewal of their liturgical musical practices. Furthermore, they are drawing attention to some of the more marginal aspects of Kreek's work, which engage Eastern Christian musical traditions, and also to Kreek's ecumenicity, by claiming his Orthodox music as their own, just as Estonian Protestants have done with his folk hymnody and large-scale concert works. In this way, the ecumenicity of Christian musics in Estonia is deeply connected to the late- and post-Soviet changes in religious, musical, and scholarly life in which Kreek has played a central role.

In addition to being an aspect of these changes, how has Estonian music scholarship responded to these changes? What sorts of disciplinary practices and institutional ideologies are shaping the study of Christian musics in Estonia today? How do religious imaginaries, geopolitical histories, discourses about national identity, and ideas about what can be called sacred and secular figure into current

Meie laulame Sulle,	We sing to You,
Oh, Puhas, Pääingli sõnu:	Oh, Pure One, the words of the Archangel:
Ole rõõmus, kes Sa armu oled saanud,	Be glad, You who have received mercy,
Issand olgu Sinuga!	the Lord be with You!

FIGURE 1 Cyrillus Kreek's arrangement of a translated *znamennyi* hymn of praise for the Virgin Mary, the Birth-Giver of God, on the Feast of the Annunciation. Photocopy from the choir of the Cathedral of St. Simeon and the Prophetess Hanna.

approaches towards Christian musics, and how does ecumenicity complicate the situation? In the discussion that follows, I will provide an overview of the significant body of late- and post-Soviet Estonian music scholarship dealing with Christian musics in order to tease out some answers to these questions.

Christian Musics in Late- and Post-Soviet Estonian Scholarship

The bulk of late- and post-Soviet scholarship on Christian musics deals with the Protestant Lutheran traditions of Estonians and Baltic Germans. That these traditions are often glossed simply as 'church music' (*kirikumuusika*) reflects the fact that the majority of institutionally affiliated Estonian Christians[2] belong to the EELC, the *de facto* national church whose public presence bolsters the mainstream association of Lutheranism and Estonianness.[3] Thus, ecumenicity is not necessarily inherent in the language of Estonian music scholarship; by and large, the study of 'church music' is the study of Protestant Lutheran music.

What is very much front and center in studies of 'church music', however, is sensitivity to and anxiety about the ways in which hymnody and religious concert music are or have become Estonian. Such sensitivities and anxieties are part of more thoroughgoing discourses emerging in the nineteenth century about Estonian national identity, Finno-Ugrianness and Europeanness that articulate a deep ambivalence about Christian, German and Russian influences of all kinds (cf. Karjahärm & Sirk 1997, 2001, 2007; Karjahärm 1998, 2003). Thus, the contributors to a 2002 volume celebrating the tenth anniversary of the new EELC hymnal each address the same provocative question: whose songs do we sing? (*Kelle laule me laulame?*) (Salumäe *et al.* 2001).

In that same volume, Toomas Siitan frames the question in a different way: does one study Estonian 'church song' or 'church song' in Estonia? (*Eesti kirikulaul või kirikulaul Eestis?*) (Siitan 2001) The ideological stakes are high in phrasing the question this way, since the derivative, non-indigenous character of the vast majority of the Lutheran hymnody he is concerned with chafes against the nationalist discourse of some Estonian music scholarship and ecclesial historiography. Siitan concludes his essay by making the necessary move toward a consideration of agency and practice – what he has elsewhere refered to as 'ethnohymnology' (2003b, p. 97) – as a way of overcoming the pitfalls of stylistic or provenance analyses and their attendant claims about authenticity: '[L]et us sing our own songs, which means the songs that have been given to us, regardless of whose they are or from where they come' ('*laulugem omi laule, see tähendab laule, mis on meile antud, küsimata kelle nad on või kust nad tulevad*') (2001, p. 44). Siitan lays the groundwork for this in his many studies of nineteenth-century Lutheran hymnody in Estonia, which expand upon the earlier work of Elmar Arro (1931, 1981, 2003). Siitan's work focuses on such important figures as Punschel and Johann August Hagen (1786–1877), the impact of the pietistic revival of the Moravian Brethren,[4] and the aesthetic, social, political, and religious bases of musical reform in the Lutheran churches of tsarist Estland and Livland (see Siitan 1994, 1995, 1998, 2000, 2003a, 2003b, 2003c, 2006).

Another scholar concerned with the aesthetic, religious, and ideological bases of renewal and reform is Anu Kõlar. Kõlar's work is notable for the ways in which it addresses questions about the ontology of 'church music' by examining musical style, social and political change, Estonian nationalism, confessional and doctrinal differences and worship practices (2004). The main body of her work is devoted to the institutions, ideological outlook, and repertoire of the Republican-era EELC in the 1930s. Kõlar shows how musical leaders and EELC elites transformed Estonian Lutheran 'church music' by taking it in a 'Christian-nationalist direction' ('*kristlik-rahvuslikus suunas*') (2002, p. 180). In keeping with the nationalist ideologies of the interwar Estonian state, the EELC sought to establish itself as an autonomous national church and divorce itself from the feudal associations of the Baltic German-dominated Lutheran Church (Kõlar 2003b, p. 59). Kõlar explores the musical, religious and social dynamics of these processes by looking at how the EELC and its Church Music Secretariat concentrated on organizing religious song festivals, revising hymnals, fostering pedagogy and raising the level of choirs, congregational singing and organ playing (2002). What emerged was a passionate discourse about indigeneity and foreignness (read: Germanness) in 'church music'. Leaders in the EELC Church Music Secretariat, like Johannes Hiob (1907–1942), for instance, pushed for the creation of identifiably Estonian 'church music' and hymnody that would echo the vernacular national romanticism of concert and secular choral music without resorting to the 'sentimentality' of Baptist and other non-Lutheran Protestant musics (Kõlar 2002, pp. 219–21). In these exhaustive studies, Kõlar elaborates the ways in which Estonian 'church music' has been and continues to be a locus of national sacrality, nativist ideology and naturalized or politicized connections between musical styles, religious institutions and confessional identities.

Another field of Christian practice that has drawn the attention of numerous music scholars is the tradition of Estonian folk hymnody. These popular variations and elaborations on Lutheran chorales are valued for their apparent indigeneity, their Scandinavianness, their vitality as the traces of a predominantly oral religious culture, their compatibility with the methodologies of Estonian folkloristics and ethnomusicology and for the different possibilities they offer to contemporary performers of traditional, jazz and improvised musics when compared to other traditional Estonian song genres like *regilaul* (cf. Bak & Nielsen 2006).[5] The ways in which folk hymnody circulates reflects these values and reveals the extent to which Christian musics have become commonplace in Estonian musical life and scholarship.

As transcribed and recorded by figures like Cyrillus Kreek in the early twentieth century, Estonian folk hymns emerged in the 1980s from the archives where, in the recent past, they were deemed inappropriate for Soviet ideological reasons and effectively silenced or, in the Republican period, obscured by the nationalist emphasis on folk materials that were considered more authentically Estonian. In addition to the scores of choirs now singing Kreek's arrangements, many active in the Estonian traditional music scene – like the ensemble Triskele or Sofia Joons, Emma Härdelin and Meelika Hainsoo – draw extensively on folk hymnody. Since the late 1980s, scholars like Mart Humal and Urve Lippus have looked to folk hymnody and Kreek's arrangements for fresh analytical opportunities (Humal 1989; Lippus 1993b), and for insight into the musical consciousness, melodic spontaneity and spiritual landscapes of Estonians and Estonian Swedes at the turn of the twentieth century (Lippus 1988, 1993a, 2003, 2006). Both Lippus and Helen Kõmmus are also interested in the social significance with which scholars invest folk hymnody. Because of its thematic content, poetic structure, strophic form, melodic ambitus and specific tonality, folk hymnody is commonly understood to represent a distinct and more recent layer of Estonian traditional music, which emerged in the eighteenth and nineteenth centuries through the influence of German-speaking and Swedish Protestantism. In questioning whether folk hymnody is a 'religious' or a 'secular' phenomenon, then, Lippus (2003, p. 20) and Kõmmus (2001, p. 77) critically reframe broader scholarly debates about Estonian identity, archaic musical and cultural forms like *regilaul*, and Protestant-inflected practices assimilated from Scandinavia and German-speaking Europe. If folk hymnody is 'religious' and genres like *regilaul* are 'secular', then the distinction between what is often championed as an authentic, pre-Christian Estonian heritage and what are viewed as derivative, imposed, or less authentic Christian traditions is maintained. However, if folk hymnody can be considered 'secular', then the situation becomes ideologically more complicated (not to mention the possibility of folk hymnody being some third thing that reflects the interdependence of the religious and secular).

Since the late 1980s, Estonian music scholars have done less work outside the Protestant Lutheran mainstream and associated vernacular practices of the nineteenth and twentieth centuries, with the exception of Heidi Heinmaa's research on Protestant cantors in sixteenth- and seventeenth-century Tallinn (1999, 2004). This is in large part due to scholars' personal involvement with the religious musics and histories they study; naturally, scholars can speak as authoritative insiders about the musics with which they worship and the religious communities in which they participate. There are social and disciplinary reasons for these currents as well. For instance, very few Estonian music scholars are Orthodox Christians, which is to be expected given the small number of Orthodox Estonians in general. Thus, with the exception of Jelena Gandšu (2002) and Kristi Sarapuu (2003), there is very little Estonian scholarly discourse about Orthodox musics. Furthermore, stereotypes about Orthodox Christianity (it is commonly glossed as 'Russian faith' or *vene usk* in everyday Estonian speech) and the absence of more Russian-speaking scholars who might bring an Orthodox perspective to Estonian scholarly discourses are other aspects of social dynamics that shape disciplinary practices.

There are also methodological challenges in working outside of the Protestant Lutheran mainstream. The rigor and comprehensiveness of Estonian music scholars' recent text-centered, structural-historical approaches (see Lippus 2004 for an overview) is difficult to translate when archival sources are few, practices are emerging, institutional affiliations are global and fluid, religious ideologies are difficult to understand or accept, or when particular religious communities are inaudible and invisible in public spaces. Therefore, scholarly engagement with the musics of Estonian evangelicals and Baptists (Paldre 2003) or with the changing liturgical musics of Estonian Catholics, Methodists, Baptists, Pentecostals and Lutherans (Jõks 2003) is noteworthy for its methodological emphasis on practice and the socio-religious dynamics of musical change. What is still much anticipated, however, is a more complete, more ecumenical consideration of Christian musics in Estonia, including the musics of Lutherans, Baptists, Methodists, and Pentecostals, Roman Catholics,

Estonian and Russian Orthodox Christians, Russian Old Believers, Ukrainian Greek Catholics and Armenian Apostolic Christians, all of whom are active in Estonia. Work with this scope would bring even greater nuance and a richer texture to late- and post-Soviet scholarship on Christian musics and the Christians for whom they are efficacious.

All of this raises the question of ecumenicity, and ecumenicity raises questions of religious ideology and the relationship of musical style, belief, theology, and sentiment. In the section that follows, I will discuss a specific congregational song whose genealogy and current relevance for Lutherans, Orthodox Estonians, evangelicals, Baptists, and Methodists illustrates the efficacy of ecumenicity and the fluidity and ambivalence of confessional categories. I do this in order to suggest some ways in which the tenacious ecumenicity of Christian musics in Estonia provides evidence of deep continuities in pre-Soviet, Soviet, and post-Soviet religious practices, and also to model a critical approach to understanding the fullest spiritual and social significance of Christian musics in Estonia.

The Genealogies and Efficacy of Ecumenicity

Around 1822, Dmitri Bortnyansky (1751–1825), the director of the Court Cappella in St. Petersburg who exercised virtually absolute control over the musical practices of the imperial Russian Orthodox Church, created the patriotic hymn 'Kol' slaven nash gospod' vo Sione' ('How Glorious Is Our Lord in Zion').

At the centers of empire, 'Kol' slaven nash gospod' vo Sione' quickly came to symbolize the sanctity of tsarist order and the military power that perpetuated empire. The elite Preobrazhensky Life Guard, buoyed by the defeat of Napoleon in 1812, adopted 'Kol' slaven nash gospod' vo Sione' as its regimental anthem, for instance. Bortnyansky's melody was chimed daily from clock towers in Moscow's Kremlin and the Peter and Paul Fortress in St. Petersburg. It served as the hymn of the imperial family and was used to accompany a host of religious and military ceremonies while having a place in everyday Russian Orthodox musical life as well.

Rumor has it that in 1813 Friedrich Wilhelm III (1770–1840) of Prussia heard Russian soldiers singing 'Kol' slaven nash gospod' vo Sione' in their camp. Impressed by the soldiers' religious and patriotic fervor, he ordered that Bortnyansky's melody be set to 'Ich bete an die Macht der Liebe' ('I Worship the Power of Love'), a text by the eighteenth-century German mystic Gerhard Tersteegen (1697–1769), and incorporated into the German military ceremony known as the *Grosse Zapfenstreich*. Following this, the story goes, 'Ich bete an die Macht der Liebe' entered into the Lutheran hymnody of the German-speaking world and took on a religious and martial significance similar to that of 'Kol' slaven nash gospod' vo Sione' (see Wittenberg 1982). While this apocryphal tale is a myth and, as Andreas Wittenberg has shown, chronologically impossible, 'Ich bete an die Macht der Liebe' had in fact appeared by 1822 in a chorale book published in Karlsruhe by Joseph Gersbach (1787–1830) (Wittenberg 1982, p. 169).

By 1844, Bortnyansky's hymn had appeared in Protestant Estland and Livland as 'Ma kummardan Sind, Armuvägi' ('I Worship You, Power of Love') in Hagen's first collection of Lutheran chorales (1844), and by 1862 in Wilhelm Bergner's later publications of Punschel's (1862) seminal chorale book.[6] In its Lutheran incarnation, the hymn made its way from the collections of Hagen and Punschel into the official 1899 hymnal of the Lutheran synods of Estland and Livland (*Uus Lauluraamat* 1900). It was also included in subsequent Republican-era and early Soviet editions of the EELC hymnal (1926, 1938, 1948, 1957). It comes as no surprise, then, that 'Ma kummardan Sind, Armuvägi' is present in the landmark 1991 edition of the EELC hymnal as well.

It is highly likely that Bortnyansky's 'Kol' slaven nash gospod' vo Sione' was also part of Russian Orthodox culture in nineteenth-century Estland and Livland, and it is at least plausible that the tune, perhaps paired with an Estonian text, was known to Estonian Orthodox converts from the 1840s onward.[7] Whatever the case, 'Kol' slaven nash gospod' vo Sione' had entered definitively into Estonian Orthodoxy by 1896, when the priest-musician Andrei Ramul (1842–1926) included it in a collection of liturgical and paraliturgical congregational songs, a page of which is shown in Figure 2 above. By 1915, 'Kol' slaven nash gospod' vo Sione' was Estonianized as 'Kui suur on Siionis me' Jumal' ('How Great Is Our God in Zion') (*Waimulikud laulud õigeusulisele Eesti rahwale* 1915) and had become one of the most popular strophic, rhymed congregational songs (*riimilaulud*) among Orthodox Estonians by the time it was published in official OCE service books during the Republican period (*Eesti Apostliku õigeusu kiriku Wiiside raamat I* 1925). It seems natural, then, that 'Kui suur on Siionis' has been included among the extensive republications and retranslations of service books that the OCE has issued since the early 2000s.

Among Estonian Baptists, Methodists, Seventh-Day Adventists, evangelicals and other Protestant groups (*usulahud*), Bortnyansky's tune, usually paired with Tersteegen's text, has circulated widely from the late tsarist period onwards, revealing the considerable extent to which 'free churches' (*vabakirikud*) and 'free congregations' (*vabakogudused*) have worked ecumenically and supported one another musically, spiritually and in other practical matters (see Paldre 2003). For instance, 'Ma kummardan Sind, Armuvägi' appeared in the International Tract Society's 1913 Estonian-language 'Songs of Zion' (*Sioni Laulud* 1913), in the Methodist Episcopal Church in Estonia's 1926 *Hymnal for the Methodist Episcopal Church in Estonia* (*Lauluraamat Piiskoplikule Metodistikirikule Eestis* 1926), and in the Estonian Union of Seventh-Day Adventists' 1928 'Songs of Zion' (*Siioni laulud* 1928). In the latter publication, there are multiple new variant texts provided for Bortnyansky's tune as well.

'Ma kummardan Sind, Armuvägi' continued to appear in Protestant publications both during and after the Second World War. In 1943, it was included in a youth hymnal that brought together the musics of Estonian and Swedish Baptists, Lutherans, Seventh-Day Adventists, Pentecostals and evangelicals (*Noortelaulik* 1943), and it also appeared in official Soviet-era hymnals for Baptists and evangelicals (*Evangeelsed laulud 1975a*, republished in 1991) and Methodists (*Evangeelsed laulud* 1975b).

In 1992, the UFEBCE, together with Estonian Methodists and Pentecostals, began work on a new hymnal whose content would better meet the Union's worship needs and reflect its members' beliefs about the propriety and efficacy of congregational singing. Given its prominent place in so many earlier Baptist, evangelical, Methodist and Pentecostal publications, it is no surprise that 'Ma kummardan Sind, Armuvägi'

FIGURE 2 'Kol' slaven nash gospod' vo Sione' (Andrei Ramul, *Waimulikud laulud, psalmid ehk waimulikud kantad, wiisidega* [Tallinn, Lindfors, 1896], p. 63).

found its way into *Sacred Songs* (*Vaimulikud laulud* 1997), the hymnal used in 92% of UFEBCE congregations as of 2002 (Paldre 2003, p. 71).

Bortnyansky's tune also circulates more generally within Eastern and Western Christianities. In the Anglophone hymnody of any number of Protestant denominations, for instance, the tune has come to be known most commonly as 'St. Petersburg' and is present in numerous hymnals. Orthodox Finns have also adopted Bortnyansky's tune for use in their paraliturgical and devotional singing (see Piiroinen 1951, p. 5), and it is popular in Serbia as well. In 2003, the Estonian Orthodox version of Bortnyansky's hymn ('Kui suur on Siionis') was included as one of the OCE's contributions to an ecumenical youth hymnal published by the Estonian Council of Churches (M.-L. Mäeväli 2003). Surrounded by representative musics of Lutheran, evangelical, Baptist, Methodist, Roman Catholic, Pentecostal, Seventh-Day Adventist, Armenian Apostolic and Russian Orthodox traditions, its appearance in this volume recognizes the ecumenical significance of Bortyansky's hymn for Christians in Estonia.

These transformations of Bortnyansky's 'Kol' slaven nash gospod' vo Sione' give just a taste of the ways in which this tune has been efficacious for Estonian Christians since the mid-nineteenth century. There are other ways as well. In the first half of the twentieth century, for instance, Orthodox Estonians frequently used the tune of 'Kui suur on Siionis' to set new texts written specifically for Orthodox feasts, burial services, or local anniversaries, which circulated on commemorative song sheets (*laululehed*). That there is no musical notation on these song sheets reveals the degree to which Bortnyansky's tune was vital to popular Estonian Orthodox oral practices at the time (in addition to the practical financial reasons for not printing notated music). In my fieldwork, I have also attended ecumenical religious song festivals where participants jointly sang both the Orthodox and Lutheran versions of this hymn.

So how might one deal with the tenacious ecumenicity of Estonian Christian music like this? How should scholars make sense of complicated musical and religious genealogies such as these? What are the ways in which music like this confounds or denaturalizes the alignment of musical styles and confessional categories? What calculus of aesthetic and theological values can explain this ecumenicity? Finally, what challenges emerge as music scholars attempt to negotiate the limits of secular methodologies?

To begin with, I would suggest that the ecumenicity of songs like 'Kol' slaven nash gospod' vo Sione' or 'Ma kummardan Sind, Armuvägi' or 'Kui suur on Siionis' and the practices they engender echo ongoing and more extensive ecumenical histories involving the interaction of different religious ideologies and confessional groups in Estonia, beliefs about the Estonian nation, and the geopolitical, imaginative, and spiritual dimensions of Eastern, Western, and charismatic Christianities. In other words, the ecumenicity of Christian musics in Estonia is a key to understanding their fullest spiritual and social significance. Ecumenicity reveals shared beliefs about the propriety and efficacy of sounds that make those sounds both Estonian and Christian.

There are any number of possible explanations for the ecumenical appeal of Bortnyansky's tune as a vessel for different religious texts—its melodic attractiveness and memorability, its impelling rhythmic character, its uncomplicated harmonic orientation around tonic–subdominant–dominant poles, its formal accommodation of textual parallelism (the *Stollen* phrases) and contrast (the *Abgesang* phrase), and its affective, august lyricism. Indeed, the ecumenicity (or ambivalence) of Bortnyansky's style, closely related as it is to secular and Western Christian vernaculars in eighteenth- and nineteenth-century Europe yet able to serve Orthodox functions, lends itself especially well to all kinds of Christians in Estonia.[8] Given its ubiquity among Estonian Christians, then, the sentiments inspired by singing Bortnyansky's hymn can be both religious and social; singing can be efficacious within the context of denominationally specific Christian worship and, at the same time, mediate experiences of national intimacy. This has considerable bearing on the ways in which the ethnolinguistic and geopolitical dimensions of the Estonian nation are often described in quasi-religious language and invested with sacred meanings, no less so today as part of the European Union and in a time of demographic change and geopolitical struggle than during the interwar Republic or the nineteenth-century 'national awakening' (ärkamise aeg).

This ecumenicity also has considerable bearing on the secular methodologies of music scholars. Text-based historical and analytical approaches may not fully reveal the ways in which music like Bortnyansky's is efficacious – not in spite of but *because* of its complicated religious and musical genealogies, its ecumenicity, and how it obscures ideological distinctions between Christian confessions and the sacred and secular. But the more profound challenge for music scholars is to deal with the sacrality of this music and the religious sentiments it engenders, both of which exceed conventional confessional and social categories. The most meaningful aspect of ecumenicity for Estonian believers may be the spiritual power it mediates and the shared, more universally Estonian practices it enables. Because of its power to forge connections across denominations and doctrines, ecumenicity may enhance the truthfulness of revealed sounds and words, and may be understood as the fuller presence of divinity, as something transhistorical, non-parochial, and cosmopolitan, or as the embodiment of values that transcend confessional categories, thereby giving voice to and making sense of other religious and social formations. For these reasons, it is incumbent on music scholars to verge on matters of belief, faith, and efficacy by analyzing the practices and discourses inspired by ecumenical musics like Bortnyansky's.

The ecumenicity of 'Kol' slaven nash gospod' vo Sione' or 'Ma kummardan Sind, Armuvägi' or 'Kui suur on Siionis' does not mean that Lutheran, Orthodox, Baptist, Methodist and evangelical Estonians have not adopted texts and transformed Bortnyansky's tune to reflect their own beliefs about the propriety and efficacy of Christian sounds. Quite the opposite, in fact. The differences between Protestant (Figures 3 and 5) and Orthodox (Figures 4 and 6) texts, for example, are fundamental. While the Protestant variants convey Tersteegen's mysticism in an insistently first-person, singular devotional voice, the Orthodox variants, though noncanonical texts, are written in a conciliar first-person plural, inflected with touches of apophatic theology, and imbued with royal imagery familiar to Orthodox Christians.

Musically, there is much that distinguishes these variants as well. The Lutheran 'Ma kummardan Sind, Armuvägi' (Figure 3) is clearly geared toward the essential, theologically symbolic liturgical practice of singing in unison to organ accompaniment. Given the proscription of musical instruments in Orthodox Christianity, however, 'Kui suur on Siionis' (Figures 4 and 6) becomes an accessible kind of Christian sound meant to foster congregational participation in a musically specialized and, at times, esoteric liturgy. Finally, the Baptist, evangelical, and Methodist version of

Jumala arm Kristuses

264   MA KUMMARDAN SIND, ARMUVÄGI

Omal viisil

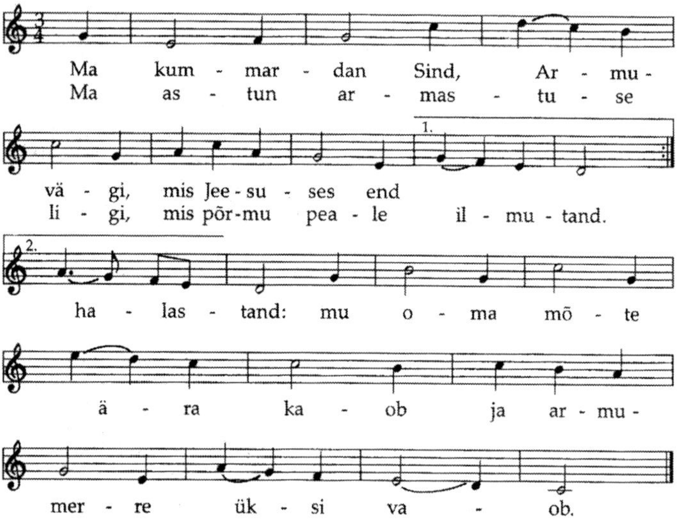

Ma kum - mar - dan   Sind,   Ar - mu -
Ma as - tun   ar - mas - tu - se

vä - gi,   mis Jee - su - ses   end
li - gi,   mis põr - mu   pea - le   il - mu - tand.

ha - las - tand: mu   o - ma   mõ - te

ä - ra   ka - ob   ja   ar - mu -

mer - re   ük - si   va - ob.

2. Kui väga Sa mind armastanud
   ja kuis Su süda nõuab mind!
   See imearm mind äratanud,
   et minu hing ka ihkab Sind.
   Mu sees Sa asu, armu võimus,
   et võrsuksin ka Sinu vaimus.

3. Su oma, Issand, on mu süda,
   Sa minu vara ja mu võit;
   mu eest Sa kandsid surmahäda,
   et mulle tõuseks elu koit.
   Sa maksid minu võla ära,
   mu hinge õnn ja kallim sära!

4. Oh Jeesus, oma püha nime
   mu südamesse kirjuta,
   et Sinu suure armu ime
   võiks hinge sisse vajuda,
   et sõna, töö ja terve elu
   siis kuulutaks Su nime ilu!

Viis: „Ich bete an dich, Macht der Liebe"
Dimitri Bortnjansky, 1751–1825.

Sõnad: Gerhard Tersteegen, 1697–1769.
Tõlge: Martin Lipp, 1854–1923.

1. Ma kummardan Sind, Armuvägi,

mis Jeesuses end ilmutand.

Ma astun armastuse ligi,

mis põrmu peale halastand:

mu oma mõte ära kaob

ja armumerre üksi vaob.

1. I worship You, Loving Power,

which was revealed in Jesus himself.

I draw near to the love,

which was spared corruption:

thought of myself vanishes

and is wholly engulfed in a sea of love.

FIGURE 3 'Ma kummardan Sind, Armuvägi' (*Kiriku laulu- ja palveraamat* [Tallinn, Eesti Evangeeliumi Luteri Usu Kiriku Konsistooriumi, 1992], p. 348).

Kiriku- ja palvelaule _____ 247

Kui suur on Siionis

V. Raska

D. Bortnjanski

1. Kui suur on Sii - o - nis me Ju - mal,
2. Oh I - sa, mõis - tust mei - le an - na
3. Sa päik - se - val - gust su - re - lis - tel
4. Oh Ju - mal, Si - nu troo - ni et - te

ei keel või ü - les rää - ki - da; ta suu - rus
Sind kii - ta, Ju - mal! Pü - ha Tall, Sa mei - e
nüüd an - nad ar - must kõi - gi - le, ja Sii - o -
nüüd tõus - ku mei - e pal - ve - hääl, ja ol - gu

pais - tab koi - du ku - mal ja mul - la - põr - must
kii - tust tae - va kan - na kui ma - gust suit - su
nis Sa o - ma las - tel teed e - lu - a - set
pan - diks Si - nu kät - te meil tä - nu - pi - sar

pais - tab ka. Ta hiil - gab kus - tu - ma - ta
Ju - ma - lal'. Nüüd võ - ta, I - sa, mei - e
hel - des - ti. Ka pa - tu - seid, Sa Ju - mal,
pal - ge peal. Mu sü - da al - ta - riks Sull'

pal - gel öö - a - jal, nii ka päe - va - val - gel.
tä - nu ja kus - tu - ta me hin - ge ja - nu.
hoi - ad ja o - ma ar - mu - lau - al toi - dad.
saa - gu, mu keel Sind kii - tes ü - len - da - gu.

1. Kui suur on Siionis me Jumal,	1. How great in Zion is our God,
ei keel või üles rääkida;	words cannot describe;
ta suurus paistab koidu kumal	God's grandeur appears in dawn's gleam
ja mullapõrmust paistab ka.	and also from the dust of the earth;
Ta hiilgab kustumata palgel	God's inextinguishable countenance
ööajal, nii ka päevavalgel.	shines
	at night, as in the light of day.

FIGURE 4 'Kui suur on Siionis' (*Õigeusu palveraamat*, Mattias Palli (ed.) [Tallinn, Eesti Apostlik-Õigeusu Kiriku Kirjastus, 2006], p. 247).

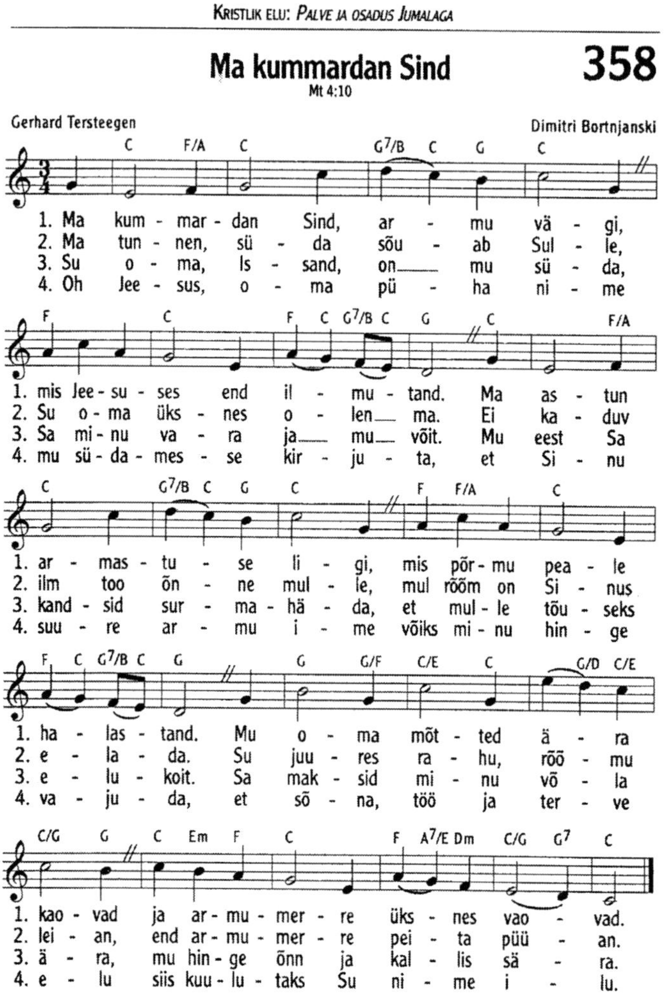

1. Ma kummardan Sind, armuvägi,	1. I worship You, loving power,
mis Jeesuses end ilmutand.	which was revealed in Jesus himself.
Ma astun armastuse ligi,	I draw near to the love,
mis põrmu peale halastand.	which was spared corruption.
Mu oma mõtted ära kaovad	Thoughts of myself vanish
ja armumerre üksnes vaovad.	and are wholly engulfed in a sea of love.

FIGURE 5 'Ma kummardan Sind' (*Vaimulikud laulud* [Tallinn, Eesti Evangeeliumi Kristlaste ja Baptistide Koguduste Liit, 1997], p. 358).

FIGURE 6 'Kui suur on Siionis' (*Oikumeeniline noortelaulik OIKU*, Mai-Liis Mäeväli (ed.) [Tallinn, Eesti Kirikute Nõukogu, 2003], pp. 130–1).

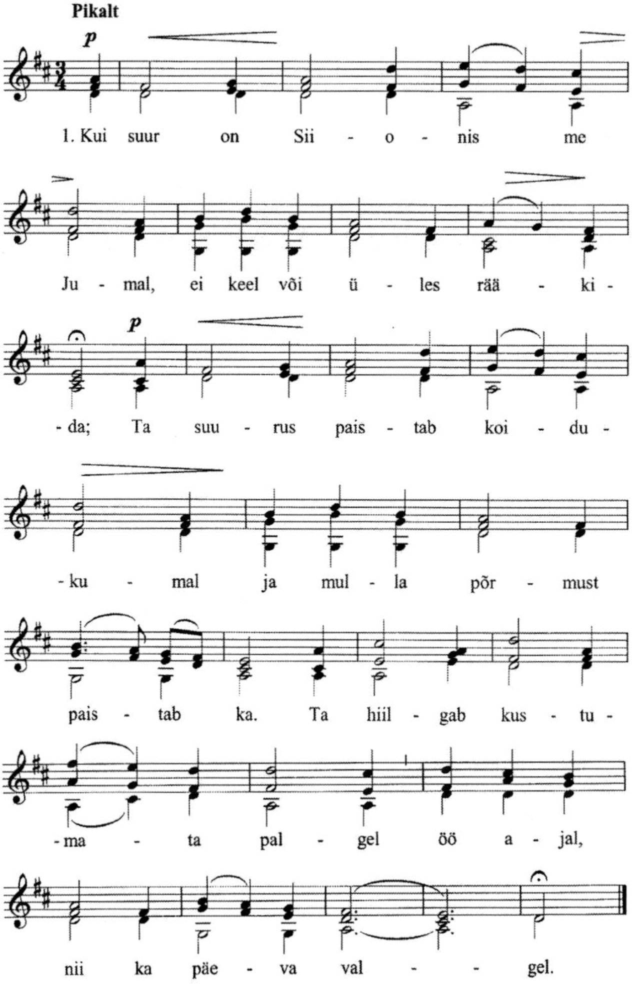

'Ma kummardan Sind, Armuvägi' (Figure 5) is suited for singing to organ accompaniment but also features chord markings to facilitate improvised accompaniment on guitar or keyboard in the context of charismatic worship.

These musical and textual differences are distillations of different attitudes towards Christian sounds and different beliefs about what makes those sounds efficacious. But instead of obscuring the ecumenicity of Bortnyansky's hymn and other Christian musics in Estonia, these differences in fact accentuate ecumenicity because of the shared practices, sentiments, and experiences they enable by being at once confession-specific and also about a more universal Christianity and sense of Estonianness. Although the ecumenicity of Christian musics in Estonia has become more publicly audible and pronounced through post-Soviet religious renewal and transformation, it also registers deep continuities in pre-Soviet, Soviet, and post-Soviet religious practices while critically recasting distinctions between confessional categories and the sacred and secular.

Conclusions

The ecumenicity of Christian musics in Estonia is tenacious, especially in light of the changes in late- and post-Soviet Estonian musical life and scholarship that I have documented here. For a host of ideological, political, and personal reasons, Christian musics once again sound in public spaces, provide creative resources for musicians of all kinds, and bring both pleasure and spiritual nourishment to listeners and worshipers. Estonian music scholarship has participated in and documented these changes, and scholars' renewed commitment to the study of Christian musics is evidence of the changing ways in which humanistic knowledge is produced in the post-Soviet era. No longer subject to ideological proscription and (self-)censorship, belief, faith, theology, socio- and musico-religious histories, and practices related to divinity have re-emerged as fields of inquiry that are redrawing and, at the same time, obscuring and overcoming disciplinary boundaries in productive ways. As I have suggested here, 'church music' has been critical in the reassessment and rewriting of Estonian music histories (see Lippus 1995a, 2002a, 2002b), and many scholars have made their careers addressing lacunae in Estonian music scholarship through the study of Christian musics, introducing new methodologies and illuminating new temporal and geographic relationships in the process.

In the wake of important work that has been done since the late 1980s, the tenacious ecumenicity of Christian musics in Estonia is becoming more explicit in music scholarship as well. What is valuable about an explicit consideration of ecumenicity is the way in which it registers the nuanced dynamics of historical change in Estonian musical and religious life, and the way in which it denaturalizes the alignment of musical styles, confessional categories, ethnolinguistic identities and religious institutions. Like those engaged in, experiencing, or studying Christian musics and religious renewal in post-Soviet Estonia, Christian sounds, ideas and believers are necessarily active within ecumenical spaces and at the fluid boundaries of the sacred and the secular in society at large. The tenacity with which musics like 'Kol' slaven nash gospod' vo Sione' or 'Ma kummardan Sind, Armuvägi' or 'Kui suur on Siionis' mediate ecumenical histories, enable ecumenical practices, and are efficacious because of their ecumenicity, then, is an essential consideration in the field of Estonian music scholarship, first and foremost because of the ways in which it challenges ambivalent secular methodologies and disciplinary practices.

In this way, post-Soviet Estonian music scholarship can no longer be considered simply post-Soviet: on the one hand, in coming to terms with the ecumenicity of Christian musics in Estonia, present-day Estonian music scholarship is dealing with methodological and ideological issues that shaped Soviet and Republican-era musicologies as well, albeit in different ways. On the other hand, in coming to terms with matters of belief, efficacy, the sacrality of sound as such, and the relationship of modernity and secularism, Estonian music scholarship is dealing with issues that concern the international musicological community as a whole. Thus, not only has Estonian music scholars' turn towards Christian musics been part of a widespread, decidedly late- and post-Soviet phenomenon, it has also been one of the ways in which Estonian music scholarship has moved beyond the post-Soviet and the essentialisms, retrograde historical interpretations, and ideas of Western 'normalcy' associated with that label to forge a vital, agentive present and future.

Notes

1   See, for example, the Estonian Evangelical Lutheran Church's *Church Song and Prayer Book* (*Kiriku laulu- ja palveraamat* 1991), the Orthodox Church of Estonia's *Orthodox Prayer Book* (*Õigeusu palveraamat*; Palli 2006), the Union of Free Evangelical and Baptist Churches of Estonia's *Sacred Songs* (*Vaimulikud laulud* 1997), and the Estonian Council of Churches' *Ecumenical Song Book for Youth* OIKU (*Oikumeeniline noortelaulik OIKUi*; M.-L. Mäeväli 2003).

2   Here I am referring to ethnic Estonians, not to the Russian-speaking population in Estonia.

3   Overall, however, Estonian society is markedly secular, and many of those living in Estonia do not identify with institutionalized religions (cf. Liiman 2001; Plaat 2002, 2003b, 2003c; Kilemit & Nõmmik 2004).

4   Also see Rudolf Põldmäe (1987, 1988) and Voldemar Ilja (1995, 2000) for late- and post-Soviet accounts of the Moravian Brethren.

5   *Regilaul* is a traditional Estonian song genre closely related to Finnish Kalevalaic song and other Balto-Finnic traditional genres. It is characterized by trochaic, octosyllabic verses, thematic parallelism, and alliteration. *Regilaul* is typically responsorial, monophonic, and cyclical; its melodies feature a limited vocal range and are generally syllabic. The earliest forms of *regilaul* probably date back to the first millennium C.E. and stand apart from the rhymed verses, strophic forms, tonally inflected melodies, and functional harmonies of later song genres arriving (along with popular Christianity) from Western Europe and taking root in the eighteenth and nineteenth centuries (see Lippus 1995c, pp. 20–7).

6   T. Siitan, personal communication, 16 May 2004.

7   On Estonian Orthodox conversion and the significance of congregational singing in Estonian Orthodoxy, see Engelhardt (2005, pp. 108–209).

8   The cosmopolitan character of Bortyansky's religious and secular music and the affinities between Russian, German, and Italian elite musical cultures in the eighteenth and nineteenth centuries have been well documented. See, for instance, Morosan (1994, p. 57–73) and Taruskin (1997, pp. xi–xiv, 105–235; 2006).

References

Altnurme, L. (ed.) (2004) *Mitut usku Eesti: valik usundiloolisi uurimusi* (Tartu, Tartu Ülikooli Kirjastus).

Arro, E. (1931) 'Baltische Choralbücher und ihre Verfasser', *Acta Musicologia*, 3, 4, pp. 112–19, 166–71.

Arro, E. (1981) *Geschichte der baltischen Kirchenmusik und geistlichen tonkunst. Versuch einer musikhistorischen Rekonstruktion*, unpublished manuscript (Estonian Academy of Music and Theatre Library Archive, RR 3 Arro/Geschichte).

Arro, E. (2003) 'Balti koraaliraamatud ja nende koostajad', Heinmaa, H. (trans.), in Priidel, E. (ed.) (2003) *Vana aja muusikud* (Tartu, Ilmamaa).

Bak, K. S. & Nielsen, S. (eds) (2006) *Spiritual Folk Singing: Nordic and Baltic Protestant Traditions* (Copenhagen, Kragen).

Eesti Apostliku õigeusu kiriku Wiiside raamat I (1925) (Tallinn, Eesti Apostliku õigeusu kiriku Sinod).

Engelhardt, J. (2005) *Singing in 'Transition': Musical Practices and Ideologies of Renewal in the Orthodox Church of Estonia* (PhD dissertation, University of Chicago).

Evangeelsed laulud: jumalateenistuse raamat (1975a) (Tallinn, Evangeeliumi Kristlaste-Baptistide Üleliiduline Nõukogu Eesti NSV-s).

Evangeelsed laulud: jumalateenistuse raamat (1975b) (Tallinn, Metodisti Kiriku Valitsus ENSV-s).

Evangeelsed laulud: jumalateenistuse raamat (1991) (Tallinn, Eesti Evangeelsete Kristlaste-Baptistide Liit).

Gandšu, J. (2002) 'Vaimuliku laulu folkloriseerumisest Värska Püha Jüri kirikus', *Lemmeleht. Pro Folkloristika*, 9, pp. 17–24.

Hagen, J. A. (1844) *Laulo-wisi-ramat: Tallinna ja Tarto ma-kele lauloramatute kõrwa ja peale sedda weel üks weikene lissa* (Reval, Lindfors).

Heinmaa, H. (1999) *Protestantlik kantoriinstitutsioon Tallinnas 16–17. sajandil* (Tallinn, Eesti Keele Instituut).

Heinmaa, H. (2004) 'Aus der Geschichte des Kantorenamtes in Reval', in Larsson, L. O. (ed.) (2004).

Humal, M. (1989) 'Vaimulikest kaanonitest Cyrillus Kreegi hilisloomingus', *Teater. Muusika. Kino*, 11, pp. 43–6.

Ilja, V. (1995) *Vennastekoguduse (herrnhutluse) ajalugu Eestimaal (Põhja-Eesti) 1730–1743* (Helsinki, Suomen Kirkkohistoriallinen Seura).

Ilja, V. (2000) *Vennastekoguduse (herrnhutluse) ajalugu Eestimaal (Põhja-Eesti) 1744–1764* (Tallinn, Logos).

Järg, T. (2003) *Cyrillus Kreek* (Tallinn, Eesti Muusika Infokeskus).

Jõks, E. (2003) 'Muutustest liturgias ja liturgilises muusikas', in Kõlar, A. (ed.) (2003).

Kalkun, A. (2001) 'Mõistus ja tunded. Protestantlik ja ortodoksne Anne Vabarna tekstides', *Klaasmäel. Pro Folkloristica*, 8, pp. 45–65.

Karjahärm, T. (1998) *Ida ja Lääne vahel: Eesti-Vene suhted 1850–1917* (Tallinn, Eesti Entsüklopeediakirjastus).

Karjahärm, T. (2003) *Unistus Euroopast* (Tallinn, Argo).

Karjahärm, T. & Luts, H.-M. (2005) *Kultuurigenotsiid Eestis: kunstnikud ja muusikud 1940–1953* (Tallinn, Argo).

Karjahärm, T. & Sirk, V. (1997) *Eesti haritlaskonna kujunemine ja ideed 1850–1917* (Tallinn, Eesti Entsüklopeediakirjastus).

Karjahärm, T. & Sirk, V. (2001) *Vaim ja Võim: Eesti haritlaskond 1917–1940* (Tallinn, Argo).

Karjahärm, T. & Sirk, V. (2007) *Kohanemine ja vastupanu: Eesti haritlaskond 1940–1987* (Tallinn, Argo).

Kilemit, L. & Nõmmik, U. (2004) 'Eesti elanike suhtumisest religiooni', in Altnurme, L. (ed.) (2004).

Kiriku laulu- ja palveraamat (1991) (Tallinn, Eesti Evangeelne Luterlik Kirik).

Kivimäe, J. (ed.) (1987) *Religiooni ja ateismi ajaloost Eestis* (Tallinn, Eesti Raamat).

Kõiva, M. (ed.) (2003) *Sator 2. Artikleid usundi- ja kombeloost* (Tartu, Eesti Kirjandusmuuseum).

Kõlar, A. (2002) 'Eesti luterlik kirikumuusika 1930. aastatel: institutsioonidest, ideoloogiast ja repertuaarist', in Lippus, U. (ed.) (2002).

Kõlar, A. (ed.) (2003a) *Artikleid ja arutlusi eesti kirikumuusikast* (Tallinn, Eesti Evangeelse Luterliku Kiriku Kirikumuusika Liit).

Kõlar, A. (2003b) 'Kolm uuendust Eesti kirikumuusikas 20. sajandi esimesel poolel', in Kõlar, A. (ed.) (2003).

Kõlar, A. (2004) 'Mis on kirikumuusika ja kuidas sellest kirjutada?' in Ross, J. & Maimets, K. (eds) (2004).

Kõlar, A. (2006) 'Kirchenmusik und Kirchenmusikforschung in Estland seit 1990', *Musik und Kirche*, 76, 3, p. 173.

Kõmmus, H. (2001) 'Vaimuliku rahvalaulu piiritlemisest', in Salumäe, E., Pikkur, T., Salumäe, I.-J. & Siitan, T. (eds) (2001).

Lankauskas, G. (2002) 'On "Modern" Christians, Consumption, and the Value of National Identity in Post-Soviet Lithuania', *Ethnos*, 67, 3, pp. 320–44.

Larsson, L. O. (ed.) (2004) *Kunst- und Kulturgeschichte im Baltikum: Hamburger Gespräche 2001–2002* (Kiel, Martin-Carl-Adolf-Böckler-Stiftung).

Lauluraamat Piiskoplikule Metodistikirikule Eestis (compiled by Söte, H.) (1926) (Tallinn, Kristliku kirjanduse agentuur).

Liiman, R. (2001) *Usklikkus muutuvas Eesti ühiskonnas* (Tartu, Tartu Ülikooli Kirjastus).

Lippus, U. (1988) 'Rahvapärane koraalide laulmine eestirootslaste külades', *Teater. Muusika. Kino*, 12, pp. 27–39.

Lippus, U. (1993a) 'The Tradition of Folk Hymnsinging in Estonia and an Introduction to the Estonian-Swedish Collections of Hymn Variants', *IAH Bulletin*, 21, pp. 68–80.

Lippus, U. (1993b) 'The Psalm Compositions by Cyrillus Kreek (1889–1962) and the Estonian Tradition of Folk Hymn Singing', *IAH Bulletin*, 21, pp. 81–5.

Lippus, U. (ed.) (1995a). *Music History Writing and National Culture* (Tallinn, Eesti Keele Instituut).

Lippus, U. (1995b) 'The Tradition of Writing on Estonian Music History', in Lippus, U. (ed.) (1995a).

Lippus, U. (1995c) *Linear Musical Thinking: A Theory of Musical Thinking and the Runic Song Tradition of Baltic-Finnish Peoples* (Helsinki, University of Helsinki).

Lippus, U. (ed.) (2000) *Valgeid laike Eesti muusikaloost* (Tallinn, Eesti Muusikaakadeemia).

Lippus, U. (2001) 'Kreek, Cyrillus', in Macy, L. (ed.) (2001) *Grove Music Online*, available at: http://www.grovemusic.com, accessed 5 March 2007.

Lippus, U. (ed.) (2002a) *Rahvuslikkuse idee ja eesti muusika 20. Sajandi algupoolel* (Tallinn, Eesti Muusikaakadeemia).

Lippus, U. (2002b) 'Omakultuur ja muusika: muusika rahvuslikke idee Eestis I', in Lippus, U. (ed.) (2002a).

Lippus, U. (2003) 'Rahvapärased koraalivariandid Eestis', in Kõlar, A. (ed.) (2003a).

Lippus, U. (2004) 'Muusikaloo kirjutamisest', in Ross, J. & Maimets, K. (eds) (2004).

Lippus, U. (2006) 'The Estonian Tradition of Folk Hymn Singing', in Bak, K. S. & Nielsen, S. (eds) (2006).

Luehrmann, S. (2005) 'Recycling Cultural Construction: Desecularisation in Postsoviet Mari El', *Religion, State, and Society*, 33, 1, pp. 35–56.

Mäeväli, M.-L. (ed.) (2003) *Oikumeeniline noortelaulik OIKU* (Tallinn, Eesti Kirikute Nõukogu).

Morosan, V. (1994) *Choral Performance in Pre-Revolutionary Russia* (Madison, CT, Musica Russica).

Noortelaulik (1943) (Tallinn, n.p.).

Paldre, E. (2003) 'Lauluvaliku kujunemine Eesti vabakiriklikees kogudustes', *Usuteaduslik Ajakiri*, 2, 52, pp. 55–74.

Palli, M. (ed.) (2006) *Õigeusu palveraamat* (Tallinn, Eesti Apostlik-Õigeusu Kiriku Kirjastus).

Piiroinen, E. (ed.) (1951) *Vaeltajan lauluja: Kokoelma yksiäänisiä hengellisiä lauluja* (Kuopio, Pyhäin Sergein ja Hermanin Veljeskunta).

Plaat, J. (1999) 'Vormsi usk: Usuliikumised Vormsi rootslaste ja eestilaste seas 1740.–1990. aastail', *Akadeemia*, 2, pp. 277–310.

Plaat, J. (2001) *Usuliikumised, kirikud ja vabakogudused Lääne- ja Hiiumaal: usuühenduste muutumisprotsessid 18. sajandi keskpaigast kuni 20. sajandi lõpuni* (Tartu, Eesti Rahva Muuseum).

Plaat, J. (2002) 'Christian and Non-Christian Religiosity in Estonia in the 1990s: Comparison of Estonians and Other Ethnic Groups', *Pro Ethnologia*, 14, pp. 97–134.

Plaat, J. (2003a) *Saaremaa kirikud, usuliikumised ja prohvetid 18.–20. sajandil* (Tartu, Eesti Rahva Muuseum).

Plaat, J. (2003b) 'Mida usuvad Eesti elanikud? Religioonisotsioloogilistest küsitlustest aastatel 1990–2000', in Kõiva, M. (ed.) (2003).

Plaat, J. (2003c) 'Eesti—luterlik või õigeusklik riik? Eestlaste ja venelaste usklikkuse võrdlus 1990–2000', *Teologinen Aikakauskirja/Teologisk Tidskrift*, 6, pp. 580–91.

Põldmäe, R. (1987) 'Hernhuutlane Christoph Michael Königseer ja tema kohtuprotsess 1767. aastal', in Kivimäe, J. (ed.) (1987).

Põldmäe, R. (1988) 'Vennastekoguduse muusikalisest tegevusest meie maal', *Teater. Muusika. Kino*, 3, pp. 67–78.

Punschel, J. L. E. (1862) *Punsli nelja heälega Laulo-wisi-ramat, mis Saksa kele, Lätti kele, ja Tallinna ning Tarto Ma-kele laulo ramatude tarwis* (Tallinn, F. Kluge).

Ramul, R. (1896) *Waimulikud laulud, psalmid ehk waimulikud kantad, wiisidega* (Tallinn, Lindfors).

Raun, T. U. (1981) 'Russification in Education and Religion', in Thaden, E. C. (ed.) (1981).

Raun, T. U. (2001) *Estonia and the Estonians*, 2d ed. (Stanford, Hoover Institution Press).

Ross, J. & Maimets, K. (eds) (2004) *Mõeldes muusikast: sissevaateid muusikateadusesse* (Tallinn, Varrak).

Salumäe, E., Pikkur, T., Salumäe, I.-J. & Siitan, T. (eds) (2001) *Kelle laule me laulame?: Hümnoloogiline kogumik 'Kiriku Laulu- ja Palveraamatu' 10. aastapäeva tähistamiseks* (Tallinn, Eesti Evangeelse Luterliku Kiriku Konsistoorium).

Salumäe, I.-J. (2001) 'Miks *Kiriku Laulu- ja Palveraamat* on selline, nagu ta on? Esimene mõtisklus', in Salumäe, E., Pikkur, T., Salumäe, I.-J. & Siitan, T. (eds) (2001).

Sarapuu, K. (2003) 'Eesti algupäraste õigeusu kirikulaulude stiilist', *Usuteaduslik Ajakiri*, 2, 52, pp. 31–54.

Sarv, V. (2000) *Setu itkukultuur* (Tartu-Tampere, Eesti Kirjandusmuuseum).

Siitan, T. (1992) 'Information über Perspektiven der hymnologischen Forschung und über Denkmäler des Kirchengesangs in Estland', *IAH Bulletin*, 20, pp. 256–60.

Siitan, T. (1994) 'Die Choral-reform im lutherischen Baltikum und Punschels Universal-Choralbuch', *IAH Bulletin*, 22, pp. 37–49.

Siitan, T. (1995) 'Das Regionale und das Allgemeine in der Choralrestauration des 19. Jahrhunderts', in Lippus, U. (ed.) (1995a).

Siitan, T. (1998) 'Zwei konkurrierende Universal-Choralbücher für die baltischen Provinzen in der Mitte des 19. Jahrhunderts', *Jahrbuch für Liturgik und Hymnologie*, 37, pp. 167–78.

Siitan, T. (2000) 'Koraaliraamatud Eesti- ja Liivimaal enne 1850. aastat', in Lippus, U. (ed.) (2000).

Siitan, T. (2001) 'Eesti kirikulaul või kirikulaul Eestis?-Identiteedist meie kirikulaulus', in Salumäe, E., Pikkur, T., Salumäe, I.-J. & Siitan, T. (eds) (2001).

Siitan, T. (2003a) *Die Choralreform in den Ostseeprovinzen in der ersten Hälfte des 19. Jahrhunderts: Ein Beitrag zur Geschichte des protestantischen Kirchengesangs in Estland und Livland* (Sinzig, Studio).

Siitan, T. (2003b) 'Koguduselaulu reformist Liivi- ja Eestimaal XIX sajandi algupoolel', *Usuteaduslik Ajakiri*, 2, 52, pp. 93–100.

Siitan, T. (2003c) 'Koraaliraamatud Eesti- ja Liivimaal 19. sajandi keskpaigani', in Kõlar, A. (ed.) (2003a).

Siitan, T. (2006) 'Das Kirchenlied in Estland', *Musik und Kirche*, 76, 3, pp. 171–7.

Sioni Laulud (1913) (Hamburg, Internationali Traktadiselts).

Sioni Laulud (1928) (Tallinn, S.P. Adv. Eesti Liit).

Taruskin, R. (1997) *Defining Russian Musically: Historical and Hermeneutical Essays* (Princeton, Princeton University Press).

Taruskin, R. (2006) '"Classicism' à la russe" [review of *The Powers of Heaven: Orthodox Music of the 17th and 18th Centuries*, Estonian Philharmonic Chamber Choir, Paul Hillier, conductor (Harmonia Mundi CD HMU 907318 [2003])]', *Eighteenth-Century Studies*, 39, 2, pp. 279–82.

Taylor, C. (2006) 'Religious Mobilizations', *Public Culture*, 18, 2, pp. 281–300.

Thaden, E. C. (ed.) (1981) *Russification in the Baltic Provinces and Finland, 1855–1914* (Princeton, Princeton University Press).

Uus Lauluraamat: kirikus, koolis ja kodus pruukida (1900) (Jurjev, K. Matthiesen).

Vaimulikud laulud (1997) (Tallinn, Eesti Evangeeliumi Kristlaste ja Baptistide Koguduste Liit).

Vallikivi, L. (2005) *Arktika nomaadid šamanismi ja kristluse vahel* (Tartu, Tartu Ülikooli Kirjastus).

Verdery, K. (1999) *The Political Lives of Dead Bodies: Reburial and Postsocialist Change* (New York, Columbia University Press).

Waimulikud laulud õigeusulisele Eesti rahwale I (1915) (Tartu, n.p.).

Wanner, C. (2003) 'Advocating New Moralities: Conversion to Evangelicalism in Ukraine', *Religion, State, and Society*, 31, 3, pp. 273–87.

Wittenberg, A. (1982) '"Helm ab – zum Gebet' – "Ich bete an die Macht der Liebe': Gedanken zum Großen Zapfenstreich', *Jahrbuch für Liturgik und Hymnologie*, 26, pp. 157–74.

Discography

Armastuse ja rõõmu laulud (2007) (self-published).

Engelhardt, J. (2004) *Eesti Apostlik-Õigeusu Kiriku Laule – Hymns of the Orthodox Church of Estonia* (Tallinn, Eesti Apostlik-Õigeusu Kirik).

Heinavanker (2007) *Estonian Religious Folk Chorales / Johannes Ockeghem* (Alba Records ABCD 237).

Johanson & Vennad (1993) *Põhja vahemäng* (self-published).

Johanson & Vennad (2000) *Päevakera* (self-published).

Mu süda, ärka üles (2005) (self-published).

Strand . . . Rand: Folk Chorales and Songs from the West Coast of Estonia (2002) (self-published).

Triskele (2000) *Eesti vaimulikud rahvalaulud / Estonian Folk Hymns* (self-published).

Triskele (2001) *Lõuna-Eesti vaimulikud rahvalaulud / South Estonian Folk Hymns* (self-published).

Triskele (2002) *Lõuna-Eesti vaimulikud rahvalaulud II / South Estonian Folk Hymns Vol. 2* (self-published).

Triskele (2003) *Kolga-Jaani vaimulikud rahvalaulud / Estonian Folk Hymns from Kolga-Jaani* (self-published).

Triskele (2005) *Ridala vaimulikud rahvalaulud / Estonian Folk Hymns from Ridala* (self-published).

Vara (2003) *Vaimulik rahvamuusika* (self-published).

LITHUANIAN MUSICOLOGY IN HISTORICAL CONTEXT: 1945 TO THE PRESENT

Vita Gruodytė

Introduction

As in Western Europe, the end of World War II in Lithuania marked the beginning of a new epoch on the musical scene – however, in an entirely different respect. One might suppose that in the field of musicology the transitions of the post-war years were not particularly painful, since it was not until that time that Lithuanian musicology first emerged as a professional scholarly discipline. However, this was hardly the case. Although there were no specialized, scholarly musicological publications prior to that time, composers and self-taught music critics had indeed published educational and pedagogical essays on various aspects of Lithuanian musical life, interpretation, historiography, and, occasionally, analysis for the lay public. Moreover, several periodical publications covering musical topics had likewise appeared prior to 1945, including *Vargonininkas* (*The Organist*), *Muzika ir teatras* (*Music and Theater*), *Muzika*, *Muzikos menas* (*The Art of Music*), *Muzikos aidai* (*Echoes of Music*) and *Muzikos barai* (*Domains of Music*). Indeed, solid conceptions of Lithuanian music historiography and criticism, as well as notions of musical modernism, had already begun to take shape. In fact, these issues provoked heated discussions of Lithuanian musical identity during the inter-war years, in which participants were divided, as they were in much of Central and Western Europe, into two opposing camps: one in favor of innovation and the avant-garde, and the other calling for the continuation of traditions and the preservation of national character. If it had not been for the Soviet occupation, these rudimentary beginnings of a Lithuanian musicological discourse would undoubtedly have played an important role in shaping the future of Lithuanian musicology, and of post-war Lithuanian music more generally.

The Institutional Beginnings of Musicology in Lithuania

Institutionally, post-war Lithuanian musicology was grounded in two structures. First of all, the Lithuanian State Conservatory, founded in 1949, was charged with training professional musicologists. In the year of its foundation, nine teachers worked in the general faculty of music history, theory and composition.[1] Independent chairs in music theory and history were established in 1953, and a chair in ethnomusicology was established in 1989. In 1948 an institute for the study of folk music had been founded at the State Conservatory's predecessor, the Vilnius Conservatory. And in 1964, an institute of scholarly research in music theory was founded at the institution.

In terms of theory pedagogy at the Conservatory, there was no radical shift between pre-war and post-war teaching practices, as the majority of teachers continued to make use of literature published during the inter-war period. As musicologist Vytautas Venckus recalled in his memoirs of the time, 'In the post-war period, the curriculum of the Vilnius Conservatory [in 1944–1949] was very close to that of the pre-war Kaunas Conservatory' (cited in Puidokienė 2001, p. 73). Or, 'Jonas Bendorius' – a composer who graduated from the Leipzig Conservatory in 1924 – 'taught musical forms from the German manual *Handbuch der Formenlehre*' (Puidokienė 2001, p. 75). To take another example, the composer Jonas Nabažas, who studied at *École Normale de Paris*, taught polyphony by way of the manuals of French authors.

The faculty of music history, on the other hand, found itself in a completely different situation, for it had neither textbooks nor reference books from the inter-war years upon which to base its work.[2] Moreover, the history of Lithuanian music had to be rewritten from a new, Marxist–Leninist perspective in order to transform music-historical study from an independent field of scholarly inquiry into a constituent part of 'scientific Communism'. Thus, books on the history of Lithuanian musics of both current and earlier periods had to be written. This work was undertaken by Juozas Gaudrimas, the first teacher of music history at the Lithuanian State Conservatory, who soon began, with the help of his students, to compile the three-volume text *From the History of Lithuanian Musical Culture* (*Iš lietuvių muzikinės kultūros istorijos*, Gaudrimas 1958–1967). In 1958 Gaudrimas published the first volume of this study, covering the history of Lithuanian music from 1861 until 1917. The choice of these dates was not accidental; they covered the period from the abolition of serfdom in Lithuania until the Great Socialist October Revolution.

By presenting the Lithuanian national movement of the second half of the nineteenth century in the Marxist–Leninist language of class struggle, and thereby downplaying the national dimensions of the movement, Soviet historians sought to legitimize their regime as its only possible, logical outcome. To conform with this narrative, the history of music too had to be presented 'in a new light', through the prism of 'the oppression of the people and their struggle for liberation'. Assuming a self-consciously objective stance – that is, 'bourgeois objectivism' – became unacceptable. Indeed, it was Lenin who formulated this approach: 'Only through the thorough knowledge of culture created throughout the entire development of humanity, only by *remaking* it, can one build proletarian culture', he proclaimed (cited in Bagušauskas & Streikus 2005, p. 261). The objective presentation of historical facts was thus treated as the 'idealisation of ancient history', and hence a manifestation of 'bourgeois nationalism'. Gaudrimas squeezed the history of Lithuanian music into this obligatory framework, setting out historical facts with scholarly precision (for this reason his study still remains one of the fundamental sources for Lithuanian musicology), and overlaying this presentation with Marxist–Leninist ideological interpretations. In 1964 he published the second volume of his study, covering the period of Republican independence (1917–1940), and in 1967, together with a group of co-authors, he completed the final installment, dedicated to Lithuanian music of the Soviet period.

The second institution that fostered musicological activity in the immediate post-war years was the Lithuanian Composers' Union. Founded with 11 members immediately after the first Soviet occupation in 1940 (when independent artists' societies had been closed), it was reconstituted after the war, in 1945. The Composers' Union was established for the purpose of organizing and controlling not only composers' and musicologists' creative activities (cultural life was totally dependent upon institutions of power acting as control mechanisms), but also their political and ideological 'education' and propaganda. Since Soviet authorities regarded culture as a principal tool of ideological and political indoctrination, they needed the help of a cadre of artists supporting the regime. The Union's first two musicologists were admitted in 1945, and an independent section of musicologists was established in 1952 (in 1971, a subdivision of music critics was established on the initiative of musicologist Jonas Bruveris). In 1954 the musicologists' section consisted of three members, in 1960 of seven, and in 1973 of 24.[3] As far as we can judge from the speech of the then-executive secretary of the Union, the composer Abelis Klenickis, delivered at the Union's second congress in 1954, the principal activities of contemporary musicologists consisted in giving public lectures and publishing critical reviews (cited in *Muzika 1940–1960* 1992, pp. 125–6). In terms of scholarship, the folklorist Jadvyga Čiurlionytė prepared pre-war collections of folklore for the press, wrote books about Lithuanian folk music (Čiurlionytė 1955) and edited the works of her brother, the composer Mikalojus Konstantinas Čiurlionis (1875–1911). Juozas Gaudrimas, in addition to writing books on the history of Lithuanian music and the music of the USSR, completed a thesis on the 'Professional Development of Lithuanian Music and Musical Life in the Period of Capitalism'. And the Russian-born musicologist Zinaida Feoktisova-Kumpienė, who arrived in Lithuania in 1944, set to work on a thesis on 'Soviet Lithuanian Songs'.

Pressure from the Center, Reactions from the Periphery

Leafing through documents from the immediate post-war years, we can see that the majority of composers and musicologists active during this period assumed an explicitly neutral position, politically speaking, in their work. From 1946 and onwards, composers were frequently reprimanded for being apolitical, for not attending the meetings of the Composers' Union, and even for not composing music at all (some of them composed secretly; for example, Konradas Kaveckas wrote religious music and even gave lectures to priests). When pressed for explanations, composers typically came up with excuses about lack of time, fatigue, or the busy schedule of their pedagogical or concert activities (Juozas Gruodis had to defend himself in the press for not being able to complete a work commissioned for the festivities of the Great October Revolution on account of illness). The situation in the Artists' and Writers' Unions was similar, and musicologists were similarly reprimanded. In 1948 the Composers' Union decried 'the almost total absence of music criticism in our press', as well as the fact that 'some teachers refuse to teach Soviet music' (*Muzika 1940–1960* 1992, pp. 87, 100). In 1954 musicologists were rebuked for their 'weak contribution to the all-Union press', for 'not showing enough initiative in studying Lithuanian musical heritage and reviewing it from a Marxist perspective', and for the fact that 'not all articles appearing in the press exhibit a sufficient ideological-political level' (*Muzika 1940–1960* 1992, p. 126).

Beginning in 1948, a new kind of pressure was exerted upon musicians and scholars, which might be regarded as initiating the coalescence of a strictly controlled Communist musicology in the Soviet Union. In a notorious speech, the official ideologist of Soviet culture Andrey Zhdanov laid out the principles of Socialist Realism in art, and pointed out intolerable ('formalist') tendencies in music. This speech presaged an official decree of the Central Committee of the Communist Party (Bolshevik) publicly denouncing the opera *The Great Friendship* by the Georgian composer Vano Muradeli, along with works by many other composers from Russia and the occupied countries. Among the Lithuanian composers accused of 'formalism' were Stasys Vainiūnas, Juozas Karosas and Juozas Gruodis (see *Muzika 1940–1960* 1992, pp. 92–109). Gruodis (1884–1948), the leading exponent of Lithuanian musical modernism, was fated to bear the most painful consequences. Deeply traumatized by his denouncement, he died two months after the decree was issued. The following year, the 'decadent' work of long-departed Mikalojus Konstantinas Čiurlionis (1875–1911) also became a target of the struggle against formalism.[4]

After 1948, Socialist Realism became the official aesthetic for all artistic work. It served as the basis for a general theory of Marxist–Leninist aesthetics, of which the aesthetics of music was a branch. It rejected everything characteristic of 'bourgeois art' – modern European and American music, individualism, subjectivity, originality, atonality, dissonance, constructivism, etc. – and legitimized everything that was contrary to it: the representation of artistic reality, the search for artistic truth, an optimistic character, comprehensibility of musical language, the folk character or melodiousness of music and the continuation of classical traditions of Western and Russian music. In all of its different treatments – as a method, an axiological category, a style, and a general artistic tendency – the aesthetic of Socialist Realism always had a political objective.

Since music criticism was considered the principal activity of musicologists throughout this period (it was also the aspect of musicological work most capable of reacting quickly to urgent issues and shifting values), it was the first to become an object of political 'education'. This same decree of 1948 announced that 'rather than dissipating the pernicious views and theories incompatible with the principles of Socialist Realism, music criticism itself is encouraging their spread by praising and proclaiming as "progressive" those composers who adhere to false creative assumptions in their work. Music criticism has ceased to express the opinion of Soviet society, the opinion of the people, and has turned into a mouthpiece for individual composers' (in *Muzika 1940–1960* 1992, pp. 34–5). Expounding this decree to the Lithuanian public, the composer Juozas Tallat-Kelpša, who died in 1949 while conducting his cantata about Stalin, defined a new function for music criticism. 'A critic', he wrote, 'is a kind of mediator between the creator and the listener; he helps the creator to understand the impression that the listener has received or will receive. Criticism must always be concrete and assist the composer, showing him the way, rather than merely pointing out the shortcomings of his work' (in *Muzika 1940–1960* 1992, p. 109). This official concept of criticism, regarded as a crucial mechanism for controlling the creator and turning an artistic result into ideologically oriented 'applied art', did not change in later times. In 1974 Juozas Gaudrimas repeated these same thoughts

> Like a sensitive dictate of conscience, music criticism must speak in time and in principle, from a correct ideological viewpoint, in a matter-of-fact and professional manner. . . . A critic should help us to understand the real function of Soviet music, its role in the aesthetic education of workers, in expanding their artistic horizons. If a composer limits himself exclusively to technology, a critic should not remain a mere onlooker, but must be a highly principled fighter for the noble ideals of Soviet art. (Gaudrimas 1985, pp. 184–5)

Within this political context, regardless of the rectification of 'certain mistakes' and the rehabilitation of 'formalist' composers during the period of the Khrushchev 'Thaw' in the late 1950s, it was rather difficult to assume an openly adverse position. Indeed, the post-war situation in Lithuania was complicated for other reasons as well; armed resistance to Soviet authority continued for more than a decade after annexation, and thus any manifestation of nationalism in art received a very negative response.

Making Decisions

The neutral attitude assumed by many musicologists in the immediate post-war years could not persist for long, as Soviet authorities did not tolerate silence; indeed, they regarded it as an expression of bourgeois nationalism, in music or any other field of culture. 'One feature of contemporary art', wrote Antanas Sniečkus, First Secretary of the Central Committee of the Lithuanian Communist Party, 'is the fact that the remaining bourgeois nationalists are secretly spreading the ideology of bourgeois nationalism under the disguise of apparent loyalty, and most often by putting on a mask of apolitical character and objectivism' (in Bagušauskas & Streikus 2005, p. 118).

As we learn from secret documents of the KGB, at some point around 1950 a number of Lithuanian intellectuals – scientists, professors, publishers, writers, and even some who had been forced to become deputies of the Supreme Council – began to discuss, in their private conversations, ways in which to preserve their culture under conditions of Soviet rule, and also actions that might taken to this end.[5] A teacher at the Vilnius Pedagogical Institute argued:

> We should take some measures for consolidating the nation's spirit and stopping the seeping of Communist views into the consciousness of Lithuanians,

particularly our youth; we should substitute our people for all non-Lithuanians [who have arrived from other parts of the Soviet Union], first of all Russians, since it is through them that the destruction of our nation is taking place. (p. 141)

A professor at Kaunas University and a member of the Lithuanian Academy of Sciences remarked:

The existing organizations – the party and its subdivisions, for example, the Komsomol – have a great significance in our life. Our youth should not avoid these organizations, but rather take part in their activity. That which cannot be said openly must be explained to our students in ways they will understand: We don't like the fact that so many Russians are coming to Lithuania, that Russian newcomers are occupying leading positions in offices and the government. (p. 141)

A deputy of the Lithuanian Supreme Council asserted:

Now we should preserve our national character and not yield to Russification, and then we'll see what happens. (p. 142)

A teacher at Vilnus Conservatory remarked:

I regard the Communist influence as an evil that cannot be avoided for the moment. (p. 144)

Another university teacher proclaimed:

We Lithuanians are a small nation that can be swept away by Moscow's 'leaders'; therefore we should be sensitive, anticipate everything, and be able to adapt ourselves. If the Komsomol needs new members, young people should enroll in the Komsomol. ... We must join all Russian organizations and even the Communist party ... because otherwise we Lithuanians will all be deported. There is no need to be afraid of repressions after the change of power, because everybody knows that people are joining Soviet organizations by force rather than of their free will. (pp. 142–3)

The field of musicology was too narrow and sparsely populated to be subjected to the same pressures that, for example, Lithuanian writers experienced. But musicology did splinter gradually into various sub-fields of interest, albeit with fluid and shifting boundaries. The general concern of all musicologists active during these years was research on Lithuanian music: studying documentary sources, processing and publishing factological material, and engaging in music analysis (combining aspects of the German and Russian schools of analysis, and focusing upon establishing harmonic and structural principles of musical composition). None of the Lithuanian-born musicologists active during this period seem to have been sincerely devoted to the ideals of Communism. For the most part, those who supported Soviet ideology seem to have done so for opportunistic reasons. In texts, this support manifested itself in quotations from the Party's directives or works by the principal authors of Marxist–Leninist aesthetics. However, it should be noted that such quotations did not always impinge upon one's scholarship. Indeed, some composers chose the titles of their works according to a similar principle: an ideologically appropriate title could serve as protection against criticism on stylistic grounds. Paradoxically, it was composers rather than musicologists who wrote some of the most strongly ideological articles on the occasions of Soviet festivals or congresses of the Composers' Union. This can be explained by the fact that composers occupied the leading posts in the Union, and thus they were subjected to inner competition for power and interests. In the absence of secret democratic elections, authorities themselves would suggest an appropriate (that is, most ingratiating) candidate for the chairmanship of the Composers' Union, who would then be endorsed by a large majority of votes.

Other musicologists devoted themselves to the hermetic field of music analysis, in which – in sharp contrast to a field like music aesthetics – ideological directives could be avoided entirely. In 1977 Algirdas Ambrazas, Antanas Venckus, Bronius Ambraziejus and Juozas Antanavičius published a comprehensive theoretical work, *Fundamentals of Analysis of Musical Compositions* (Ambrazas *et al.* 1977).[6] Antanas Venckus formulated theories of multi-harmony and multi-tonality, the composer Julius Juzeliūnas explored new theoretical foundations for chordal constructions, and Rimantas Janeliauskas embarked upon research into the theory of functional dynamics.

Those musicologists who chose, at first, to focus upon relatively apolitical subjects such as the influence of folk music on professional music, the activity of local performers, conductors, orchestras, or Lithuanian composers of various generations should be divided into two groups. The opportunism of the first group was expressed by the fact that they wrote about works promoting the spread of Soviet ideology (mass songs, oratorios for the Party, etc.), or else described objects of research having nothing to do with Marxist–Leninist aesthetics through the prism of Socialist Realism. In turn, the resistance of the second group manifested itself in a cautious choice of themes and analytical perspectives. From this we can conclude that conscious choice was indeed possible; it is quite obvious in retrospect. The ideological positions assumed in one's scholarship were determined solely by one's personal standpoint with regard to the regime. Indeed, some scholars focused upon the most unwelcome of themes, such as contemporary Western European music, analysis of the work of Lithuanian composers of the pre-Soviet period, the history of organ music (in which otherwise forbidden religious music could be included), and the study of themes related to the musical life of the Grand Duchy of Lithuania. Although sketchy and episodic, these explorations were particularly important for the formation of Lithuanian musicology. However, they could exist only within a more or less predetermined framework.

With the shifts in Moscow's policy (turning stricter or milder) came shifts not only in the themes of musicological articles, but also in the style of writing by some authors. Rimantas Gučas, Edmundas Gedgaudas, and particularly Vytautas Landsbergis developed an elaborate, literary, allegorical-metaphorical style of writing, well protected from faultfinding. A similar situation existed among composers. Some ceased their creative work or died (for instance, in 1948 a young composer by the name of Juozas Pakalnis died under strange circumstances that still remain unsolved). Others began to compose politically engaged works out of either conviction or opportunism. Still others sought ways to engage the Lithuanian avant-garde during the years of its prohibition, or at least to compose music that was distinctly modern stylistically. It should be noted that supporting the dominant political line was, for both musicologists and composers, not so much (and not only) a political act, but also a pragmatic decision. The Composers' Union was an important provider of material welfare, which distributed, according to one's merits, apartments, cars, trips, and refrigerators; offered larger or smaller prices for composers' works; organized performances of their works; and so forth. As Vytautas Landsbergis recalled in his memoirs:

> Very often, indeed nearly always, you were compelled to make decisions. Even while writing an article of music criticism, you had to choose whether to be reticent and enjoy its advantages, or, overcome with indignation, to speak your mind. And then you would remain without a refrigerator. . . . One had to choose between conformism and non-conformism; it was the basic dividing line. We could risk crossing it without being fired from our work or deported to Siberia, but then we would face troubles of local significance and acquire enemies. And these 'enemies' of our own lot could hinder us from going abroad. (Landsbergis 1997, pp. 98, 97)

Periods of Political Restrictions and Thaws: In the Maze of Soviet Prohibitions and Permissions

From a theoretical perspective, the Soviet system was a fairly well structured organism, foreseeing appropriate means of resolving every situation encountered. However, it was in reality a kind of maze, in which one had to learn to walk without getting stuck. A single composition might be criticized at the Composers' Union but defended by the Central Committee of the Communist Party and even nominated for an award. The same text could be rejected by one publishing house or newspaper and accepted by another. And, once published, it might be denounced *post facto*. For example, one of the earliest pre-war folklore collections, Jadvyga Čiurlionytė's *Juška Brothers' Selected Folk Songs* (in three volumes), remained unpublished until 1954. After publication in that year (Juška 1954), however, the collection was criticized in a secret KGB secret document, dated 1955, which read: 'The publishing house has left some ideologically alien and artistically weak songs, imposed on the people by the exploiting classes, among them some songs extolling priests and propagating religious views'. (Paradoxically, it was the institution that prepared the text for printing rather than Čiurlionytė herself that was accused.) At the meeting convened for the occasion of discussing the collection, the senior staff of the publishing house and the Ministry of Culture were made aware of the 'grave mistakes' that they had committed. 'The employees of the publishing house', the record of the meeting explained, 'have exhibited a certain amount of *objectivism* that is alien *to us* in assessing some important issues of our cultural legacy . . . the publishers were supposed not simply to present the songs collected by the Juška brothers to readers, but to provide a key *to their proper understanding*' (emphasis added; in Bagušauskas & Streikus 2005, pp. 211–12, 217).

In the second half of the 1950s, advantage was taken of Moscow's weakening control in Lithuania, and more Lithuanians were successfully installed in the Party and administrative apparatus. (The majority of positions dealing with cultural issues were, significantly, occupied by persons well aware of the importance of preserving Lithuanian culture.) Thus, under the pretext of legitimizing the regime, certain national symbols and traditions were revived, and some important though remote historical plots, like the struggles of Lithuanians with the Teutonic knights, were publicized. In 1956 the composer Vytautas Klova wrote the opera *Pilėnai* (*Castle Defenders*) on the latter topic and even received the State Award, despite the fact that he found himself on the verge of being fired from the Vilnius State Conservatory for 'nationalism'.

Musicologists also reacted quickly to the advantages of the period of the Khrushchev 'Thaw', which manifested themselves in the field of scholarship first of all in a broadening of available research methodologies. Soon, musicologists were attempting to revive the forcefully disrupted links between Lithuanian musical culture and Western musical traditions, and to reconsider crucial facts of Lithuanian music history. In the first issue of the magazine *Kultūros barai* (*Domains of Culture*), which appeared in 1965, Vytautas Landsbergis published an article about aleatoric and visual music (Landsbergis 1965), and continued his studies of Mikalojus Konstantinas Čiurlionis' work on the synthesis of music and the arts, begun in 1956. In 1965 Adeodatas Tauragis published a monograph – the first in the Soviet Union – about Benjamin Britten (Tauragis 1965); wrote on Hindemith, Bartók, Stravinsky, Gershwin, Berg, the *Groupe des Six*; and published the book *Lithuanian Music: Past and Present* in English (Tauragis 1971) and German (Tauragis 1972). In 1960 Algirdas Ambrazas published the first feature article about Juozas Gruodis (Ambrazas 1960), to be followed by several large publications dedicated to that composer's work (e.g. Ambrazas 1981). Nine years later he completed the book *Muzika ir dabartis* (*Music and the Present Time*), which considered the twentieth century's principal techniques of composition (Ambrazas 1969). In 1966 Vytautas Jurkštas published an article about the beginnings of Lithuanian musicological thought at Vilnius University, as revealed in the volume *Ars et praxis musica* (1667) by Professor Žygimantas Liauksminas (Jurkštas 1966). Ona Narbutienė compiled a collection dedicated to the early twentieth-century Lithuanian composer Juozas Naujalis (Narbutienė 1968a) and in 1969 published a book about Antanas Kučingis, the outstanding bass vocalist of the inter-war period (Narbutienė 1969).[7] Antanas Venckus wrote about Naujalis' religious music (Venckus 1968), and Dana Palionytė compiled a collection dedicated to Stasys Šimkus, another Lithuanian composer of the early twentieth century (Palionytė 1967).

In addition to these new avenues of research, the political 'Thaw' opened the way for the first professional trips abroad. This was vitally important for musicologists interested in contemporary music, since in 1959–1961 a system of controlling the influx of goods from foreign countries to Lithuania was established, and thus the primary source for the newest books and recordings was travel abroad.[8] (Apart from what was acquired through travel, Lithuanian musicologists had access only to a handful of specialized foreign periodicals in libraries, such as the Polish musical magazine *Ruch muzyczny*, which published some material on various issues concerning contemporary music, and the British *Musical Quarterly*.)

Thus, in 1963 the musicologists Algirdas Ambrazas and Vytautas Landsbergis, together with the Estonian composers Arvo Pärt and Veljo Tormis, went on their first trip to Poland, to the contemporary music festival *Warsaw Autumn*. The latter festival remained the main source for information about the newest Western European musics for Lithuanian composers and musicologists until the restoration of Lithuania's independence. It was thanks to literature and recordings brought from Poland that Ambrazas was able to write his above-mentioned book *Muzika ir dabartis*, and Landsbergis was able to complete his first article on aleatoric and visual music. Incidentally, upon his return from Warsaw, Landsbergis gave a lecture based upon material acquired in Warsaw for a clandestine circle of musicians at the Vilnius Art Institute, whose 'unhealthy' activities drew the attention of the KGB. Soon, this circle was forcibly disbanded.[9]

In 1969, the period of thaw came to an end, and Moscow gave orders to subject printed material to increasingly strict control. These orders reached Lithuania in 1972, after the young Romas Kalanta's political act of self-immolation to protest the Soviet occupation. On this occasion, the chief editors of the most liberal cultural publications – the magazines *Kultūros barai* and *Nemunas* – and at the publishing house Vaga lost their jobs, accused of 'liberalism', 'publishing politically harmful articles', and 'deviating from the requirements of Socialist Realism' (Bagušauskas & Streikus 2005, pp. 389–90). These events had a direct impact upon musicologists, as both of the above-mentioned periodicals and Vaga provided major forums for musicological discourse. In 1973, Čiurlionis' *Letters to Sofija*, a collection of letters to his wife compiled by Landsbergis, came out, as they had already been prepared for printing. However, the publication of another book by Landsbergis, about the composer and organist Česlovas Sasnauskas (1867–1916), likewise already included in the publishing house's program for that year, was stopped.[10]

Following a decision of the Central Committee of the Lithuanian Communist Party in 1977, bilingualism and Soviet internationalism were widely encouraged in the Republic, as they were in other parts of the Union. The aim of these programs was not only closer collaboration between Soviet peoples, but also the unification of the musics of different republics. These programs received a very weak response among Lithuanian musicologists, who produced very few works along these lines, mostly compiled from pedagogical lectures given at the Vilnius Conservatory. These included Adeodatas Tauragis' edited textbook *Rusų muzikos literatūra* (*The Literature of Russian Music* 1982), and Kazys Jasinskas' *TSRS tautų muzikinė kultūra* (*Musical Culture of the Nations of the USSR* 1982b) and *Latvijos ir Estijos TSR muzikinė kultūra* (*Musical Culture of the Latvian and Estonian SSRs* 1982a). Cooperation with the republics of Central Asia and the totally Russified Belorussia, which officials insistently attempted to impose upon Lithuania, failed. At the same time, links with Latvia and Estonia, considered undesirable by Soviet officialdom, were further consolidated. The three republics defended their geo-political distinctness and their right to hold the Conferences of Baltic Musicologists. Launched in 1965, these conferences played a very important role in the formation of musicological thought in the three Baltic countries. In the words of the Estonian musicologist Mart Humal, they performed two basic functions: 'First of all, they have had an exceptional social value in preserving and reinforcing our Baltic identity and solidarity. And secondly . . . they have formed an important milieu for us, Baltic musicologists, where we were able to make each other acquainted with the achievements of our musicological thought' (Humal 2001, p. 250). Issues concerning the traditions, history and national character of Baltic musics were frequently discussed in these conferences, and conference surveys of new musical works allowed for the discussion of contemporary compositional techniques and idioms.

Despite one final attempt from Moscow to place restrictions on Lithuania's cultural life (in 1982, when Yuri Andropov came to power), the gap between the positions assumed by Lithuania's cultural elite and the standards of official culture and ideology propagated in Moscow was steadily increasing. By that time, the regime was no longer able to impede artistic experimentation and, in music, the spread of original and modern works.

Traces of the Soviet Regime in Lithuanian Musicology

The turning of art into an ideological instrument and the politicization of science eventually made musicologists realize that they could no longer remain neutral in their scholarly work. The constant demand for political engagement (ousting profession-alism to second place!) and the necessity of finding a way around the cycle of permissions, prohibitions and intercessions gradually deformed the scholarly landscape of the period. Even against its will, musicology, and particularly music criticism, became an important vehicle for the implementation of Soviet cultural policies, and few individuals realized the real damage that was inflicted as a result of this.

A closer study of some of the urgent issues confronting musicians and musicologists of the period will enable us to identify several of the primary influences of the Soviet regime and its policies upon Lithuanian musicology.

Personality Cult

The world of music was characterized by the same kind of hierarchy that existed in the Soviet army and political culture. In short, one's superior was always right, and thus sensitivity to criticism was particularly high. Moreover, one's 'superiors' were those who belonged to the Communist Party, or those who bore some honorary name. (In ascending order of importance, artists were conferred the titles of Honored Artist of the LSSR, Honored Art Worker of the LSSR, People's Artist of the LSSR, and ultimately People's Artist of the USSR; other orders and medals existed as well.)

We can assume – though admittedly without documentary evidence – that objective criticism was disadvantageous for artists from the periphery (as opposed to the center: Moscow), who feared that they would be refused important concerts elsewhere in the Union, or that they would not be allowed to go on concert tours abroad because of bad reviews of their activities in the local press. Therefore, music critics found it very difficult to write about performers who considered themselves right and unerring. They had either to make compromises or to write 'between the lines', since after publishing several negative reviews a critic might be 'taught a lesson' by the Composers' Union, or one's editors might simply delete one's statements if they were deemed 'not corresponding to society's opinion'. This was one of the reasons why the musicologist Rūta Naktinytė, who was among the first to write openly about what she heard and thought, quit her work as a music critic, in which she had been engaged from 1975 to 1980. Here, for example, is an excerpt from her review of the Second Festival of Chamber Orchestras in Vilnius, held in 1978, in which the real target of her invective, Saulius Sondeckus, conductor of the Lithuanian Chamber Orchestra and founding director of the festival, is not mentioned by name. The identity of her target, however, is immediately clear to all who are familiar with the surrounding context:

> The final concert of the festival has left an unpleasant aftertaste – its program could have been compiled more discreetly (the same can be said about the first festival [of 1975]). The excellent composition *Cantus* by Arvo Pärt, dedicated to the memory of [Benjamin] Britten, simply did not suit the mood of this festive evening, particularly when juxtaposed with the dance from the ballet *Eglė, žalčių karalienė (Eglė, Queen of Serpents)* by Eduardas Balsys. The joint chamber orchestras of Weimar, Azerbaijan and Lithuania presented an interesting rendition of the *Adagio* by S[amuel] Barber (conductor: Juozas Domarkas), whereas the execution of Haydn's 28th Symphony, which ended the whole event, was far from praiseworthy. This final concert further confirmed the doubts already raised by the last festival, about whether joining several good chamber orchestras into one bad symphony orchestra for the whole evening was really such a good idea. (It is only natural that musicians performing unfamiliar works will 'read' them from notes for lack of rehearsal time.) Besides, it contradicts the style and idea of a festival of chamber music. In the final concert, each orchestra could play one work that is most successful or characteristic of its artistic style. (Naktinytė 1979, p. 132)

And here is what the supervisor of Naktinytė's graduation paper, Vytautas Venckus, said at a meeting of the Composers' Union in 1979 with regard to Naktinytė's highly critical review of a concert by the pianist Birutė Vainiūnaitė:

> From the outset, Naktinytė demonstrated a unique critical style, looking at the performer's art and the interpretation of compositions from a new angle. Her precise, courageous and often categorical remarks were acclaimed by the readers and the editorial board, which rewarded her for the urgency of her articles. She is a truly interesting and promising critic, though her youthful zest sometimes allows her to forget that her articles are read not only by music lovers but also by the performers themselves, to whom – especially if they are young – forthright criticism, however valid it may be, might do harm as well as good. (Puidokienė 2001, p. 397)

The most obvious example of the personality cult or 'personification of sound politics' in Lithuania was that which surrounded the founder and conductor of the Lithuanian chamber orchestra, Saulius Sondeckis. Sondeckis became an influential figure on the Lithuanian cultural scene, favored by Moscow and thus sensitive to criticism. He tried more or less diplomatically to silence quite a few musicologists who had 'unjustly' criticized him, including Naktinytė, Rimantas Gučas, and others.

The personality cult in the world of music made it very difficult for Lithuanian music critics to express their views openly. Music criticism did exist, but it failed to perform its function. More often than not, it stated rather than assessed the facts.

Totalitarianism

Totalitarianism left its imprint on musicology through the elimination of differences in opinion. The beginnings of this phenomenon can be traced to 1948, in a report by Abelis Klenickis, Executive Secretary of the Organizational Committee of the Lithuanian Composers' Union, delivered at the First Congress of Soviet Composers of the Lithuanian SSR:

> An unheard-of thing has happened: In the same newspaper one composition received two diametrically opposed reviews – in one review Konstantinas Galkauskas' quartet was praised lavishly, and in the other it was reproved, and rather inconsiderately. True, the reviews were written by two different people, who have the right to state their opinions. But the newspaper is one and the editorial board is one, and by publishing two opposing reviews of the same work, it has disoriented the reader, particularly when we consider the fact that these reviews were not intended as fodder for discussion. When I pointed out this fact – as well as non-objectivity of other reviews – to the editors . . . they took the path of least resistance; they cancelled and liquidated the reviews, and peace was restored. (Kiauleikytė & Tumasonienė 1992, p. 88)

The obligatory expression of a single 'official opinion', regarded as the exclusive opinion of the editorial board, meant nothing else than the prohibition of *subjectivity* in critical assessment. In turn, this resulted in the emergence of non-critical texts, an avoidance of oppositional thinking, and the absence of public dialogue. At the same time, this trend also affected musicology as a branch of scholarship; the fear of voicing one's opinions impeded the formation of an authentic musicological discourse. Musicologist Jonas Bruveris recalls that at one point, a section of critics was established at the Composers' Union in an attempt to revive the tradition of expressing different opinions on a given issue, but it soon it withered away because of the small number of professional music critics active in Lithuania.[11] It was not until the restoration of independence that a plurality of opinions began to flourish. Even now, however, it manifests itself in the press only when the most significant of musical events is discussed.

The Hermetic Nature of the System

Limited contacts with foreign scholars and literatures and the limited nature of public discussion hindered the development of interdisciplinary and sociologically oriented approaches to music study, and lent Lithuanian musicology as a whole a hermetic, parochial quality. This was evident in scholars' teaching activities as well as their focus upon narrow fields of research. Moreover, inadequate methods of teaching music-historical subjects at university level (with, for example, an obligatory emphasis on Russian repertoires) prevented young musicologists from acquiring an objective understanding of historical processes. In addition, the ever-intensifying official criticism of 'bourgeois art' was rapidly erasing from society's memory not only the musical history of pre-war Lithuania but also the post-war legacy of Lithuanians in exile. Such topics as the music culture of the Grand Duchy of Lithuania, liturgical music, and the legacy of Lithuanians in exile found their place in Lithuanian musicology only after the restoration of independence.

For these reasons, it was very difficult for Lithuanian musicology to retain a truly scholarly orientation. Instead, it acquired a descriptive character, relating rather than analyzing, narrating rather than assessing and presenting rather than criticizing. Indeed, the spread of such unscholarly tendencies was noticed by Jadvyga Čiurlionytė as early as 1956: 'I would like to mention some methods of work, particularly typical of young musicologists. They often stick to description and are not able to generalize, to bring out key ideas and reveal the essence of their objects of research' (Čiurlionytė 1956).

The Period of Breakthrough

Strange as it may seem, the major breakthrough in Lithuanian musical life took place around 1970, rather than after the restoration of independence in 1990 as one might expect. Several composers who had previously dissociated themselves from the mainstream (Bronius Kutavičius, Feliksas Bajoras and Osvaldas Balakauskas) began to form an alternative trend in Lithuanian music, which soon came to be realized as a new (or true, versus conditioned by the regime) identity of Lithuanian music.

Balakauskas devised and used in his works a new compositional technique, a kind of dodecaphony that he called 'dodecatonics'. Kutavičius and Bajoras, in turn, worked in line with the break with the tonal tradition that originated with Claude Debussy and Manuel de Falla at the beginning of the century, which sought to reinterpret various pre-tonal and geographically 'exotic' idioms within the context of local tradition. The return to modal thinking and combination of tonal, pre-tonal and atonal elements in their work signaled a paradigmatic shift in Lithuanian music. Modernist trends that were able to develop only briefly during the inter-war period (in Vytautas Bacevičius' work, for instance, which he continued in America after the Second World War), finally caught the train of Western post-modern developments. Kutavičius' new minimalist approaches, which drew upon aspects of the archaic polyphonic genre of Lithuanian folk music called *sutartinės*, resonated quite unexpectedly with the repetitive music of Philip Glass, Steve Reich and Terry Riley in America. And the new concept of tonality, conventional narrative forms, and consonance typical of what Juozas Antanavičius has called the Lithuanian 'generation of neo-romanticists' of the 1980s – Vidmantas Bartulis, Mindaugas Urbaitis, Algirdas Martinaitis, Onutė Narbutaitė – had affinities with a variety of contemporaneous musical trends in America, Britain and Germany (Antanavičius 1982).

Soon, Kutavičius became an emblematic figure in Lithuanian music. Having turned to the past for musical inspiration (to themes evoking the pagan period of Lithuania's history in his *Panteistinė oratorija* [*Pantheistic Oratorio* 1970], *Paskutinės pagonių apeigos* [*The Last Pagan Rites* 1978], *Iš Jotvingių akmens* [*From the Jatvingian Stone* 1983], *Pasaulio medis* [*The Tree of the World* 1986], *Magiškas sanskrito ratas* [*The Magic Circle of Sanskrit* 1990], etc.), he was considered a herald of the Lithuanian musical revival and of national consciousness more generally – a decade before the founding of the *Sąjūdis* national revival movement. Indeed, Kutavičius' music quickly took root in the modern social discourse in a remarkable way: presented to listeners as a continuation of tradition, it not only became widely popular but also came to be regarded as standing in opposition to the Soviet occupation. And Soviet authorities could not disregard this situation. When the Composers' Union nominated the composer in 1982 for the title of Honored Worker of Culture and Art of the Lithuanian SSR, the honor was conferred upon him – despite the fact that Kutavičius had not composed a single ideological work though insistently urged to do so. In the composer's opinion, he was conferred this award because compromised composers with much weaker work already bore various titles, and if he had not received it after having become one of the most famous Lithuanian composers, the name itself would have lost its meaning in the public's view.[12]

In turn, the heterogeneous tendencies of Kutavičius and other post-modern composers encouraged musicologists to expand the purview of their own research. Some began to experiment with sociological, psychological, acoustic, philosophical and semiotic approaches to research, and to forge new vocabularies and modes of argumentation. Indeed, musicologists played a leading role in this breakthrough in Lithuanian music that occurred during this period. The great majority of musicologists immediately showed critical support for composers who had dissociated themselves from Soviet ideology. This is how Vytautas Landsbergis described the situation in his memoirs:

A large group of our composers . . . was growing more and more independent of the notion of 'Soviet music'. Dissociation was taking place among composers. Some of them were not able to create for themselves strong and original artistic personalities: They adapted to state commissions, to producing compositions for song festivals, official concerts, and other kinds of music on demand, which was always bought by the Ministry of Culture. . . . More talented artists composed distinct works, often large-scale, for which they had to be remunerated more generously according to the established rates. In this way the common money pot was always decreasing, and the influence of the talented ones was growing. Indeed, they seized upon possibilities of representing Lithuanian music outside of Lithuania.

For these reasons modern music was a cause of indignation for some. Scandals would flare up, when some higher official of the Communist Party would come to a concert of contemporary Lithuanian music and not understand anything at all. We used to take precautions to avoid this kind of thing. When festivals or performances of works on the occasion of a congress of the Composers' Union were to be held, we would invite the party leaders to a concert of choral music, in which a cantata about the party or something of the sort would be included. Usually we did not invite them to concerts of symphonic music, as we knew that they would not like and understand it, and would only become irritated.

Thus, the leaders naturally reacted against our modern music. They would become indignant at the fact that some critics and musicologists praised it, when 'the people' did not understand it. Other composers – friends of the leaders – used this to their advantage; they composed more banal music and asserted that their music was good and necessary, because people understood it.

They provided themselves with their own critics and writers of articles, who would 'prove' the good qualities of more primitive musics even on a scholarly basis . . . There was public talk that 'all' composers, rather than 'select' talented modernists, should be praised. . . . Certain pressures were applied. Articles were rejected by the press, or parts of them would be crossed out so that the authors themselves would refuse to publish them. For our part, we had to fight against articles making rude and stupid assaults on composers who composed good and meaningful contemporary music. (Landsbergis 1997, pp. 98–9)

It was, in the end, musicologists who finally suppressed this official tendency, as the great majority simply stopped towing the official line. However, this was not an easy transition. In the words of the musicologist Rūta Gaidamavičiūtė, 'As soon as critics took an interest in [post-modernist] composers, the editors would place restrictions on the publishing of articles dedicated to the work of Bajoras, Balakauskas, and Kutavičius, and even mentioning these names more than twice in a review was deemed undesirable' (Gaidamavičiutė 2005, p. 15). Nonetheless, a shift of values had begun to take place in the field of musicology, whose first sign was a wave of public discussions of problems related to new musical languages. These discussions played an important role in dissociating the discourse from Soviet ideology, as essential notions of musical form, content, ideas, perception, assessment, and so forth, which had been imposed upon Lithuanian musicology by Soviet officialdom, were revised.

In Lieu of Conclusions

During the Soviet period, Lithuanian musicology had to operate under conditions that did not allow it to become a branch of collective scholarship. There was not a single center of scholarly research, and not a single publication specializing in academic musicology. For these reasons, Lithuanian musicology was forced to develop according to an individualistic model: one author, one theme. Thus marginalized within both the academy and society as a whole, musicologists found it difficult to grasp the breadth and potential of the field as a whole. And while the musicological discourse has been greatly enriched by the creative developments of the 1970s, 1980s and 1990s, many institutional problems persist. In the words of Rūta Goštautienė, 'the weak network of scholarly institutions does not create sufficient possibilities for employment for young specialists, and thus many young musicologists opt for teaching work . . . or a career in cultural institutions' (Goštautienė 2004, p. 191). Along these lines, it should be noted that musicology remains one of the most poorly paid fields of academic study in Lithuania.

As it happened, the restoration of independence did not mark a radical shift in either Lithuanian music or musicology. Rather, the restoration of independence should be regarded as providing a newly opened space in which to work, and in which new priorities had to be found. As the state ceased dictating topics of musicological study, musicologists ceased thinking about whether to adopt an oppositional stance or to attempt to fill quietly the topical gaps overlooked by the system. Instead, they were compelled to adopt a more purely scientific perspective with regard to musical realities, to find new topics of interest, to take part in international projects, and to cultivate links with foreign scholars. This transition, productive and still ongoing, is probably the greatest challenge posed to Lithuanian musicology since the beginning of its existence, and its success will depend not only upon the energy of individual musicologists but upon the state's policy with regard to humanistic research as well.

Despite the increasing attention paid to cultural issues (Rūta Goštautienė, Rūta Gaidamavičiūtė, Vita Gruodytė), questions of aesthetics and interpretation (Jonas Bruveris, Donatas Katkus, Lina Navickaitė), psychology (Vida Umbrasienė) and semiotics (Inga Jasinskaitė-Jankauskienė, Goštautienė, Lina Navickaitė, Gruodytė), it should be said that 'sub-products', to use Joseph Kerman's term (structuralism, post-structuralism, anthropology, feminism, hermeneutics, criticism of ideologies, gender studies) – that is, 'new musicology' – has only made fragmentary inroads into the Lithuanian musicological discourse (cited in Bent 2004, p. 625). Although such approaches to musicological work might be of significant interest and use for the lay public, in recent years musicologists have been occupied almost entirely with large-scale, fundamental works that could not be undertaken during the Soviet period. These include *Muzikos enciklopedija* (*Encyclopedia of Music*, Ambrazas 2000–2003); a revised *Lietuvos muzikos istorija* (*History of Lithuanian Music*, 2002); a study guide for schools of higher education, *Muzikos kalba* (*The Language of Music*, Palionytė-Banevičienė and Daunoravičienė 2003, 2006); the *Sisteminis norminamasis muzikos terminų žodynas* (*Systematic, Prescriptive Dictionary of Musical Terms*, Gustaite *et al.* 2006); and a history of the Lithuanian Opera and Ballet Theater by Jonas Bruveris (2006).

Let us hope that the first manifestations of interdisciplinarity in Lithuanian musicology, as well as the abundance of international scholarly conferences and the beginnings of cooperative, international scholarly projects, will help bring to a close the present era of 'laying the foundations' for Lithuanian music study. May we also hope that these activities and phenomena will encourage a paradigmatic breakthrough, enabling more radical changes and greater freedom in formulating new approaches to research, the development of new methodological tools, and the formation of new musicological languages.

Acknowledgements

The author is very grateful to musicologists A. Ambrazas, J. Bruveris and R. Goštautienė for their valuable comments on this article; and to musicologists V. Landsbergis, R. Naktinytė, V. Gerulaitis and J. Antanavičius, and composers A. Martinaitis and B. Kutavičius, for sharing their reminiscences. Thanks also to Aušra Simanavičiūtė for translating from the Lithuanian, with support from the Musicological Section of the Lithuanian Composers' Union and the Lithuanian Music Information and Publishing Centre (www.mic.lt).

Notes

1   The Lithuanian State Conservatory was founded in 1949 by joining the Kaunas Conservatory (established in 1933) and the Vilnius Conservatory (established in 1944). In 1992 it was renamed the Lithuanian Academy of Music; in 2004 it became the Lithuanian Academy of Music and Theatre. The original faculty of the Lithuanian State Conservatory included the composers Antanas Račiūnas, Jonas Bendorius, Konstantinas Galkauskas, Jonas Nabažas, Zigmas Aleksandravičius, and Povilas Tamuliūnas, and the musicologists Juozas Gaudrimas, Jadvyga Čiurlionytė and Konstantin Tchernetsov.

2   Only a single book-length musicological study was published during the inter-war years, Juozas Strolia's *Trumpa muzikos istorija* (*A Short History of Music* 1936).

3   In 1945, the Union's composers were Jadvyga Čiurlionytė and Zinaida Feoktisova-Kumpienė. Juozas Gaudrimas was admitted in 1954. These three were joined by Stasys Yla, Vytautas Karpavičius, Vytautas Venckus and Julius Špigelglazas in 1960.

4   It was not until 1955, the 80th anniversary of Čiurlionis' birth, that musicologists were permitted to mention his name in their work. The composer Julius Juzeliūnas and the musicologists Juozas Gaudrimas and Jadvyga Čiurlionytė were the first to write about him (Gaudrimas in the Lithuanian press, Čiurlionytė in the Russian press).

5   The discussions are documented in the secret 'Report of the Minister of State Security of the LSSR, Pyotr Kapralov, on Statements Made by Lithuanian Intellectuals Regarding the Destruction of the Nation's Spiritual Life' (1950; in Bagušauskas & Streikus 2005, pp. 136–45; the passages cited are taken from this source).

6   For this work, Ambrazas and Venckus received the State Award in 1979.

7   Work on an earlier monograph on Juozas Naujalis by Narbutienė was halted around 1960 by the Ministry of Education, which apparently disapproved of the Narbutienė's treatment of Naujalis' activities as an organist. It was not until 1989 that this study was published (Narbutienė 1989).

8   From 1958 onward, control over printed material in Lithuanian received by mail from abroad was entrusted to the Glavlit of the Lithuanian SSR. In 1961 a list of institutions that could use confiscated material with 'anti-Soviet contents' was compiled (see Bagušauskas & Streikus 2005, pp. 266, 286).

9   In a meeting of this circle held in 1963, Landsbergis was reputed to have been 'talking about contemporary trends of modernist music in the West, illustrating his speech with tape recordings; excerpts from dodecaphonic music were performed' (quotation from a KGB report of 1965, in Bagušauskas & Streikus 2005, p. 343).

10   In this book, Landsbergis referred to the composer's archive, which had been brought from St. Petersburg to Kaunas, where it was secretly held after the Revolution. (In 1967, Landsbergis had published an article based upon some of this material in *Muzika ir teatras*.) When publication of the book was stopped, the author divided its contents into three parts and published the first – a Sasnauskas bibliography – as a teaching aid for schools in 1978. In 1980 the publishing house, having failed to find a way to justify the advance paid for the book, was compelled to publish the biographical part as well; in this matter, Landsbergis was also helped by intercession from the head of the Culture Department of the Central

Committee. (Some 'ideologically unacceptable' facts were removed from the biography, and the image of a cross that appeared in a photograph of a prayer book owned by the composer's mother was retouched.) The third part of Landsbergis' book, including the composer's own writings, was not published until 2002 (Landsbergis 1967, 1978, 1980, 2002).

11   Bruveris, interview with the author, April 2006, Vilnius.
12   Kutavičius, interview with the author, April 2006, Vilnius.

References

Ambrazas, A. (1960) *Kompozitorius Juozas Gruodis* (Kaunas, Pedagoginės literatūros leidykla).

Ambrazas, A. (1969) *Muzika ir dabartis* (Vilnius, Vaga).

Ambrazas, A. (1981) *Juozas Gruodis* (Vilnius, Vaga).

Ambrazas, A. (ed.) (2000–2003) *Muzikos enciklopedija*, Vols 2 (Vilnius, Lietuvos muzikos akademija, Mokslo ir enciklopedijų leidybos institutas).

Ambrazas, A., Venckus, A., *et al.* (1977) *Muzikos kūrinių analizės pagrindai* (Vilnius, Vaga).

Antanavičius, J. (1982) 'Pastarųjų metų lietuvių tarybinės muzikos stilistiniai poslinkiai', *Muzika*, 3, pp. 5–9.

Antanavičius, J. (1988) 'Kad liepsnotų kūrybos žaizdras', *Muzika*, 8 7.

Bagušauskas, J. R. & Streikus, A. (eds) (2005) *Lietuvos kultūra sovietinės ideologijos nelaisvėje 1940–1990 (dokumentų rinkinys)* (Vilnius, Lietuvos gyventojų genocido ir rezistencijos tyrimų centras).

Bent, M. (2004) 'Le métier de musicologie', in Nattiez, J.-J. (ed.) (2004) *Musiques. Une encyclopédie pour le XXIe siècle*, Vol. 2 (Paris, Actes Sud/Cité de la musique).

Bruveris, J. (2006) *Lietuvos nacionalinis operos ir baleto teatras* (Vilnius, Mokslo ir enciklopedijų leidybos institutas).

Čiurlionytė, J. (1955) *Lietuvių liaudies dainos* (Vilnius, Valstybinė grožinės literatūros leidykla).

Čiurlionytė, J. (1956) 'Mintys apie mūsų darbus', *Literatūra ir menas*, 18 February, pp. 28–30.

Daunoravičienė, G. (ed.) (2003) *Muzikos kalba*, Vol. 1, *Viduramžiai, Renesansas* (Vilnius, Lietuvos Mokslų akademijos leidykla).

Daunoravičienė, G. (ed.) (2006) *Muzikos kalba*, Vol. 2, *Barokas* (Vilnius, Leidykla Enciklopedija).

Gaidamavičiūtė, R. (2005) *Nauji lietuvių muzikos keliai* (Vilnius, Lithuanian Academy of Music and Theatre).

Gaudrimas, J. (1958–1967) *Iš lietuvių muzikinės kultūros istorijos*, (Vilnius, Mintis), Vol. 3.

Gaudrimas, J. (1985) *Muzikologijos baruose* (Vilnius, Vaga).

Goštautienė, R. (2004) 'Muzikologija', in *Lietuvos humanitarinių ir socialinių mokslų plėtros problemos* (Vilnius, LII).

Gustaite, J., Ambrazas, A., Kalinauskas, A., Mikuleviciute, I., Nomicaite, R. & Vitkauskas, V. (2006) *Sisteminis norminamasis muzikos terminų žodynas* (Vilnius, Lithuanian Academy of Music and Theatre).

Humal, M. (2001) 'Thirty Conferences of Baltic Musicologists: Some Recollections and Results' in *Music of the Twentieth Century within the Horizons of Musicology* (Vilnius, Lithuanian Composers' Union).

Jasinskas, K. (1982a) *Latvijos ir Estijos TSR muzikė kultūra* (Vilnius, Lietuvos TSR aukštojo ir specialiojo vidurinio mokslo ministerijos Leidybinė redakcinė taryba).

Jasinskas, K. (1982b) *TSRS tautų muzikinė kultūra* (Vilnius, Lietuvos TSR aukštojo ir specialiojo vidurinio mokslo ministerijos Leidybinė redakcinė taryba).

Jurkštas, V. (1966) 'Senieji lietuvių muzikai', *Kultūros barai*, 6, pp. 51–3.

Juška, A. (1954) *Lietuviškos dainos*, 3 Vols, Jadvyga Čiurlionytė (ed.) (Vilnius, Valstybinė grožinės literatūros leidykla).

Kiauleikytė, L. & Tumasonienė, L. (eds) (1992) *Muzika 1940–1960 (dokumentų rinkinys)* (Vilnius, Alka).

Landsbergis, V. (1965) 'Šis tas apie aleatorinę ir regimają muziką', *Kultūros barai*, 1, 2, pp. 38–9, 35–7.

Landsbergis, V. (1967) 'Česlovo Sasnausko gyvenimo ir veiklos bruožai', *Muzika ir teatras*, 4, pp. 91–9.

Landsbergis, V. (1978) *Česlovas Sasnauskas. Bibliografija* (Vilnius, Aukštojo ir spec. vid. moklso ministerija).

Landsbergis, V. (1980) *Česlovo Sasnausko gyvenimas ir darbai* (Vilnius, Vaga).

Landsbergis, V. (1997) *Lūžis prie Baltijos (politinė autobiografija)* (Vilnius, Vaga).

Landsbergis, V. (ed.) (2002) *Česlovas Sasnauskas. Tekstai: gyvenimas ir kūryba* (Vilnius, Katalikų akademija).

Naktinytė, R. (1979) 'Antrasis kamerinių orkestrų festivalis', *Muzika*, 1, pp. 130–2.

Narbutienė, O. (1968a) *Juozas Naujalis* (Vilnius, Vaga).

Narbutienė, O. (ed.) (1968b) *Juozas Naujalis. Straipsniai. Laiškai. Dokumentai. Amžininkų atsiminimai. Straipsniai apie kūrybą* (Vilnius, Vaga).

Narbutienė, O. (1969) *Antanas Kučingis* (Vilnius, Valstybinis leidybos centras).

Narbutienė, O. (1989) *Juozas Naujalis* (Kaunas, Šviesa).

Palionytė, D. (1967) *Stasys Šimkus* (Vilnius, Vaga).

Palionytė-Banevičienė, D. (ed.) (2002) *Lietuvos muzikos istorija*, Vol. 1, *Tautinio atgimimo metai 1883–1918* (Vilnius, Kultūros, filosofijos ir meno institutas, Lietuvos muzikos akademija).

Puidokienė, S. (ed.) (2001) *Vytautas Venckus* (Vilnius, Tyto alba).

Tauragis, A. (1965) *Benjamin Britten* (Leningrad, Muzyka).

Tauragis, A. (1971) *Lithuanian Music: Past and Present* (Vilnius, Gintaras).

Tauragis, A. (1972) *Litauische Musik: gestern und heute* (Vilnius, Gintaras).

Tauragis, A. (ed.) (1982) *Rusų muzikos literatūra*, Vol. 2 (Kaunas, Šviesa).

Venckus, A. (1968) 'J. Naujalio mišios, giesmės, motetai ir kantatos', in Narbutienė, O. (ed.) (1968b).

SOVIET MUSICOLOGY AND THE 'NATIONALITIES QUESTION': THE CASE OF LATVIA

Kevin C. Karnes

With its annexation by the Soviet Union in the spring of 1940, Latvia became the latest testing ground for the array of cultural and political policies by which Soviet authorities had long sought to negotiate the Union's persistently troublesome 'nationalities question' (*natsional'nyi vopros*). At the heart of the matter was a problem familiar to Soviet officials from their knowledge and experience of Russia's old regime: how to maintain political control over a multinational empire during a period famously described by Eric Hobsbawm as the 'apogee' of European nationalism (Hobsbawm 1992, p. 131). Having gained independence from imperial Russia in the wake of the Revolution of 1917, Latvia was reabsorbed, during World War II, into a new multinational empire. And as was the case in much of the rest of the former imperial territory, the problems of control that had dogged Romanov officialdom for centuries in the non-Russian provinces newly confronted the Bolshevik inheritors of the Latvian lands.

In the months immediately following Latvia's annexation to the USSR, the republic's new leaders sought to quell local resistance with a show of force (Misiunas & Taagepera 1993; Plakans 1995). But they understood that future unrest would never be averted if they did not also win over Latvian hearts and minds. To this end, they embarked upon an ambitious cultural program that Stalin, as Lenin's Commisar of Nationalities, had broadly described as 'nativization' (*korenizatsiya*) in the immediate post-Revolutionary years. By deliberately imbedding Soviet symbols and ideology within the cultural artifacts and rituals of the Union's minority peoples, Stalin argued, those peoples would be encouraged to regard the present Sovietization of their societies not as a foreign (Russian) imposition, but as a reflection of autochthonous traditions and values. The goal, as Stalin wrote in 1934, was to help the residents of minority republics recognize that 'Soviet power and its organs are the affair of their own efforts, the embodiment of their desires' (cited in Martin 2001, p. 12). The means by which this nativization program was pursued in Latvia were diverse and largely beyond the scope of this article (see Misiunas & Taagepera 1993; more generally, Martin 2001, pp. 9–15; Suny 1993, pp. 102–6). But in a republic where popular notions of cultural identity were so entwined with images of its musical heritage that many Latvians had taken to identifying their community as a 'Nation of Singers' (*dziedātājtauta*) nearly a century before (Bula 1996, 2000; Karnes 2005), it comes as no surprise that musicology figured prominently in the Soviet nativization campaign. This is the subject of the present essay.

In the pages that follow, I will attempt three things. First, I will analyze the imposition of Soviet authority upon Latvia's musicological discourse in the immediate post-war years, as evidenced in the popular and academic press of the period. In doing so, I will argue that the Stalinist policy of nativization provided a principal ideological foundation – one not acknowledged previously – for the discipline's Soviet-era refashioning.[1] Second, I will examine the impact of two pivotal events in Soviet cultural life upon the subsequent development of Latvia's learned discourse on music: the scandalous premiere of Vano Muradeli's opera *The Great Friendship* (*Velikaya druzhba*) in 1948, and the Twentieth Party Congress of 1956. Considering closely the academic discourse on the life and work of the Latvian composer Jāzeps Vītols (1863–1948) in light of these events, I will argue that Stalin-era prescriptions for scholarly work continued to shape the Latvian musicological discourse for decades after Stalin's death and the attendant political 'Thaw'. Third, I will examine briefly the musicological literature on Vītols published since 1991, in an attempt to assess the degree to which Latvian musicology has moved beyond the boundaries of Soviet-era academic discourse in the decades since the collapse of Soviet rule. I will conclude by suggesting that significant continuities persist alongside meaningful departures, and that the intellectual legacy of the Soviet era has, in the case of Latvian musicology, proven doggedly difficult to transcend.

Nationalities Policy and the Soviet Musicological Program

At the heart of Soviet thinking about the phenomena of nation and nationalism lay the Marxist-inspired conviction that neither is perennial or reflective of innate qualities of the human psyche. Rather, Soviet intellectuals regarded both as bourgeois phenomena, products of the urge toward cultural and individual particularism peculiar to capitalist societies (Smith 1990a; Suny 1993, 1998; Smith 1999; Martin 2001; Suny & Martin 2001). As Stalin argued as early as 1918, the explosion of nationalist rhetoric that accompanied the Revolution in many non-Russian parts of the Romanov Empire was little more than a smokescreen, fomented by counter-Revolutionary elements seeking to hide from working peoples the fact that their true enemies were not their fellow workers in neighboring republics (especially the Russians) but the scions and institutions of capitalist society. In Stalin's view, the potentially destabilizing power of nationalist sentiment and rhetoric would eventually dissipate on its own, as the working peoples of all nations came to recognize their deceptive purpose and banded together in struggle against their common, bourgeois enemies. At that point, Stalin predicted, the 'merging' (*sliyanie*) of the proletariat of all socialist nations would occur.

Significantly, however, the merging of the Union's peoples that Stalin foresaw was not something for which he felt one must idly wait. Rather, he argued that their 'drawing together' (*sblizhenie*) be encouraged by aggressively promoting the cultural heritage of each as 'national in form and socialist in content' (cited in Frolova-Walker 1998, p. 331). By demonstrating overt respect for – and even encouraging – the celebration of local traditions and modes of creative expression, Stalin reasoned, the culturally particularist ambitions of the Empire's constituent peoples might be channeled in such a way that their sympathies toward the Bolsheviks' ostensibly anti-imperialist cause could be won. At the same time, invoking in cultural artifact and ritual images and ideas that resonated with the shared experiences of working peoples throughout the Union would enable those peoples to recognize their common interests and values, to overlook their cultural differences, and to unite together in struggle to build a supranational socialist society. Taken together, these endeavors constituted an ambitious attempt to implant the political and cultural values of the new regime within the national consciousness of the Union's minority groups. In Stalin's terms, those Soviet values would, in these ways, be 'nativized'.[2]

In recent years, thanks to the work of Frolova-Walker, Maes, Taruskin and others, we have begun to understand the ways in which Soviet composers worked to encourage the 'drawing together' of the Union's peoples through musical means (Taruskin 1997; Frolova-Walker 1998; Maes 2002). From the Central Asian Republics to the Caucasus and the Baltic, composers were alternately encouraged and compelled to produce works whose musical language hinted at traditional and local custom, but whose texts and musical imagery reflected upon the shared experiences of the Soviet peoples: Stalin's Five-Year Plans, collectivization, capitalist oppression and so forth. Even in those republics annexed to the Union as late as the Second World War, attempts to 'internationalize' the 'content' of their musics were hastily undertaken. The goal, in the words of Stalin's deputy Vyacheslav Molotov, was 'to initiate' them, as quickly as possible, 'into the Soviet system' (cited in Misiunas & Taagepera 1993, pp. 25–6).

Less than two months after Soviet tanks entered Riga in June 1940, an editorial ran in the newly founded daily *Brīvais zemnieks* (*The Free Peasant*) explaining the need for operatic reform. 'Henceforth', its anonymous author declared, 'the task of the theater will be to cultivate a dramatic art and to build a culture that is national in form but socialist in content' ('Teātri un opera' 1940, p. 7). When their hold upon the territory was solidified at the end of the war, Soviet authorities called upon the Georgian composer Aram Khachaturian to elaborate on this point – to explain to his Latvian colleagues that their music must be 'internationalized' if the Latvian people were ever to be brought into cultural communion with other the Soviet peoples. Khachaturian, who had earlier played an integral role in engineering the Sovietization of musical life in the Caucasus and Central Asia (Frolova-Walker 1998), declared the following in a lecture to the newly founded Union of Soviet Latvian Composers in the spring of 1946:

> The Great Russian school has demonstrated that music can be national and at the same time attain worldwide significance. And it is our good fortune that in our music there are united the national styles of the various peoples of the Soviet Union, who are dissimilar with regard to their histories but nonetheless assimilated into a unified and integral brotherhood of friends. Latvian music possesses all the elements necessary to enable it to overcome its narrow provincialism – without losing anything of its national character – and to weave itself into the fabric of the broad, Union-wide musical arena. ('Pervyi plenum' 1946, pp. 32–3)

From this point forward, 'national in form, socialist in content' would be the guiding principle for artists and musicians working in the newly annexed republic.

Alongside attempts to 'internationalize' the contemporary musical cultures of minority nations, another program, less familiar to Western scholars, was simultaneously undertaken by Soviet officials in an effort to integrate minority peoples into a spiritually united Soviet community: the refashioning of cultural history (Tillett 1969; Litvin 2001). As historians of Soviet culture have frequently observed, the writing of history in the USSR was, since the mid-1920s, an affair tightly controlled by the Communist Party (Mazour 1971; Litvin 2001; Markwick 2001). Treated as ideological 'weapons' in the struggle to build socialism, historical narratives were carefully crafted by academics and political figures in an attempt to ground Party policy and ideology within the historical consciousness of the Union's citizenry (Tillett 1969, p. 44). In Latvia and other minority republics, historians, including musicologists, were charged with refashioning local historical narratives so as to make them read like variations on canonical Soviet tellings of Russian cultural history. In this way, just as composers were instructed to infuse their 'national' works with a universal, 'socialist' spirit, so too were historians charged with elucidating the 'socialist content' posited to underlie the diverse national forms of their peoples' histories.[3]

In Latvia, the first attempts at 'truthfully reconstructing' the republic's history – as the task was described in a *Bol'shevik* editorial of 1945 (Tillett 1969, p. 90) – took place just months after the republic's annexation in the spring of 1940. As an essay published in the journal *Karogs* (*The Flag*) explained in September of that year, the Latvian people were henceforth charged with refashioning their nation's historical narratives in accordance with the guiding wisdom of Soviet society's leading intellectuals. In this article, entitled 'Work is Beginning', Žanis Spure, Second Secretary of the Latvian Communist Party, proclaimed:

> Our history awaits true scholars, poets, and writers, who will study and write about all the beautiful things, heroism, and suffering that our people have experienced in the past. . . . But this reflection cannot consist of a mere registry of facts; writers and artists must be able to provide perspective as well. The content [of their work] must be deeply principled and artistic. Its foundation and guide must be the teaching of Marx, Engels, Lenin, and Stalin. (Spure 1940, p. 4)

Another *Karogs* essay of that year elucidated the essential tenets of Soviet Socialist Realist aesthetics for Latvia's largely uninitiated intellectual community (Vipers 1940). Yet another stressed the need for writers to adhere to the principles of Marxist–Leninist historical analysis so as not to be 'left behind' (*paliktu iepakaļ*) by their colleagues working in other republics (Upīts 1940). Soon, the fruits of such efforts would be brought before the public – not only in writings on literary and political history but also, and prominently, in the form of musicological research.

'Work is Beginning': Transformation of a Discipline

Khachaturian's speech cited above was delivered at the inaugural meeting of the Unions of Soviet Latvian Composers, a local branch of the central Union established in 1932 in order to monitor and control the activities of composers and musicologists working throughout the USSR (on the latter, see Taruskin 1997, pp. 94–8; Maes 2002, pp. 254–5). Khachaturian's speech was reprinted, in its original Russian, in the central organization's monthly journal, *Sovetskaya muzyka* ('Pervyi plenum' 1946). A report on the meeting's proceedings appeared simultaneously, in Latvian, in *Literatūra un māksla* (*Literature and Art*), a collective publication of the Union of Soviet Latvian Composers, Artists, and Writers ('Atklāts' 1946). In the latter, an anonymous correspondent explained the ways in which new creative work must exhibit the 'international' qualities of which Khachaturian spoke. And he or she also suggested some principal lines of academic inquiry for music scholars in the new Soviet republic.

Henceforth, this anonymous author explained, scholars of music would be responsible, first and foremost, for cultivating their readers' appreciation for the 'deep ties' posited to exist 'between Latvian and Russian music' ('Atklāts' 1946, p. 1). Topics to be studied included the historical relatedness of Russian and Latvian musical languages, the historical indebtedness of Latvian musical culture to Russian cultural models, and evidence of broader cultural exchanges preserved in historic musical repertoires.[4] Like their colleagues working in other fields of historical inquiry, Latvian musicologists were charged, in the words of Lowell Tillett, with projecting the 'alleged friendship of Soviet peoples ... to tsarist times, even to ancient and medieval times'. They were called upon to emphasize those peoples' 'common struggle against enemies, both foreign and domestic', and to make clear that 'all peoples of the future Soviet state' had recognized the 'leadership' displayed by the Russian people throughout the preceding centuries (Tillett 1969, pp. 3–4). The goal of such historiographical endeavors, Tillett continues, was to construct an image of a 'historic commonwealth of peoples, fated by history to a common struggle which reached its victory in the October Revolution' – or, in the case of Latvia, in the republic's recent annexation to the USSR (Tillett 1969, p. 4).[5]

The first round of musicological work along these lines focused upon an obvious source: the vast corpus of Latvian folksong texts that had been collected and studied since the mid-nineteenth century as evidence of the Latvian people's historic cultural identity (Bula 1996, 2000; Vīksna 1996; Karnes 2005). In an essay of 1942 entitled 'Latvian Folksongs about German Lords, Backsliders, and Friends of the People', Jānis Niedre adduced the text of supposedly ancient Latvian folksong – without telling his readers where he found it – that appeared to attest to the sort of age-old friendship between the Latvians and other Soviet peoples for which evidence was desired:

> I gave my sister to a Russian,
> and I myself took a Lithuanian bride.
> Among the Russians, among the Lithuanians,
> everywhere I find friends and relatives.
>
> (Krievam devu sav māsiņu,/Pats apņēmu leišu meitu./Iem krievos, iem leišos,/ Visur manim draugi, radi.) (Niedre 1942, p. 162)

In another essay, the ethnographer Roberts Pelše published the text of another supposedly ancient Latvian folksong (again without specifying his source), apparently suggesting that the Latvian people had received help from the Russians in their medieval struggles against the Teutonic Knights:

> Russians, Russians, what are you waiting for?
> The Germans are invading our land!
> Sharpen your spurs, put on your boots,
> saddle up your horses!
>
> (Krievi, krievi, ko gaidāt,/Vāci nāca šai zemē!/Triniet piešus, auniet kājas,/ Seglojiet kumeliņus!) (Pelše 1947, p. 3)

Another essay from these years announced that Jēkabs Graubiņš, one of the leading Latvian musicologists of the inter-war Republican period, had recently embarked upon a search for evidence of ancient cultural ties between Latvians and Russians in the melodic structures of their traditional songs (Zālīte 1946).

This quest for musical evidence of an enduring friendship between Russians and Latvians was not limited to the study of ancient folksongs, however. As Jānis Sudrabkalns made clear in an essay of 1945, the Latvian people were also indebted to the Russians for their classical ('art' or 'professional') music-making traditions. Nearly every accomplished Latvian composer of the last half-century, Sudrabkalns reminded his readers, had been trained at the conservatories of St. Petersburg or Moscow. At those institutions, he explained, 'Russians, with all their hearts, encouraged and enabled the representatives of all other peoples to cultivate their own national traditions'. In St. Petersburg, Nikolai Rimsky-Korsakov, professor of composition and an eminent figure in Russian musical life, 'taught this to Andrejs Jurjāns and [Jāzeps] Vītols', both of whom went on to become pioneering composers of Latvian choral and symphonic music. 'Armed with the knowledge acquired at St. Petersburg and inspired to patriotic work', Sudrabkalns reported, Jurjāns and Vītols 'applied themselves with great passion' to their creative endeavors. 'From their desire to raise Latvian music up to a place of honor and light . . . and from out of traditions inspired in St. Petersburg and the most wide-ranging ideals of Russian social humanism, there arose the greatest, most enlightened, and most distinguished works that had been created in a quarter-century, which enabled one to speak truly of a distinctly Latvian tradition' (Sudrabkalns 1945, p. 1). In essays such these, we find the first statements on Latvian music and its history published in the post-war years. As we will see, such essays laid the ideological and rhetorical foundations for musicological writing in the new Soviet republic, not only in its early years but throughout the course of the half-century that followed.

An Unexpected Turn: 'The Great Friendship' and the *Zhdanovshchina*

Significantly, Latvian musicologists trained and active in the inter-war Republic hardly contributed, initially at least, to the transformation of the academic discourse that we have sketched so far. None of the authors cited above – neither Niedre, Pelše, nor Sudrabkalns – had any formal musicological training.[6] And Jēkabs Graubiņš, a trained musicologist who earnestly struggled, out of fear, to meet the Party's demands, fell out of favor before his promised study was published and was deported to Siberia in 1950 (Boiko 1994, p. 51; Bērziņa 2006, pp. 204–26; Boiko 2008). The other leading historical musicologist of Latvia's Republican period, Jēkabs Vītoliņš, was principally occupied, in the immediate post-war years, with writing and publishing critical essays on Riga's contemporary musical life (for example, Vītoliņš 1946a, 1946c). Soon, however, the musicological discourse received a powerful revivifying jolt, which encouraged not only the broader participation of trained musicologists but also a more thorough consideration of Latvia's classical musics from the pre-Soviet past. The impetus for this expansion of the discourse came from an unexpected source: the events of the so-called *Zhdanovshchina*, which was first felt within the musical sphere in February 1948.

In the prevailing present-day historiography of Soviet musical life, the period of the *Zhdanovshchina*, inaugurated by official reaction to the opera *The Great Friendship* by the Georgian composer Vano Muradeli, is depicted as an abrupt end to the relative freedom of cultural expression that had been tolerated during the war years (Taruskin 1997, pp. 489–91; Fay 2000, pp. 154–65; Maes 2002, pp. 308–17). After similarly condemning recent developments in Soviet literature (Suny 1998, pp. 369–75), Stalin's deputy Andrei Zhdanov publicly denounced the 'formalism' (traces of modernist musical languages) and 'falsification of historical facts' that he detected in Muradeli's opera (Maes 2002, p. 310). From there, Zhdanov embarked upon a scathing critique of recent works by the Union's most prominent composers, including Khachaturian, Dmitri Shostakovich, Sergei Prokofiev and Nikolai Myaskovsky. Five days after Zhdanov delivered his speech on *The Great Friendship* in Moscow, a Latvian translation of his address was published in *Literatūra un māksla* ('Par V. Muradeli operu' 1948). Mirroring what had happened a week earlier in the Moscow press, the publication of Zhdanov's speech in Riga was accompanied by denunciations of recent works by Latvia's leading composers (for example, Grīnfelds 1948; Vītoliņš 1948a). In March, Latvian musicologists were likewise implicated in the purported decline in musical standards, in an essay charging that they had failed to ground their scholarship and teachings sufficiently in Marxist–Leninist theory (Zviedris 1948; for a summary of Latvian responses to Zhdanov's speech, see Butulis 2004).

In a recent essay on twentieth-century Baltic music historiography, Urve Lippus has argued that the *Zhdanovshchina* was 'the most forceful event to establish Soviet official demands and jargon' in the region (Lippus 1999, p. 58). To be sure, one can hardly deny the truth of Lippus' assertion. But in Latvia, this same event also marked the start of something else. For in their attempts to make the stylistic retrenchment and artistic populism for which Zhdanov called compatible with the broader program of cultural 'nativization' already well underway, those charged with implementing Soviet nationalities policies in Latvia found themselves in the paradoxical position of calling upon the republic's composers to examine more carefully and internalize more completely those musics already familiar to and beloved by the Latvian populace. They called, in other words, for a more thorough study of Latvia's pre-Soviet musical heritage. Twelve days after Zhdanov launched his attack against Muradeli and others, the journal of the Latvian Composers' Union described the new artistic climate in a manner that had provocative implications for the republic's musicological community. Referring to the series of political decrees that followed Zhdanov's proclamations, the anonymous author of this essay declared:

> In the decrees of the Central Committee of the Communist Party (Bolshevik) and the corresponding decrees of the Central Committee of the Latvian Communist Party (Bolshevik), the people's demands of composers are formulated clearly and unambiguously: to create profound and ideologically saturated music, and to speak in a natural and effective musical language that the people can understand. To fulfill these demands requires that one turn to the best traditions of Russian and Western European classical music. . . . In addition, the experience of our Latvian classical masters and their connectedness to the people must also be taken as a model. The music of [Latvian composers] A. Jurjāns, E. Dārziņš, J. Vītols, A. Kalniņš, and E. Melngailis, while quite diverse stylistically, contains clear-sounding melodic and harmonic characteristics that are beloved by the entire populace. ('Mūsu lielajam laikam' 1948, p. 3)

In this way, the beginning of the *Zhdanovshchina*, recently described by one historian as marking the 'climax' of 'Great Russian chauvinism' in the post-war years (Markwick 2001, p. 40), was interpreted in the Latvian press as necessitating a closer look at the 'national forms' of the republic's own classical music-making traditions.

The first musicologist to answer this unexpected challenge posed by Zhdanov's declarations was Jēkabs Vītoliņš, who, along with Jēkabs Graubiņš, had been one of the leading musicologists trained and active in the inter-war Republic. Two years earlier, Vītoliņš had published an essay on 'Some Strands in the Development of Latvian Music', in which he had identified the composer Jāzeps Vītols (1863–1848) as the founder of a 'New Latvian National School' of composition. In that essay, Vītoliņš, like Sudrabkalns before him, had grounded his assertions of Vītols' significance solely in the fact that Vītols had studied at the St. Petersburg Conservatory and had assimilated there the 'progressive tendencies' of the 'New Russian School' of Rimsky-Korsakov and others (Vītoliņš 1946b). Four months after the publication of Zhdanov's speech in February 1948, Vītoliņš published a second essay focusing largely on Vītols. And in the latter, the substance of his discussion differed in some important respects from what he had published two years earlier. Beginning his 1948 essay by repeating many of his earlier assertions, Vītoliņš went on to elaborate a sketch of Vītols' creative life and work that was unprecedented in Soviet times for its detail. He discussed important events in the composer's biography and described a number of Vītols' compositions. He assessed the impact of Vītols' teachings upon his Latvian and Russian students, and he even discussed the composer's participation in the All-Latvian Song Festival of 1888 (Vītoliņš 1948b).

To be sure, Vītoliņš still framed his discussion within the context of a broader consideration of Vītols' 'tremendous significance as a forger of deep ties between Latvian and Russian music' (Vītoliņš 1948b, p. 5). And there was nothing in his 1948 essay that might be counted as the product of new, source-based research (none of the biographical assertions in his 1948 essay departed from those he had published during the inter-war years; cf. Vītoliņš n.d., pp. 529–49). But whereas previous Soviet-era discussions of Latvia's historic musicians and repertoires had trumpeted the latter as providing evidence of Latvia's historic indebtedness to Russian culture and its institutions exclusively, Vītoliņš' essay considered, in however limited and tentative a manner, Vītols' life and work as objects of historical interest in themselves. Its publication in the wake of the Muradeli scandal marked a watershed moment in the evolution of Latvia's musicological discourse. And significantly, Vītoliņš' new approach to writing on Latvian musical history went unchallenged in the press. Indeed, the thumbnail biographical sketch of Vītols that he published in 1948 was fleshed out with further historical details in the second volume of the official *History of the Latvian SSR*, completed in 1955. There, nearly a third of the discussion of the republic's musical heritage was dedicated to Vītols, with Vītoliņš apparently supplying the bulk of the discussion (*Latvijas PSR Vēsture* ii, 1955, p. 194).[7]

The Ambivalent Legacy of the Twentieth Party Congress

In his essay on Vītols of 1948, Jēkabs Vītoliņš pioneered an approach to musicological writing that would dominate the learned discourse on the art over the course of the four decades that followed. While the immediate post-war years had seen a concerted effort to demonstrate the 'socialist' or 'international' (in effect, Russian) 'content' of Latvian musics and musical institutions, Vītoliņš strove to balance that emphasis with a careful look at the 'national forms' of those musics themselves. Further impetus for historical explorations along these lines came in the months that followed Nikita Khrushchev's famous denunciation of the Stalin personality cult at the Twentieth Party Congress in the winter of 1956. In an article entitled 'The Problem of National Form in Music', the young musicologist Oļģerts Grāvītis, recently appointed to the faculty of the Latvian Conservatory, challenged his colleagues to examine more closely the events, figures, and repertoires that had shaped their republic's pre-Soviet musical history. Citing a cardinal tenet of Soviet Socialist Realist aesthetics reiterated in Zhdanov's 1948 decrees, Grāvītis declared that 'one of the most significant things that makes a work "of the people" – that is, its dearness to the masses, its comprehensibility, and its deep rootedness in their broad strata – is the national form that contains the ideologically rich content' (Grāvītis 1956a, p. 3).

Four months later, Grāvītis published a remarkable follow-up essay, in which he proclaimed and endeavored to exemplify a new *modus operandi* for his Latvian colleagues. In this article, entitled 'Musicologists Must Step into the Avant Garde',

Grāvītis framed his discussion of methodological issues around a discussion of the cantata *Tēvijai* (*To the Fatherland*, 1886) by the Latvian composer Andrejs Jurjāns (1856–1922). With respect to cultural policy in the Latvian SSR, Jurjāns' cantata made for a particularly problematic discussion for two reasons. First, the central portion of the cantata's text is overtly religious, taking the form of a prayer to God for the material and spiritual renewal of the Latvian nation. And second, the work, like its composer, had long ago become emblematic of the so-called 'national awakening' (*tautas atmoda*) of the 1850s through the 1870s, which was widely associated in the popular imagination with the birth of the modern Latvian nationalist movement.

Grāvītis began his consideration of Jurjāns' cantata with what sounded, at first, like a commonplace call for a more thoughtful elucidation of musical works according to the tenets of Socialist Realist aesthetics. But when he turned his attention to the music and text of *Tēvijai* itself, his provocative ideological agenda immediately became clear. Tackling first the work's religious imagery, he wrote:

> Here one must note that religion does not always erupt wherever the word 'God' is mentioned. It is true that in the middle portion of the cantata the soloist intones a prayer to God, but with respect to the musical character this prayer reaches far beyond the bounds of the church. It is the deeply human, deeply heartfelt longing of the simple working man for better times, for freedom. Indeed, if an orphan can sing 'Go, sun, to God' (*Ej, saulīte, drīz pie dieva*) in a folksong, then why can't 'My God, I pray to you' be sung in Jurjāns' cantata? (Grāvītis 1956b, p. 3)

After this, Grāvītis turned to the thorniest problem posed by Jurjāns and his work: their status in the popular imagination as representatives of so-called 'bourgeois' Latvian nationalism. He wrote:

> We have good reason to denounce Jurjāns for remaining caught up in the ideals of the period of national awakening while all around him life was rumbling with the stormy waves of revolution. But we have no right whatsoever to disparage a distinguished figure of Latvian music because he did not know how to think like a Marxist. The musical heritage of the past must be accepted as it was. If reactionary tendencies are readily apparent in it, then we are obligated to unmask them unflinchingly. If we see contradictions in it, we must clarify them. But to be satisfied with simply declaring 'this is acceptable' or 'this is unacceptable' is to misunderstand the past, to fail to comprehend what is greatest and most instructive in it. (Grāvītis 1956b, p. 3)

With these lines, Grāvītis came close to turning the means of Stalin's nativization campaign against its own desired ends. In his discussion, the search for a 'socialist content' underlying the 'national forms' of Latvian music became little more than a pretext for studying those national forms themselves. Indeed, Grāvītis even seemed to suggest that the presence or absence of socialist content must not be taken as a primary criterion for the critical evaluation of a work. In effect, musicological inquiry became, for the musicologist, an exercise in which the logic and rhetoric of Marxist–Leninist cultural criticism were harnessed for the purpose of advancing knowledge of and appreciation for the republic's pre-Soviet musical past.

With respect to both methodology and political subtext, Grāvītis' essays of 1956 were emblematic of the wave of optimism that passed among Soviet scholars in the wake of the Twentieth Party Congress, of which many historians have written previously (Litvin 2001, pp. 21–2; Markwick 2001, pp. 47–9). Indeed, Grāvītis' articles inspired a flurry of essays by his Latvian colleagues eager to follow his lead. One, writing on 'The Problem of Cultural Inheritance and Latvian Choral Music', reminded her readers of Lenin's conviction that a socialist future must be founded upon the feudal and capitalist past. For this reason, she wrote, 'We must be mindful of the fact that classical works must be evaluated historically. To attempt to subject past masters to the same demands that we impose upon our Soviet artists is to approach one's work from an improper perspective' (Albiņa 1956, p. 3). Another scholar sought to rehabilitate – as Grāvītis had done with Jurjāns – another maligned and problematic composer from the period of Latvia's national awakening, Jānis Cimze (Bērziņa 1956). Such optimism about the future course of musicological research reached its peak toward the end of the decade. The year 1958 saw the launch of *Latviešu mūzika* (*Latvian Music*), the first post-war forum for the publication of original musicological research in the Soviet republic. And the following year brought yet another hopeful development: the publication of the final installment of the *History of the Latvian SSR*, which included the first substantial post-war discussion of musical life in the inter-war Republic (*Latvijas PSR Vēsture* iii, 1959, pp. 365–7; cf. Vītoliņš & Grīnfelds 1954, pp. 26–7).

Yet as Aleksandrs Ivanovs has recently argued with respect to Soviet historiography of Latvia's wartime annexation, the Khrushchev 'Thaw', viewed in hindsight, seems not to have marked the birth of an age of radical change in historical scholarship so much as the beginning of a new period of stability and even, ultimately, stagnation. Following a brief period of liberalization in the late 1950s, Ivanovs observes, the principal components of most narratives of Latvia's history became essentially fixed. Thereafter, scholars worked not to revise or to challenge those narratives but to 'fill them in' (*papildināt*) with documentary evidence (Ivanovs 2003a, p. 78), to 'fashion them into an academic guise' (*zinātniski noformēt*) (Ivanovs 2004, p. 393).[8] Indeed, as we have already seen with respect to the musicological literature, even Grāvītis' essay on Jurjāns' cantata only elaborated upon an approach to historical inquiry pioneered by Jēkabs Vītoliņš in 1948. And while a new era in music scholarship seemed to be signaled by the launch of *Latviešu mūzika*, the limits of musicologists' new-found freedoms were made clear in that journal's inaugural essay. There, Nilss Grīnfelds, Conservatory professor and founding Secretary of the Latvian Composers' Union, called for intensive research into Latvia's pre-Soviet past, and even into musical developments of the 'bourgeois' Republican period. But Grīnfelds also made clear to his colleagues that they must never lose sight of the political goals of their historical inquiries. 'Historical truth and an understanding of the decisive power of a period's social structures are helping our present-day working people to understand the musical works of Jāzeps Vītols', Grīnfelds wrote, reminding his readers of their duty to adhere to tenets of Marxist–Leninist historical analysis, and of their responsibility to undertake their work in the service of the Party and its propaganda efforts. The musicologist, Grīnfelds continued, must never lose sight of the essential fact that Vītols' compositions 'are tied to the people's healthy and optimistic view of the world, and to the serene founts of the people's art' (Grīnfelds 1958, p. 8). Three years later, Grīnfelds fomented a scandal that cost Jēkabs Vītoliņš his professorship at the Latvian Conservatory after the latter had failed to vet his publications carefully enough for ideological 'errors' (Braun 2002, pp. 327–9; Boiko 2008). In doing so, Grīnfelds left little doubt about the consequences of transgressing the ideological boundaries of acceptable musicological research.

Barometer of a Discourse: The Case of Jāzeps Vītols

From the mid-1950s until the collapse of Soviet authority in 1991, the literature produced by Latvian musicologists was marked by what Roger Markwick has characterized more generally as 'constant tension between what was historiographi-cally possible and what was politically permissible' (Markwick 2001, p. 49). If Grāvītis' essays of 1956 sought to codify a new paradigm of musicological research and writing in the post-Stalin years, then Grīnfelds' preface to *Latviešu mūzika* and his subsequent administrative actions against Vītoliņš made clear that scholars' new-found freedoms still had limits that could not be breached. And the post-Thaw Latvian musicological discourse was marked by ambivalence of another kind as well. On the one hand, the increasing accessibility of primary source materials fostered a highly productive academic culture with respect to archival research and the publication of archival materials (Ivanovs 2004, p. 398). But on the other hand, this substantial production of historical knowledge was not accompanied by any significant reevaluation of post-war narratives and views. To gain a sense of how the musicological discourse evolved during the remaining years of Soviet rule, we may consider briefly four decades of scholarship on the composer Jāzeps Vītols. Vītols makes for an apposite case study, for he was the most studied musician of Latvia's pre-Soviet musical past, in both the Republican and the Soviet periods. His position in the historical canon was secured not only by his artistic achievements, but also by the roles he played – as founding director of both the Latvian National Opera and the Latvian Conservatory – in Latvia's Republican history.

Among the first musicological fruits of the post-Stalin years was Oļģerts Grāvītis' pioneering life-and-works study, *Jāzeps Vītols and Latvian Folksong* (1958). In conducting research for this book, Grāvītis made extensive use of a broad array of primary source materials previously unavailable to Latvian historians. These included scholarship published in the nineteenth century and the inter-war years, as well as letters, memoirs, and other unpublished sources located in Latvian and Russian archives (see Grāvītis 1958, pp. 248–50). The bibliographical apparatus of Grāvītis' study was unprecedented in Soviet Latvian scholarship for its thoroughness and specificity. And the volume included the most detailed treatment of Vītols' biography ever published in any language (Grāvītis 1958, pp. 13–59). With regard to all of these issues, Grāvītis' work was a significant achievement, and truly a reflection of its time. But as a product of its time, *Jāzeps Vītols and Latvian Folksong* is also a deeply problematic text. Its problems are apparent not only in its biographical chapters, but also in its analytical discussions. For Grāvītis' analyses of Vītols' music are deeply ideological, collectively elaborating a portrait of the artist as an anachronistic adherent to central tenets of Soviet Socialist Realist aesthetics, and of the composer himself as a model proto-Soviet artist.

In Grāvītis' portrayal, Vītols was, in Soviet parlance, a progressive realist, who could not resist the urge to comment in his music upon the oppressive pre-Soviet political milieu in which he spent most of his life. Indeed, Grāvītis wrote, 'The composer demonstrates', in his vocal works, 'his desire not to suppress the realities of life, but . . . to reveal the social causes of the experiences of the Latvian people, and to show just how much this profoundly oppressed people despised the Baltic German baronial class that ruled over them with fire and bared teeth' (Grāvītis 1958, p. 97). Considering one of Vītols' folksong arrangements, 'Aijā, Ancīt, aijā' (Sleep, little Ancis, sleep), from his *200 Latvian Folksongs* (1906–19), Grāvītis observed the following about the 'progressive' nature of Vītols' musical language and world-view:

> It seems that the composer often found expressions of social protest even where the text at first glance does not suggest such an interpretation. This is demonstrated clearly by the cradlesong 'Aijā, Ancīt, aijā'. The text speaks about the child's future, yet the dark, heavy-hearted mood of the melody seems to contradict the character of the text. But this contradiction merely reflects the realities of life. In the mother's cradlesong there are indeed many pleasant wishes. However, the singer's wishes cannot possibly come true. For this reason there is a great deal of darkness in the cradlesong. The tendency of the melody to rise at the beginning of the song is muffled in the second measure, as if covered over by dust. The second half of the melody comprises a hopeless, downward-slinking intonation [*intonācija*]. (Grāvītis 1958, pp. 97–8)

In composing 'Aijā, Ancīt, aijā', Grāvītis argued, Vītols did more than craft a musical setting appropriate to the overt message of his chosen text. Indeed, he recognized, in the apparent contradiction between the happy poetry and the decidedly darker character of the traditional melody, an element of protest presumably voiced by a historical Latvian folk singer against the pre-Revolutionary conditions under which she lived. In response to his realization that the mother's dreams for her child would never be fulfilled so long as her land was ruled by Baltic Germans, Vītols created a musical accompaniment that highlights the ironic pairing of emotional messages conveyed by the textual and melodic components of the folksong. In this way, Grāvītis suggested, Vītols revealed his sympathies with the Latvian peasantry in their historic plight. Indeed, Grāvītis suggested, Vītols' musical 'distortion' of the singing mother's 'bright, dream-like fantasies about the future' mirrored the tragic way in which generations of Latvians' hopes for a brighter future were undermined by centuries of Baltic German oppression (Grāvītis 1958, pp. 98–9). The latter circumstance came to an end, of course, only with the Revolution of 1917.

Throughout the remaining years of Soviet rule, Vītols' music would repeatedly be subjected to this sort of analytical explication (for example, Grīnfelds 1978, pp. 47–54). But music, as is well known, is notoriously susceptible to widely divergent readings and interpretations, and so making a convincing case for Vītols' proto-Soviet convictions required corroborating biographical evidence.

Here musicologists faced greater difficulties, since Vītols had openly expressed his opposition to the Bolshevik Revolution in memoirs and letters, and he fled to Germany just prior to the Soviet rout of German troops from Latvian soil in the fall of 1944. In the years immediately following Latvia's annexation to the USSR, these complicating aspects of Vītols' biography were either ignored by Latvian scholars or else portrayed as the tragic outcome of Nazi machinations (Sudrabkalns 1945, p. 1; Pelše 1951, p. 222 n.). Even Grāvītis attributed Vītols' emigration to the effects of German propaganda upon the composer's elderly mind (Grāvītis 1958, pp. 43–5). But as historical archives were opened to an increasing number of historians in the late 1950s, and as the new climate of intellectual openness encouraged the publication of archival materials, scholars of Vītols were eventually compelled to confront these aspects of Vītols' history directly.

The first attempt at such a confrontation was made by Jēkabs Vītoliņš, who published a transcription of extensive portions of Vītols' previously unpublished memoirs in the first volume of *Latviešu mūzika* (Vītols 1958b). (Vītols had penned his memoirs, in fits and starts, between 1936 and 1943, and had left them with a friend in Riga immediately prior to his emigration in 1944.)[9] Those portions of the memoirs that Vītoliņš selected for publication in 1958 did not touch upon politically sensitive issues. But four years later, Vītoliņš undertook the task of preparing further selections from the memoirs for publication, and here he encountered a different and troubling situation. For in what was left of Vītols' manuscript source, the composer recorded his despair over the Revolutions of 1905 and 1917 and recounted his flight from Bolshevik-controlled St. Petersburg for the newly independent Republic of Latvia in the summer of 1918 (Vītols 1962b).

Vītoliņš' solution to the problem he faced was vividly revealing of the tensions between scholarly ambition and political feasibility felt by many musicologists of his generation. He heavily edited his manuscript source, excising from his published edition all passages from Vītols' text that might belie the composer's supposedly proto-Soviet political sympathies. In Vītoliņš' edition of the composer's discussion of his departure from St. Petersburg, the musicologist omitted Vītols' remarks about the hardships of life in Bolshevik-controlled Russia (Vītols 1962b, pp. 165, 166, 167; cf. Vītols n.d., pp. 103–4, 105, 108). Vītoliņš likewise excised Vītols' characterization of Bolshevik soldiers as the 'enemy' (*ienaidnieks*), and the composer's account of the great 'mirth' (*jautrības*) he felt upon his departure by train from St. Petersburg in 1918 (Vītols 1962b, p. 167; cf. Vītols n. d., pp. 108, 106).

The most extensive cutting of material, however, is found at the end of Vītoliņš' edition. In a single rich passage, the composer recounted his experience of the 1917 Revolution, his resignation from the director's post of the Latvian National Opera in the fall of 1918, his thoughts on the founding of the sovereign Republic of Latvia on 18 November of that year, and his response to the storming of Riga by Bolshevik forces in January 1919. Below, I have provided a translation of the entirety of this passage from Vītols' memoirs. The complete text of Vītoliņš' edition, published in 1962, is given in the left-hand column; the ellipses are Vītoliņš'. The text as it appears in the composer's manuscript is provided in full on the right. In that column, I have italicized those passages omitted from Vītoliņš' published edition.

My resignation went almost entirely unnoticed. Arbeņins wondered, 'why are you going?' The attention of all the others was focused upon the ... political events of the new year: The occupying German army had left, as had the English warships. ...	My resignation went almost entirely unnoticed. Arbeņins wondered, 'why are you going?' The attention of all the others was focused upon the *bleak* political events of the new year: The occupying German army had left, as had the English warships. *In the dreadful glow of the burning opera house, control of Latvia fell into [the Bolshevik] Stučka's hands.* The theater where the Latvian opera had begun its work was still smoking, in ruins. A Phoenix rose up from the ashes! *But the sublime act of 18 November will nevertheless forever be connected to the theater on Kronvalds Boulevard. It is not my intention to say too much about that eternally unforgettable day. Will we ever see another 18 November? − −*

The theater where the Latvian opera had begun its work was still smoking, in ruins. A Phoenix rose up from the ashes! ...

*	*In the Fatherland*
I left behind a musical culture that had grown to one of monumental significance. ...	I left behind a musical culture that had grown to one of monumental significance. *The Bolshevik regime had still not been able to destroy it. The calls for serious support of the PROLETKULT had still not been taken up.* When I left St. Petersburg, I never thought that I would not see it again in my lifetime; my leave from the St. Petersburg Conservatory was limited to half a year, and my ties to it have still not been severed. *But now there is no doubt, even for an instant. I feel that my proper place now is in Latvia. Indeed, the invasion by the Bolsheviks [Stučka, et al.] put our beautiful hopes in perilous jeopardy and threatened to shake our faith in the future. But the news received from St. Petersburg was every bit as wicked: anarchy constantly on the rise, even at the Conservatory; hunger becoming unbearable. I was sorry for my friends.* (Vītols n. d., pp. 110–11)[10]
When I left St. Petersburg, I never thought that I would not see it again in my lifetime; my leave from the St. Petersburg Conservatory was limited to half a year, and my ties to it have still not been severed. ... (Vītols 1962b, p. 169)	

Over the course of the next two decades, Vītoliņš and his colleagues would edit and publish a large corpus of archival materials related to Vītols and his work (for example, Vītols 1958a, 1962a, 1966). But to borrow a term from Ivanovs, the effect of all of this archival research was largely to achieve the 'filling out' of narratives and interpretive positions elaborated years and even decades earlier. In spite of continuous discoveries of archival materials that significantly complicated the image of Vītols as a model proto-Soviet artist, the image of the composer advanced in Grāvītis' 1958 book remained largely unchanged through 1991. In the first attempt at a comprehensive post-war history of Latvian music, published in 1972, Lija Krasinska, like Grāvītis before her, accounted for Vītols' emigration to Germany as an elderly response to Nazi propaganda (Vītoliņš & Krasinska 1972, p. 266). In another attempt at a comprehensive history, published in Russian in 1978, Nilss Grīnfelds attributed Vītols' departure from St. Petersburg to his failure to 'comprehend the historical significance' (*ne ponyal istoricheskogo znacheniya*) of the Bolshevik Revolution (Grīnfelds 1978, p. 41). Even as late as 1988, when an attempt was finally made to publish the text of Vītols' memoirs in its ostensible entirety, Grāvītis, the editor of the volume, retained many of the cuts to the composer's text made by Vītoliņš a quarter of a century earlier (Vītols 1988).[11] And he too argued, once again, that Vītols' unsympathetic statements about the Bolshevik government 'indirectly reflect the impressions made by the anti-Soviet propaganda of the period, approaching a ferocious pitch on radio and in the press, upon Vītols' elderly mind' (Vītols 1988, p. 323 n. 170).

The Landscape Since 1991

As the Vītols case vividly demonstrates, the Stalinist policy of nativization provided a principal ideological foundation for musicological research and writing throughout the entire period of Soviet rule. To be sure, the scholarly discourse did evolve in tandem with the broader vicissitudes of Soviet cultural life, as we have seen with respect to responses to the Muradeli affair and the Twentieth Party Congress. But from Sudrabkalns' statements of 1945 through to Grāvītis' edition of Vītols' memoirs published in 1988, the study of Latvia's historical musicians remained tightly enmeshed with a political effort to demonstrate the historical rootedness of contemporary Soviet ideology and cultural policy in the republic's historic cultural artifacts and experience. In this respect, it is important to note that Vītols was not an isolated figure. Nearly every pre-Soviet composer and musician to receive significant post-war scholarly attention was treated in this same manner (Grāvītis 1953 [on Andrejs Jurjāns]; Lūse 1969 [on Ernests Vīgners]; Klotiņš 1977 [on Emils Dārziņš]). Given this situation, it seems fitting to conclude our investigation with a look at the scholarly landscape as it stands nearly two decades after the collapse of Soviet rule, in an attempt to assess the degree to which Latvian musicology has transcended the boundaries of Soviet historical discourse. To this end, we may turn once again to the exemplary but hardly singular case of Vītols.

To begin with, it is notable, given the intense focus on Vītols by scholars of both the Republican and the Soviet periods, that little work has been undertaken on the artist in the post-Soviet years. In a decade and a half, the sum total of published interpretive scholarship on the composer consists of two books, both authored by Oļģerts Grāvītis. The first consists of a collection of photographs with an accompanying introductory essay (Grāvītis 1995). The second is an extensive volume of reminiscences of the composer recorded by students, colleagues, and friends, likewise accompanied by copious editorial explication (Grāvītis 1999). To be sure, both volumes make attempts to correct the image of Vītols advanced in Soviet-era scholarship. But neither offers a clearly documented reassessment of Vītols' political sympathies, and neither confronts directly the biographical distortions perpetuated in a half-century of Soviet scholarship.

To take one example: in the introduction to his photographic collection, Grāvītis acknowledges that Vītols emigrated to Germany in 1944 'seeking to escape the threat of new repressions' (*glāboties no jauniem represiju draudiem*) (Grāvītis 1995, p. 7). But this statement, provided without reference to either archival materials or other published studies, only raises further questions. Most importantly, if the composer sought, as Grāvītis asserts, to flee *new* (*jauni*) repressions in 1944, then what *prior* repressions had he already witnessed or suffered under the Soviets, presumably in 1940–1941? Grāvītis provides no further commentary on this issue. The publication of the scholar's second post-Soviet book on Vītols, the 1999 documentary volume, would seem to have provided an ideal venue in which to address this subject in greater detail. But there the musicologist's account of the composer's emigration is even more ambiguous, for it recapitulates a common Soviet-era refrain: that Vītols himself had never wanted to emigrate at all, but had been pressured, in his mentally weakened elderly state, by his wife and friends to do so. 'The third and final period of [Vītols'] life', Grāvītis wrote in 1999,

> was marked by the mournful day of 7 October 1944, when, persuaded [*pierunāts*] by his friends and supported by his wife, J. Vītols boarded a passenger ship overloaded with refugees in Riga's harbor. With tears in his eyes he bid *adieu* to his homeland in silence, like hundreds of thousands of others similarly orphaned by fate, believing in the War's end, in the driving off of the Bolsheviks, and in their own speedy return. The dreams of this loyal Latvian son did eventually come true. But, tragically, not in his lifetime. (Grāvītis 1999, p. 11)

Exculpated from responsibility for his own actions and decisions (he was persuaded by friends; his anti-Bolshevik sympathies were merely – and no more specific than – those of the masses), Vītols is reduced, in this account, to the status of a passive actor in the unfolding of his own destiny. But more significant than this problem of interpretation is an accompanying problem of documentation. For the musicologist does not cite a single study or archival document as the source for the account just quoted. The reader is asked to accept the validity of this narrative solely on the basis of his or her faith in the musicologist's trustworthiness and status as a well-informed scholar. But as we have seen, numerous hints are readily apparent elsewhere – including in the mention of 'new repressions' in Grāvītis' own 1995 book – that the situation surrounding Vītols' emigration was far more complicated than this most recent contribution to the literature suggests. In the end, the correctives offered in recent Vītols scholarship to Soviet-era narratives of the composer's emigration provide nothing in the way of clarification or insight into Vītols' motives. Indeed, all that they offer is further obfuscation.

Since 1991, significant musicological work has been undertaken on Latvian topics all but inaccessible to Soviet-era scholars, especially regarding the crucial role played by Baltic German musicians and institutions in the historical evolution of Latvian musical life. Much of this work has been archival in nature, and much of it has met the highest standards of bibliographical transparency (for example, Lindenberga *et al.* 1997; Lindenberga *et al.* 2004; Jaunslaviete 2007). Yet the fact that Vītols – a figure whose work has played such a central role, for over a century, in the construction of both popular and academic notions of Latvian cultural identity – remains in the shadows of

Soviet obscurantism makes clear just how much work remains to be done.[12] Unquestionably, to confront anew the favored artists of Soviet-era music scholarship will prove to be a difficult and painful task, for it will require a confrontation with that scholarship itself, many of the authors of which are still writing today. But to do so will be liberating as well. For it will mark an important step toward freeing the Latvian musicological discourse of the still-oppressive weight of the Soviet nativization campaign.

Acknowledgements

The author wishes to thank Martin Boiko, Joachim Braun and Silvio dos Santos for their invaluable comments on earlier versions of this article; the staff of the Misiņš Library (Riga) and the Library of the Jāzeps Vītols Latvian Academy of Music for their kind assistance with primary source materials; and both Emory College and the University of South Carolina Research Foundation for financial support of this project. Unless otherwise noted, all translations in this essay are his own.

Notes

1   Though there has recently been intense interest in the general topic of Latvian historiography of the Soviet and post-Soviet years (for example, Buholcs 2003; Ivanovs 2003a, 2003b, 2004; Strods 2003), there exists no post-Soviet literature on Latvian music historiography specifically. The only published consideration of the subject remains Joachim Braun's 'Some Preliminary Considerations on the Present State of Baltic Musicology', first published over a quarter of a century ago (Braun 1982; reprinted in Braun 2002, pp. 238–55).

2   What changed between 1918 and 1989 with respect to Soviet nationalities policy was, primarily, the degree to which the leadership at various times emphasized the *sliyanie* (merging) or the *sblizhenie* (drawing together) of the Soviet peoples as the immediate goal of their efforts, and the degree to which it granted autonomy to local leaderships with regard to economic and cultural planning. These vacillations in policy and rhetoric are usefully summarized in Smith (1990b).

3   The canonical text that provided the model upon which minority histories were fashioned was, from 1938 through to the mid-1950s, the *History of the Communist Party of the Soviet Union (Bolshevik): A Short Course* (*Istoriya vsesoyuznoi kommunisticheskoi partii [bol'shevikov]: kratky kurs*) (Moscow, Gos.uchebno-pedagog. izd-vo, 1938). On the *Short Course*, see Markwick (2001, pp. 42–7). On its use in the framing of non-Russian histories, see Litvin (2001, p. 124); Mazour (1971, pp. 288–90); and Tillett (1969, pp. 40–9). With respect to the situation in Latvia specifically, see Ivanovs (2003a, 2003b).

4   It should be noted that the historiographical transformations described here were accompanied by radical structural reforms at the Latvian Conservatory and the University of Latvia. These included the dismissal and deportation of scholars employed during the inter-war years, administrative restructuring (the founding of chairs in Marxism–Leninism and Communist Party History), and the importing and promotion of Russian and ethnic Latvian scholars trained and formerly

    residing in the Soviet Union (Ivanovs 2003a, pp. 78–9; Stradiņš 2004; Bērziņa 2006, pp. 210–17; Boiko 2008).

5   As Ivanovs has recently shown, this historiographical strategy had roots in Russian imperial historiography, one line of which argued that ancient ties between ethnic Russians and Latvians 'justified Latvia's annexation to imperial Russia' (Ivanovs 2003b, pp. 64–5). It should also be noted that to demonstrate the 'internationalism' of Latvian music (in the parlance of Khachaturian and other Party officials) typically meant, in practice, to demonstrate its indebtedness to Russian historical models. In this respect, the musicological discourse in Latvia reflected broader currents of Soviet thinking about the nationalities question – with Russia regarded as the 'first among equals' in the Soviet 'family of nations' – that prevailed in the Soviet cultural discourse from the late 1930s through to the late 1950s (see Martin 2001, pp. 451–5).

6   Niedre, who studied history and economics at the University of Latvia, served as secretary of the Union of Soviet Latvian Writers in 1941–1943. Pelše, a folklorist, was director of the Ethnography and Folklore Section of the Latvian Academy of Sciences from 1946 to 1955. Sudrabkalns, a poet, authored numerous propagandistic works and held a series of prominent Party appointments in the post-war years (Stašulāne & Rožkalne 2003, pp. 423–4, 440, 569–70).

7   The text of all entries on cultural topics in the volume is credited to the literary historian Emma Andersone. The volume's preface, however, indicates the participation of Jēkabs Vītoliņš in its compilation. Given that Andersone had no training or record of publication on music-related topics and the fact that Vītoliņš is the only musicologist whose name appears on the list of contributing scholars, it seems likely that Vītoliņš was responsible for supplying – or at least suggesting – much of the volume's musical content (*Latvijas PSR Vēsture* ii, 1955, pp. 3–4; Stašulāne & Rožkalne 2003, p. 28).

8   On the essential stability of historical scholarship in Latvia from the 1950s through to the mid-1980s and its continued dependence upon *Short Course* paradigms, see Ivanovs (2003a, 2004). As recent studies by Markwick and Litvin make clear, the situation in Latvia paralleled that in much of the rest of the Union with respect to this issue; see Litvin (2001, pp. 16–17, 21–2); and Markwick (2001, pp. 46–7).

9   The principal source for the memoirs, upon which Vītoliņš based his edition, is a manuscript preserved in the Rare Book and Manuscript Section (Reto grāmatu un rokrakstu nodaļa) of the Misiņš Library (Riga), Kārlis Egle fond, item 159 (hereafter cited as Vītols n.d.). This manuscript contains 23 chapters or parts thereof as designated by the composer. An additional chapter is preserved, in manuscript, in the Vītols archive at the Jāzeps Vītols Latvian Academy of Music in Riga. A copy – apparently incomplete – of the Misiņš manuscript, made by the composer's wife Annija and presently in private collection, was published in Sweden in 1963 in an edition by Jānis Rudzītis (Vītols 1963; I have not been able to examine Annija Vītols' copy of the manuscript). For a more detailed discussion of the sources, see Grāvītis' introduction to Vītols (1988). Transcriptions from the memoirs cited in the present article are my own, taken from manuscript held in the Misiņš Library (Vītols n.d.).

10   The text as it appears in the manuscript is as follows (Vītols n.d., pp. 110–11):

    Mana demisīja palika gluži nepamanīta. Vienigi Arbeņins brīnījās: kamdēļ ejot? Visu citu prāti bīja saistīti pie Jaunā gada drūmiem politiskiem notikumiem: aizgāja vācu okupācijas armija, aizbrauca anglu kaŗa kuģi. Degošā operas nama drausmīgājā blāzmā, vara Latvijā pārgāja Stučkas rokās. ~~Operas~~ ^Teatŗa^ namam pa daļai vēl drupās kūpojot, ~~turp parvietojām [illeg.]~~ tur uzsāka Latvju opera savu nākamo posmu. Fēnikss cēlās no pelniem!

Bet celais 18. novembra akts tomēr uz visiem laikiem saistīts pie teatra Kronvalda bulvārā. Nav mans uzdevums lieku reizi stāstīt par šo mūžigi neaizmirstamo dienu. Vai vēl piedzīvošu jaunu 18. novembri? – –

Tēvzemē

Aiz muguras bīju atstājis kalna galos pacēlušos muzikālu kultūru. Vēl lielinieku režīms nebīja paspējis to ārdīt; sauciens pēc proletkulta nopeitna atbalsta vēl atradis nebīja. Kad pemetu Peterpili, nebīju tais domās ka to vairs savu mūžu neredzēšu; mans atvaļinājums bīja norobežots uz pusgadu – saites[corr.] ar Pēterpils konservatoriju nebūt raisītas vēl nebīja. Bet gan ne acumirkļa nešaubījos. Jutu ka mana vieta ~~[illeg.]~~ ^tagad^ Latvijā. Gan iestājies lielinieku starprežims bīstami apdraudēja jaukās cerības, varēja saškobīt pārliecību par nākotni. Bet tikpat ļaunas bija arī direkti un indirekti no Pēterpils saņemtās ziņas: anarķija arī konservatorijā pastāvīgi pieaugot, bads topot nepanesams. Bīj man savu dragu žēl.

11   Grāvītis preserved, for instance, almost all of the cuts made to Vītols's text shown in the long passage just quoted in the present essay (Vītols 1988, pp. 263–4; cf. Vītols 1962b, p. 169). The only lines that Grāvītis returned to this passage, in comparison with Vītoliņš' 1962 edition, are 'In the dreadful glow of the burning opera house, control of Latvia fell into Stučka's hands'; and 'But now there is no doubt, even for an instant. I feel that my proper place now is in Latvia'. The other cuts made by Vītoliņš in this passage are preserved by Grāvītis in Vītols (1988).

12   This work should be substantially aided in the coming years by the recent publication of a large selection of the composer's letters in an edition by Uldis Siliņš (Vītols 2006).

References

Albiņa, D. (1956) 'Klasiskā mantojuma problema un latviešu kora dziesma', *Literatūra un māksla*, 13 October, p. 3.

'Atklāts Latvijas Padomju Komponistu Savienības jaunrades plēnums' (1946) *Literatūra un māksla* 31 May, p. 1.

Bērziņa, D. (1956) 'Jānis Cimze 1814. g. 3. VII – 1881. g. 22. X', *Literatūra un māksla*, 20 October, p. 3.

Bērziņa, V. (2006) *Daudz baltu dieniņu. Jēkaba Graubiņa dzīvesstāts* (Riga, Atēna).

Boiko, M. (1994) 'Latvian Ethnomusicology: Past and Present', *Yearbook for Traditional Music*, 26, pp. 47–65.

Boiko, M. (2008) '*Muzikoloģija/Mūzikas Zinātne:* A Critical History of Latvian Musicology', Karnes, K. C. (trans.), *Journal of Baltic Studies*, 39, 3, pp. 325–40.

Braun, J. (1982) 'Some Preliminary Considerations on the Present State of Baltic Musicology', *Journal of Baltic Studies*, 13, 1, pp. 40–52.

Braun, J. (2002) *Raksti: Mūzika Latvijā*, Boiko, M. (ed.) (Riga, Musica Baltica).

Buholcs, J. (2003) '1940. gadā notikušās valsts iekārtas pārveides Latvijā vēstures interpretācijas maiņa (1988–1989)', *Domino*, 1, pp. 195–215.

Bula, D. (1996) 'The Singing Nation: The Tradition of Latvian Folksongs and the Self-Image of the Nation', *Humanities and Social Sciences Latvia*, 11, pp. 4–32.

Bula, D. (2000) *Dziedātājtauta. Folklora un nacionāla ideoloģija* (Zinātne, Riga).

Butulis, I. (2004) 'Padomju kultūrpolitikas aspekti dažos latviešu padomju preses izdevumos (1945–1949)', in Caune, A., Feldmanis, I., Strods, H. & Šneidere, I. (eds) (2004) *Latvijas Vēsturnieku komisijas raksti 13: Totalitārie okupācijas režīmi Latvijā 1940–1964 gadā* (Riga, Latvijas vēstures institūta apgāds).

Fay, L. E. (2000) *Shostakovich: A Life* (Oxford and New York, Oxford University Press).

Frolova-Walker, M. (1998) '"National in Form, Socialist in Content": Musical Nation-Building in the Soviet Republics', *Journal of the American Musicological Society*, 51, 2, pp. 331–71.

Grāvītis, O. (1953) *Jurjānu Andrejs* (Riga, Latvijas Valsts izdevniecība).

Grāvītis, O. (1956a) 'Nacionalās formas problema mūzikā', *Literatūra un māksla*, 28 April, pp. 3–4.

Grāvītis, O. (1956b) 'Muzikas zinātnei jāsoļo avangardā', *Literatūra un māksla*, 1 September, p. 3.

Grāvītis, O. (1958) *Jāzeps Vītols un latviešu tautas dziesma* (Riga, Latvijas Valsts izdevniecība).

Grāvītis, O. (1995) *Jāzepa Vītola mūžs fotoattēlos* (Riga, Jāzepa Vītola fonds).

Grāvītis, O. (1999) *Jāzeps Vītols. Tuvinieku, audzēkņu un laikabiedru atmiņas* (Riga, Zinātne).

Grīnfelds, N. (1948) 'Vairāk paškritikas', *Literatūra un māksla*, 29 February, p. 5.

Grīnfelds, N. (1958) 'Padomju Latvijas muzikas kultura', *Latviešu mūzika*, 1, pp. 5–26.

Grīnfelds [Gryunfel'd], N. (1978) *Istoriya latyshskoi muzyki* (Moscow, Muzyka).

Hobsbawm, E. J. (1992) *Nations and Nationalism since 1780: Programme, Myth, Reality*, rev. ed. (Cambridge, Cambridge University Press).

Ivanovs, A. (2003a) 'Latvijas PSR historiogrāfija (konceptuāls pārskats)', *Latvijas Vēsture*, 51, 52, pp. 75–83, 69–77.

Ivanovs, A. (2003b) 'Vēstures zinātne kā padomju politikas instruments: historiogrāfijas konceptuālais līmenis', in Caune, A., Feldmanis, I. & Kļaviņa, D. (eds) (2003) *Latvijas Vēsturnieku komisijas raksti 9: Padomju okupācijas režīms Baltijā 1944–1959. gadā: politika un tās sekas* (Riga, Latvijas vēstures institūta apgāds).

Ivanovs, A. (2004) 'Latvijas sovetizācija 1944–1956. gadā Latvijas padomju historio-grafijā', in *Latvijas Vēsturnieku komisijas raksti 13: Totalitārie okupācijas režīmi Latvijā 1940–1964 gadā* (Riga, Latvijas vēstures institūta apgāds).

Jaunslaviete, B. (2007) 'Ieskats vācbaltiešu dziesmu svētku vēsturē', *Mūzikas akadēmijas raksti*, 3, pp. 33–52.

Karnes, K. C. (2005) 'A Garland of Songs for a Nation of Singers: An Episode in the History of Russia, the Herderian Tradition and the Rise of Baltic Nationalism', *Journal of the Royal Musical Association*, 132, 2, pp. 197–235.

Klotiņš, A. (1977) 'Emila Dārziņa estētika', *Latviešu mūzika*, 12, pp. 17–52.

Latvijas PSR Vēsture (1953–9) 3 Vols (Riga, Latvijas PSR zinātņu akadēmijas izdevniecība).

Lindenberga, V., Torgāns, J. & Fūrmane, L. (1997) *Gadsimti skaņulokā* (Riga, Zinātne).

Lindenberga, V., Torgāns, J., Fūrmane, L. & Čeže, M. (2004) *Skaņuloki gadsimtos* (Riga, Zinātne).

Lippus, U. (1999) 'Baltic Music History Writing: Problems and Perspectives', *Acta Musicologica*, 71, 1, pp. 50–60.

Litvin, A. L. (2001) *Writing History in Twentieth-Century Russia: A View from Within*, Keep, J. L. H. (ed., trans.) (Basingstoke and New York, Palgrave).

Lūse, L. (1969) 'Vīgneru Ernesta estētiskie uzskati', Latviešu mūzika, 7, pp. 124–42.

Maes, F. (2002) A History of Russian Music: From Kamarinskaya to Babi Yar, Pomerans, A. J. & Pomerans, E. (trans.) (Berkeley and Los Angeles, University of California Press).

Markwick, R. D. (2001) Rewriting History in Soviet Russia: The Politics of Revisionist Historiography, 1956–1974 (Basingstoke and New York, Palgrave).

Martin, T. (2001) The Affirmative Action Empire: Nations and Nationalism in the Soviet Union, 1923–1939 (Ithaca and London, Cornell University Press).

Mazour, A. G. (1971) The Writing of History in the Soviet Union (Stanford, Hoover Institution Press).

Misiunas, R. J. & Taagepera, R. (1993) The Baltic States: Years of Dependence 1940–1990, rev. ed. (Berkeley and Los Angeles, University of California Press).

'Mūsu lielajam laikam cienīgu muziku' (1948) Literatūra un māksla, 22 February, p. 3.

Niedre, J. (1942) 'Latviešu tautas dziesmas par vācu kungiem, atkritējiem un tautas draugiem', Karogs, pp. 157–62.

'Par V. Muradeli operu "Lielā draudzība": VK(b)P CK 1948. gada 10. februara lēmums', (1948) Literatūra un māksla, 15 February, pp. 1–2.

Pelše, R. (1947) 'Latviešu un krievu kulturas sakari', Literatūra un māksla, 6 June, p. 3.

Pelše, R. (1951) Latviešu un krievu kulturas sakari (Riga, Latvijas Valsts izdevniecība).

'Pervyi plenum Soyuza sovetskikh kompozitorov Latviiskoi SSR' (1946) Sovetskaya muzyka, July, pp. 25–41.

Plakans, A. (1995) The Latvians: A Short History (Stanford, Hoover Institution Press).

Smith, G. (ed.) (1990a) The Nationalities Question in the Soviet Union (London and New York, Longman).

Smith, G. (1990b) 'Nationalities Policy from Lenin to Gorbachev', in Smith, G. (ed.) (1990a).

Smith, J. (1999) The Bolsheviks and the National Question, 1917–23 (New York, St. Martin's Press).

Spure, Ž. (1940) 'Darbu sākot', Karogs, 1, pp. 3–4.

Stašulāne, I. & Rožkalne, A. (eds) (2003) Latviešu rakstniecība biogrāfijās, 2d ed. (Riga, Zinātne).

Stradiņš, J. (2004) 'Totalitāro okupācijas režīmu represijas pret Latvijas zinātni un akadēmiskajām aprindām (1940–1945)', in Caune, A., Feldmanis, I., Strods, H. & Šneidere, I. (eds) (2004) Latvijas Vēsturnieku komisijas raksti 13: Totalitārie okupācijas režīmi Latvijā 1940–1964 gadā (Riga, Latvijas vēstures institūta apgāds).

Strods, H. (2003) 'Baltijas valstu okupācija: ieskats terminoloģijā, periodizācijā, izpētē', in Latvijas Vēsturnieku komisijas raksti 9: Padomju okupācijas režims Baltijā 1944–1959. gadā: politika un tās sekas (Riga, Latvijas vēstures institūta apgāds).

Sudrabkalns, J. (1945) 'Latviešu mūzikas svētki', Literatūra un māksla, 9 February, p. 1.

Suny, R. G. (1993) The Revenge of the Past: Nationalism, Revolution, and the Collapse of the Soviet Union (Stanford, Stanford University Press).

Suny, R. G. (1998) The Soviet Experiment: Russia, the USSR, and the Successor States (Oxford and New York, Oxford University Press).

Suny, R. G. & Martin, T. (eds) (2001) A State of Nations: Empire and Nation-Making in the Age of Lenin and Stalin (Oxford and New York, Oxford University Press).

Taruskin, R. (1997) Defining Russia Musically: Historical and Hermeneutical Essays (Princeton and Oxford, Princeton University Press).

'Teātri un opera sāk jaunu darbu' (1940) Brīvais zemnieks, 15 August, p. 7.

Tillett, L. (1969) *The Great Friendship: Soviet Historians on the Non-Russian Nationalities* (Chapel Hill, University of North Carolina Press).

Upīts, A. (1940) 'Marksistiskā literātūras zinātne un kritika', *Karogs*, 1, pp. 261–9.

Vīksna, M. (1996) 'The History of the Collection of Folklore in Latvia', *Humanities and Social Science Latvia*, 11, pp. 85–101.

Vipers, B. (1940) 'Sociālistiskais reālisms mākslā', *Karogs*, 1, pp. 437–42.

Vītoliņš, J. (n.d.) *Mūzikas vēsture* (Riga, Grāmatu draugs).

Vītoliņš, J. (1946a) '"Tautu draudzība": Jauns vokāli instrumentāls ansamblis', *Literatūra un māksla*, 5 April, p. 5.

Vītoliņš, J. (1946b) 'Dažas līnijas latviešu mūzikas attīstībā', *Literatūra un māksla*, 24 May, pp. 2–3.

Vītoliņš, J. (1946c) 'Aktivizēt mūsu koru darbu', *Literatūra un māksla*, 23 August, p. 2.

Vītoliņš, J. (1948a) 'Pretī jaunam padomju muzikas uzplaukumam', *Literatūra un māksla*, 22 February, p. 4.

Vītoliņš, J. (1948b) 'Rimskis-Korsakovs un latviešu nacionalās muzikas tapšana', *Literatūra un māksla*, 20 June, p. 5.

Vītoliņš [Vitolin'], J. & Grīnfelds [Gryunfel'd], N. (1954) *Latviiskaya SSR* (Moscow, Muzgyz).

Vītoliņš, J. & Krasinska, L. (1972) *Latviešu mūzikas vēsture* (Riga, Liesma).

Vītols, J. (n.d.) *Manas dzīves atmiņas* (unpublished manuscript; Misiņš Library [Riga], Rare Book and Manuscript Section, Kārlis Egle fond, item 159).

Vītols, J. (1958a) 'Jāzepa Vītola vēstules Kārlim Kalējam', *Latviešu mūzika*, 1, pp. 353–407.

Vītols, J. (1958b) 'Manas dzīves atmiņas', *Latviešu mūzika*, 1, pp. 241–351. Article ed. by Vītoliņš, J.

Vītols, J. (1962a) 'Jāzepa Vītola vēstules Kārlim Kalējam', *Latviešu mūzika*, 2, pp. 179–223.

Vītols, J. (1962b) 'Manas dzīves atmiņas. II. Nobeigums', *Latviešu mūzika*, 2, pp. 139–77. Article ed. by Vītoliņš, J.

Vītols, J. (1963) *Manas dzīves atmiņas. Ar papildinājumiem no Annijas Vītolas atmiņām*, Rudzītis, J. (ed.) (Uppsala, Daugava).

Vītols, J. (1966) 'J. Vītola vēstules Alfrēdam Kalniņam', *Latviešu mūzika*, 5, pp. 229–86.

Vītols, J. (1988) *Manas dzīves atmiņas*, Grāvītis, O. (ed.) (Riga, Liesma).

Vītols, J. (2006) *Dziesmai vieni gala nava. Jāzeps Vītols savās un laikabiedru vēstulēs. 1918–1944*, Siliņš, U. (ed.) (Riga, Nordik).

Zālīte, M. (1946) 'Jēkaba Graubiņa jaunākie pētījumi muzikas folklorā', *Literatūra un māksla*, 22 November, p. 5.

Zviedris, O. (1948) 'Nepieciešami nopietni pārkārtojumi Valsts konservatorijas darbā', *Literatūra un māksla*, 21 March, p. 4.

MODERNIST TRENDS IN ESTONIAN MUSICOLOGY IN THE 1970s–1980s AND THE STUDY OF FOLK MELODIES

Urve Lippus

Introduction

Estonian musicology as an academic field of research is rather young, but the tradition of contemplating and writing about music in the Estonian language goes back to the formative period of Estonian national culture in the second half of the nineteenth century. Several aesthetic ideas concerning Estonian national music developed in the decades immediately after 1900, and some have remained in broad circulation. One of these ideas concerns the role of folk music in the development of Estonian classical music. In the early twentieth century, many musicians, composers among them, considered it important to collect folk melodies. This was certainly inspired by nineteenth-century views about national character in music, going back to Johann Gottfried von Herder and the German Romantics, but later the Hungarians Béla Bartók and Zoltán Kodály also became important models for Estonian artists. In the 1930s, such an attitude was widespread throughout much of Europe, but it largely disappeared after the Second World War. In Soviet musical aesthetics, however, it once again became central, and it was officially supported throughout the second half of the century. As a result, folk music research in the Soviet Union remained closely tied not only to general musicology but also to the activities of the Composers' Union; it belonged to the curriculum of conservatories and it enjoyed greater support than many other fields of musicological inquiry. This article will trace the development of musicology in Estonia, focusing especially upon some research problems and methods used for investigating folk music in the 1970s and 1980s. In folk music research, as we will see, it was possible to apply a variety of new ideas and analytical methods derived from structural linguistics and semiotics, mathematical modeling, phonetics and perception studies.

The influence of structuralist thinking, interest in scientific approaches to research, and the use of quantitative methods, all widespread in the humanities since the late 1950s, influenced both musicology and folklore studies in Estonia. Such approaches typically derived from linguistics (generative linguistics and experimental phonetics were represented at the University of Tartu and at the Estonian Academy of Sciences) and semiotics (the Tartu school of semiotics became famous in the 1960s). Common to researchers with otherwise different academic backgrounds was a striving after scholarly strictness and formalization in opposition to official Soviet musicology's persistent insinuation of 'formalism' as a means of condemning both musical works and writings about them. Significantly, the vocabulary of this latter Soviet rhetorical tradition – like the underlying concept itself – was sufficiently vague that one could regard mathematical formalization in folk music research as entirely unrelated to such ideological criticisms, rooted as they were in aesthetic considerations. Indeed, the authority of 'science' was so high in the 1970s that statistical analysis and other mathematical approaches could find high academic recognition as progressive research methods, at least in music analysis and in describing folk music repertories. And if the mainstream musicological audience responded with suspicion or reserve toward such approaches, those responses were typically prompted by the surplus of tables and graphs in this kind of musicological writing, or by the discursive fireworks that such writing initiated, rather than by any aesthetic or ideological considerations. The conferences of the Folklore Committee of the Soviet Composers' Union (*Vsesoyuznaya fol'klornaya komissiya*) in Moscow offered a supportive forum for presenting such studies, at least in 1975–1980. Interdisciplinary endeavors often reflected collaboration between mathematicians and musicologists, and the strong German basis of Soviet musicology in musical folkloristics (*vergleichende Musikwissenschaft*), with its interest in large text collections, provided a good starting point for such work.

In Estonia, cooperation with linguists and phoneticians became increasingly important in the 1970s and 1980s. Some attempts were made to develop formal methods for analyzing art music, but for the most part such endeavors used folk melodies as their objects of investigation. There were, in part, institutional reasons for this choice: the study of folk music enjoyed the support of well established academic institutions, including the international network of researchers studying Finno-Ugric languages and folk culture. Moreover, this choice of material reflected an awareness of possible attacks. To measure and quantify aspects of art music could very well be labeled formalism. But to explore quantitative methods, formal modeling, and means of automatic transcription of large folk music collections was generally regarded as a non-ideological task. Indeed, it was a positivist, practical science.

Background: Musicology in Estonia at the End of the 1930s

The Soviet period is usually regarded as constituting a break in Estonia's cultural traditions, and in many aspects this is true. In some academic fields, a majority of leading scholars were either repressed by authorities or forced to flee to the West during the Second World War. After the war, most well established academic institutions made an attempt to resume their pre-war work, and many succeeded, albeit typically reformed and renamed according to Soviet patterns. Unfortunately, musicology had not yet been institutionalized in Estonia before World War II.

In the 1930s, two scholars active in Tartu could very well have become university-level teachers and the founders of Estonian academic musicology had not the war interrupted the natural growth of musicological work and thought. Dr Elmar Arro (1899–1985) graduated from the University of Vienna under Guido Adler. His most important studies were written in Tartu in the 1930s, and he also participated in publishing the journal *Eesti Muusika Kuukiri* (*The Monthly Journal of Estonian Music*). His main interest was the history of music and musical life in Estonia and Latvia, and he undertook extensive archival research in the city archives of Tartu and Riga. Arro's working language was German, and that was certainly an obstacle for his integration into Estonian academic life during the Republican period, when developing university-level curricula in Estonian was a high priority. The other musicologist was Karl Leichter (1902–1987), who later became an important teacher of young musicologists at the Tallinn Conservatory. Leichter graduated from the University of Tartu as a Master of Philosophy, and from the Tartu Higher Music School as a composer. His interests included music criticism and aesthetics, and after the war he also studied nineteenth-century Estonian musical life. If Leichter could have continued his studies abroad, he would have become a good candidate for a chair in musicology.

Still a third young scholar, Herbert Tampere (1909–1975), an ethnologist who worked at the Estonian Folklore Archives from 1929, specializing in folk music, could have become a potential candidate for an academic position in musicology. At that time, while the number of works composed by Estonian composers was still not very large, folk music was considered a very important research area and a source for the creation of a new and original form of national music. The close relationship that Estonian folklorists enjoyed with the famous Finnish School of folkloristics enables one to imagine a possible start for musicology at the University of Tartu, as *vergleichende Musikwissenschaft*.

To better understand the musicological situation in Estonia during this period, we should compare it with the institutional organization of musicology in Finland and Sweden. Since the middle of the nineteenth century, Estonian national movements had often received inspiration from the Finns, and several national institutions were founded following Finnish models. Around 1900, several Estonians interested in the humanities chose to study at the University of Helsinki instead of at Tartu. Throughout the nineteenth century, the University of Tartu had been predominantly a Baltic German institution, although the Russification that occurred toward the end of that century had raised the proportion of Russians on the faculty. After Estonia became independent in 1918, the University of Tartu was thoroughly reformed so as to make it a national university with Estonian as the language of instruction. Several new chairs were founded for the purpose of studying and teaching national subjects, and several Finnish professors were brought in to fill them, further strengthening academic contacts with Helsinki in many areas. However, musicology was, at that time, still not an independent academic discipline in Helsinki, and many of its Finnish pioneers, like Ilmari Krohn (lecturer on music history and theory, 1900–1918; extraordinary professor, 1918–1935), Armas Launis (lecturer on music analysis and folk music, 1918–1922) and Armas Otto Väisänen (lecturer, 1940–1957; full professor 1957–1959), were recognized more as scholars of Finnish folk music than as musicologists in the broader, modern sense of the term. Only in 1957 was a full professorship in musicology established at the University of Helsinki. In Sweden, the first chair in musicology was established in 1947 at the University of Uppsala, with Carl Allan Moberg as professor. To be sure, musicological teaching and research had begun much earlier than the founding of these chairs would suggest, with some musicologists working as lecturers and associate professors.[1] Nonetheless, we can – given the situation in Finland and Sweden – regard it as quite normal that Estonian institutions of higher learning still lacked the resources to support musicology formally in the 1930s, and that the University of Tartu employed only an instructor of music, not a professor of musicology, during that decade.

Given this situation, it is remarkable that, in an article published just a few months before the Soviet invasion, Leichter envisaged the establishment of musicology as an academic discipline at the Tallinn Conservatory (in Leichter 1982, pp. 73–6).[2] According to Leichter, Estonian musicians had long felt the need for academic research and higher-level musicological thinking, and leading figures in the Republic's musical life had already, for quite some time, been expecting the University of Tartu to establish a chair in musicology. Evidently, no resources could be found for the establishment of an independent chair (faculty, library, finances), and the demand for graduates in musicology was limited. Thus Leichter proposed the establishment of a chair at the Tallinn Conservatory and, moreover, the teaching of musicological subjects to all music students. Moreover, the teaching of music history, aesthetics, and the history of art at the Conservatory would require significant retooling, as the new goal of the institution would be to balance practical training with general intellectual education. I do not know whether (or to what degree) Leichter was aware of the institutional organization of musicology in the Soviet Union, where the teaching musicology was, as he suggested, carried out at conservatories rather than at universities. But the proposal that he drafted was certainly not informed by any Soviet ideology. Rather, it was a local, practical response to what Leichter perceived as a distinctly local need. A year later, a chair of music history and theory was indeed founded at the Conservatory – but already in accord with Soviet curricula for higher musical education.

Teaching Musicology at the Tallinn Conservatory

The teaching of musicology as a specialty at the Tallinn Conservatory started after the war, in 1945–1946; the first two students in the field graduated in 1951. Throughout the period of Soviet rule, this academic specialty remained very small, with an average of two to three students per year. Such a limited number of students certainly helps to explain why musicology, as a field of research, scarcely developed in comparison to the study of art or literature. At first, Leichter was appointed Dean at the Conservatory, and he invited Herbert Tampere to assume the chair in musicology

(Topman 1999, pp. 46–58). Evidently, Leichter and Tampere hoped to realize their old ideas for developing musicology in Estonia, as they had articulated them during the Republican period. After the war, the first years of Soviet rule were confused in many respects, and there was still some local initiative shown in cultural life. Struggling with everyday necessities, people tried to restore pre-war institutions and to get over wartime losses. That situation changed in 1948, with the declarations by the Central Committee of the Communist Party about the opera *The Great Friendship* by the Georgian composer Vano Muradeli, and with the subsequent local decisions made about music making and writing about music within Estonia itself. At the Conservatory, the department of musicology was attacked as several of its faculty members had been recognized critics and writers on music during the Republican period, and had continued to publish throughout the subsequent period of German occupation. Leichter was fired in 1949 (he returned to teaching in 1956 and retired in 1968), and Tampere was dismissed in 1951 (he returned to teaching in 1961 and was active until his death in 1975).

From 1949 until 1965, a young choral conductor, Artur Vahter, served as head of the musicology section at the Conservatory. As a draft-age man, Vahter had served in the Soviet army in 1941, and thus he was deemed an acceptable figure by the new authorities. However, he was certainly not an ideological party-soldier. His writings resonated, in broad outline, with earlier views about Estonian national music and culture, couched within patches of Soviet rhetoric and obligatory passages as demanded by the authorities. Unfortunately, Vahter himself had no academic training, and so he could not lend significant support to the development of musicology as a scholarly discipline. The next generation of teachers in musicology included a composer, Leo Normet (1922–1995), who later earned a Candidate of Arts degree in musicology at the Moscow Conservatory with a dissertation on the symphonies of Jean Sibelius. Normet became a lecturer of music history and theory in 1954 and retired as a professor in the spring of 1995. His interests were wide-ranging; he was, first and foremost, a critic, penning hermeneutic essays about composers, works and musical styles. In 1965, Johannes Jürisson (1922–2005) was appointed lecturer in music history. His main interest was Estonian cultural history.

In 1966 the Conservatory's departments of composition and musicology were joined, since both were regarded as small specialties with largely overlapping curricula. The Soviet program for musicological study, like that for composition, included a large amount of practical training and music theory, and graduates of both programs received qualifications as music teachers. Besides teaching, an area of intense interest for graduates in musicology was music journalism; some took regular jobs as editors or producers, and all were expected to write, occasionally, surveys, program notes and even concert reviews. Training in research methods and other things necessary for a career in academic research was considered secondary. Moreover, there were almost no positions available for musicologists in the Estonian system of research institutions.[3] A larger group of young musicologists joined the Conservatory's faculty in the 1980s, but only in 1990 were they able to form an independent academic department.

Research on Estonian Music History

In 1946, several research institutes were founded at the Estonian Academy of Sciences. Over the course of the next 50 years, these became the principal centers of Estonian humanistic research of all kinds. By contrast, the universities engaged mainly in teaching. This obviously involved an element of research as well. Nonetheless, faculty members at university-level schools maintained high teaching loads in addition to their research projects, while the staff of a research institute could devote all of its time to research. At one point, plans were drawn up to found an independent research unit specifically for musicology at the Academy of Science's Institute of History. In 1946, Leichter sent a letter to the president of the reorganized Estonian Academy, Hans Kruus, with a detailed proposal for such a unit.[4] Thus we can only imagine the situation in which Estonian musicology would have found itself had Leichter's plan been approved, and if a number of research positions had been created for musicologists at the Institute. Leichter's proposal included a list of scholars and research areas, together with financial calculations and a list of necessary equipment. However, his plan did not include any 'Soviet' research topics, and most of the persons he mentioned in his proposal were later attacked as 'bourgeois nationalists'. Thus, his proposal was not very realistic in its time. Moreover, Leichter's list of scholars included several persons who were already active at the Conservatory, and thus the lack of human resources required for two independent musicological institutions was evident.

And so, the academic discipline of musicology remained institutionally isolated at the Tallinn Conservatory. For a long time, writing a history of Estonian music was the central subject for research and discussions among scholars at that institution. In 1968, a rather compressed first book was finally published, covering the subject from the very beginnings up to 1917. In 1975 a much thicker volume continued this survey up to 1940 (Vahter 1968–1975).[5] However, the many plans and articles left in manuscript that survive in the archives of Leichter and other musicologists, now deposited at the Estonian Museum of Theatre and Music (TMM), provide interesting insights into these scholars' discussions and struggles to find a compromise between their views about Estonian national culture and the demands of Soviet authorities. In several respects, the earlier narratives of Estonian music history meshed well with the framework established by the Soviets – they started with the rise of musical life among Estonian peasants in the nineteenth century (with the founding of choruses in the countryside, song festivals and the rise of an Estonian classical repertoire) and continued with the professionalization of musical activities, the founding of musical institutions and the composition of original works in most genres of art music. Moreover, the deeply anti-German attitude expressed in many earlier writings was strongly supported by the new Soviet authorities. The basic ideological conflict between the old and new narratives derived from the Soviets' requirement that the achievements of the independent Republic of Estonia be diminished, and that Estonia's Sovietization be presented as the flourishing of all forms of cultural life in the republic. As a defensive reaction against this pressure, images of pre-war Estonia actually became – ironically – canonized as a paradise lost. This attitude resonated even in published Soviet-era writings, sometimes in conflict with the official rhetoric found in introductory paragraphs and titles.[6]

Such a situation, however, blocked any objective analytical and critical discussion of Estonian music history, and encouraged thinking about Estonian music in isolation, without consideration of the broader context of European musical life or even of the local multicultural reality. And although writings on music history from the Soviet period are often considered to be Marxist, the situation was in fact confused, as local musicologists were unfamiliar with Marxism as a systematic methodology of thinking about history but knew well a set of popular schemes and obligatory Marxist–Leninst phrases.[7] Writers had to conform to certain official models in order to get their works published. Yet at a deeper level, their work was governed by intuitive mixing of earlier historiographical models; the general approach of style history, with its concentration on works and compositional novelties, was merged with a descriptive approach to local musical life.

Folk Music Studies at the Academy of Sciences

As we have seen, composition based on folk melodies was already supported by authorities in independent Estonia, where it was regarded as a crucial component of 'our own' – that is, Estonian – national culture (Viires 1986). It thus seems paradoxical that this latter view, so strongly loaded with national emotions, survived the Soviet campaign against 'nationalism and bourgeois formalism'. During the Soviet period, compositions using folk melodies were indeed viewed positively, as opposed to the modern, dissonant and nervous language of 'bourgeois formalist' music. Following the model of Soviet Russian institutions, the Tallinn Conservatory introduced a course of folk music study into its curriculum, and students of both composition and musicology had to participate in a fieldwork expedition. Apart from any ideology, it was certainly positive that young musicians came to know Estonian folk traditions. In general, folk music research in Soviet Estonia had more luck than traditional musicology. And the field continued to enjoy institutional support from a number of institutions established before the war, whose activities were allowed to continue afterwards. The Estonian Folklore Archives, for instance, founded in 1927, was an academic institution with a few researcher positions of its own. Their collections included a large amount of music, mostly transcribed, but also recorded.

Both Leichter and Tampere studied those collections and had published a number of articles about them in the 1930s (Leichter 1932; Tampere 1932, 1934, 1937). Tampere had also compiled, edited, and published some scholarly folksong collections (Tampere 1935). After the war, Tampere continued his work at the Archives for years, while simultaneously teaching in Tallinn.[8] The Estonian Folklore Archives, which constituted an independent section of the Estonian National Museum, was reorganized by Soviet authorities as the Department of Folklore at the Fr. R. Kreutzwald Literary Museum. Although called a museum, this institution was more like a literary archive governed administratively by the Academy of Sciences. The primary task of the Museum was to collect, arrange and preserve materials, and to make them available for researchers. It also sponsored research and publishing.

In the 1960s, Ingrid Rüütel joined Tampere as a researcher in folk music at the Literary Museum, and she succeeded, in 1978, in founding a Department of Folk Music at the Institute of Language and Literature of the Academy of Sciences. In truth, hers was the first official research institution in Estonian musicology, though by that time several musicologists had already been engaged by other departments, at both the Institute of Language and Literature and at the Institute of History.[9] Most people involved in folk music studies during this period had a background in philology; Rüütel and Olli Kõiva, both active since the 1960s, studied folklore at the University of Tartu.[10] This philological tradition has continued. Even today, more Estonian ethnomusicologists have a background in philology than in musicology or other disciplines, and this fact is reflected in their selection of research problems and methods. In cooperation with the Composers' Union, Rüütel launched, in 1976, the Soviet Finno-Ugric Folk Music Conferences, which until 1989 were held every third year. Along with sponsoring a series of concerts and publishing papers,[11] those conferences became highly attractive for scholars – including members of the Moscow-based Folklore Committee of the Soviet Composers' Union – investigating a wide diversity of peoples.

The Network of Finno-Ugric Studies

International relations between musicologists were tightly controlled throughout the Soviet period, with the hierarchy of power centered in Moscow. Soviet musicologists had to seek approval for their research topics and professional activities from the Composers' Union. Research institutions had to look to the Academy of Sciences for funding. Still, there was one large, heterogeneous and international 'network' of scholars in which Estonian scholars were allowed a degree of independence, and that was Finno-Ugric studies.

Years ago, I happened to read an article by Juhani Lehtonen reflecting upon the pioneering work of the Finnish scholars Johan Reinhold Aspelin, Uuno Taavi Sirelius and Matian Aleksanderi Castrén on Finno-Ugric ethnology (Lehtonen 1981). This gave me a strong impulse for thinking about the place of Finno-Ugric studies in Estonian culture in general. Lehtonen, discussing some ideas that were widespread in Finland around the turn of the twentieth century, wrote:

> According to J. R. Aspelin, professor of archaeology and the most important figure in early Finno-Ugric archaeological research, to study Finno-Ugric topics was a task that all of mankind expected the Finnish people to undertake. In reality, this demand was made only by a small group of Finnish intelligentsia, first opening its eyes during the awakening of national pride [in the nineteenth century]. The *Kalevala* had earlier demonstrated that the Finns had a highly developed culture behind them. Now, Finno-Ugric research was to prove that the Finns were not a lonely, minuscule folk but part of a great family of peoples that had once inhabited vast regions of northern Eurasia. Finno-Ugrianism, then, guarantees the Finns the right to a great antiquity and a great history. ... To the Hungarians, who were at least as interested in a great antiquity as the Finns, this Finno-Ugric alternative did not, at first, seem

adequate. They would rather have seen themselves as the descendents of great Eastern cultures, or at least of the Scythians or the Huns. . . . For the Finns, there was only the Finno-Ugric alternative, and they set out, all the more gratefully, to follow the way pointed out by Castrén. (Lehtonen 1981, pp. 18–19)

Lehtonen concluded:

Despite difficulties and methodological problems of application, however, the Finno-Ugric branch of ethnology became established though Sirelius's efforts. And ever since his day the debate has continued – now fierce, now mild, in both Finland and Hungary – about the extent to which this branch of ethnology is or is not justified. It is not necessary to take a stand on the issue here; let it suffice to note that the University of Helsinki's chair in ethnology is still a chair in Finno-Ugric ethnology, and, as such, the only one of its kind in the world. (Lehtonen 1981, p. 20)

During the Soviet period, Estonian scholars took a leading role in many areas of Finno-Ugric studies. Most of the Finno-Ugric peoples lived in the Soviet Union, and strict control over the movements of foreigners in that country made it difficult for Finnish scholars to conduct fieldwork. Together with linguists, ethnographers and folklorists organized expeditions, studied materials, and published under the broad rubric of Finno-Ugric studies. The idea of finding common characteristics of Finno-Ugric peoples in their folk culture, beliefs, folk music, etc., was very strong and spread into different areas of cultural research, and even into the creative arts. Like recomposing elements of our own folk art or music, the use of Finno-Ugric elements in one's creative work was related to more general ideas: to supporting an ecological lifestyle, to going back to nature and one's roots, and to protesting against the broader homogenizing tendencies of Soviet culture. (Such ideas are evident, for example, in the music of Veljo Tormis and the graphic art of Kaljo Põllu.)

The international network of Finno-Ugric studies also provided a channel for international academic communication between Finnish, Hungarian, Estonian and other Soviet research institutions. Actually, it was not necessary to study, explicitly, a broadly Finno-Ugric problem to be considered a member of this network. Anything concerning Estonian language and culture was, by default, regarded as a part of the Finno-Ugric field. Since 1960, congresses of the International Finno-Ugric Society, held every fifth year, brought together not only scholars from countries with large Finno-Ugric populations but also scholars of Finno-Ugric topics (mostly linguists) from throughout the world (including those Estonian war refugees working in Western universities). The third congress, held in 1970, took place in Tallinn; it marked the first time that many foreign scholars had visited Soviet Estonia and met with colleagues who were often not allowed to travel abroad. The existence of such a network and its sponsorship of regular international academic events, publications, and research projects greatly stimulated research in Finno-Ugric folk musics. Selecting folk music as one's research material enabled one to relate rather theoretical musical problems to broader studies of Finno-Ugric folklore, and thus to participate in this international network of scholars.[12]

As for the methodological aspect of folk music research, participating in the interdisciplinary network of Finno-Ugric studies fostered strong relationships with scholars of linguistics. (On an institutional level, such a relationship was already evident in the affiliation of those two fields at the Institute of Language and Literature.) The 1970s were just the time when the influence of structural linguistics, generative grammars, and various quantitative methods of analysis using formal characteristics and formal modeling became important both in American ethnomusicology and East European musical folkloristics or musical ethnography. The application of modern methods for investigating Estonian folk music was a relatively smooth and natural process, nurtured by the general research environment described above.

Throughout the Soviet period, publishing in Russian was recommended, and in Soviet conferences, including the meetings of Baltic scholars, Russian was the only official language. After the reform, in 1975, of the Higher Attestation Committee in Moscow (the body that confirmed all academic degrees – Candidate, Doctor – and assigned academic titles – Docent, Professor), all dissertations that were not written in Russian had to be submitted together with a complete Russian translation. To avoid double work, most Estonian dissertations defended in Estonia after 1975 were written in Russian, even those considering problems regarding the Estonian language itself. On the other hand, participating in the International Finno-Ugric Society provided opportunities for regular publication in German, English and Finnish. Browsing the bibliographies of Finno-Ugric studies, publications related to various Finno-Ugric congresses and conferences, and reports from the regular Finnish–Estonian symposia is remarkable, and points to the strong motivation of Estonian scholars to participate in this international community and to present their work, in various European languages, at its forums. Indeed, compiling the voluminous *Bibliographia Studiorum Uralicorum* (1990) was itself one of the great projects of this network.

Generative Linguistics and Experimental Phonetics in Musicological Research

Due to the rising popularity of semiotics, the metaphor of music as language became widely used in the 1970s. Both semiotics and structural linguistics had roots in Russian philology of the early twentieth century, though in the Soviet Union they were treated as dangerously dissident fields. During the Soviet period, one of the most important centers for study in these fields was the Department of Russian Philology at the University of Tartu, headed by Professor Juri Lotman. The department's conferences in the 1960s and 1970s brought together open-minded scholars from the Soviet metropoles, though their activities were closely watched by the authorities. In the early 1970s, a lecturer in the department, Boris Gasparov (presently Professor of Russian Philology at Columbia University in New York), who was interested in music and had earned a degree as a musicologist (at Moscow's Gnessin Institute of Music Pedagogy), wrote a handful of articles describing classical harmony by way of linguistic structural analysis (Gasparov 1975, 1979).

The link between this Russian-speaking group of linguists and a group of Estonian musicologists gathering at the Institute of Language and Literature was Mart Remmel (1944–2000). Remmel had graduated in Estonian philology at the University of Tartu in 1969, and had participated both in Lotman's seminars and in the seminars of the Group for Generative Grammar (a group of Estonian linguists consisting of younger faculty and students, who gathered with the aim of studying new developments in general linguistics that had not been introduced into official courses of study at the universities). Owing to Remmel's special combination of interests, his studies touched upon both mathematics and computing, fields that had recently become more and more central for new developments in linguistics. Remmel was, moreover, deeply interested in music and had some experience in music theory. In 1968 he became a researcher at the Laboratory of Experimental Phonetics at the Institute of Language and Literature. There, he showed great enthusiasm for applying his skills in formal modeling to different areas, and he actively sought out collaborators. In 1975, when I graduated from the Tallinn Conservatory as a musicologist specializing in the analysis of folk music, Remmel invited me to join the Laboratory of Experimental Phonetics to continue my research. Upon his initiative, we organized a series of seminars in music analysis, informal meetings open for everyone interested in thinking about music. Our first guest lecturer was Gasparov.[13] The first period of the seminar's existence lasted a handful of years. Its very active first season concluded with a seminar in collective analysis following the model of 'monographic analysis' as practiced by Lotman's group for the purpose of analyzing poetry (concentrating on a single work, with participants analyzing it from different perspectives and using different analytical methods).[14]

Remmel's ambitious plan to reorganize the Laboratory of Experimental Phonetics into a Department of Computational Linguistics and to purchase a computer (at that time, a small number of computing centers served many institutions simultaneously, and it was not an easy task to argue persuasively that linguists needed such equipment) was realized in 1977. In designing the new department, Remmel was eager to draw together researchers active in different fields in an endeavor to identify suitable problems for computer analysis. A group of phoneticians comprised the core of the department; new areas added were grammatical analysis, formal analysis of folklore materials (proverbs, folk melodies) and music perception. Common denominators for different computational tasks included automatic pattern recognition and classification and computing distances between different groups of input material. As for analyzing music, the resources of experimental phonetics and computational linguistics were both used, and the projects were not limited to folk music analysis. Indeed, the methods employed were highly effective for analyzing diverse sets of structurally similar and simple musical items.

Remmel himself had already had some earlier experience collaborating with musicologists. Together with the computer engineer Raivo Sule, he had devised a system for the automatic recognition of pitch contours using the computer owned by the Institute of Astrophysics in Tõravere. At first, a system was designed for the phonetic analysis of word intonations. Later, an application of this system for the automatic notation of folk melodies was developed. In the latter project, Remmel's musical collaborators were Ingrid Rüütel and Jaan Sarv, a sound engineer at Estonian Radio with a special interest in recording and studying folk music. The work of these scholars resulted in several publications in 1975–1976 (Remmel *et al.* 1975; Remmel & Rüütel 1976), but their system itself had a short life. A more stable system for detecting pitch contours was developed after the Department of Computational Linguistics received its own computer in late 1979, but by that time the idea of automatic notation had lost its attractiveness for many. To be sure, the possibility of attaining not only pitch contours but also various acoustic analyses via computational methods was later actively pursued for the purpose of investigating folk singing. The aim, however, was no longer to develop an automatic system of notation but to investigate different features of prosody in singing.[15]

Throughout this period, the formal classification of folk melodies was of interest in a number of countries, and in 1975 a group working at the Institute of Art in Yerevan, Armenia, organized a conference on the formalized analysis of musical texts (Goshovskii 1977). The leader of this project group was Vladimir Goshovskii, whose own work focused upon Slavic melodies. The group included Armenian musicologists and computer specialists, whose goal was to work out an analytic chart for codifying the characteristics of a melody, and then to develop algorithms for the automatic processing of that data. Together with Ingrid Rüütel, Mart Remmel presented, at a meeting of this group, the Estonian system of automatic notation and his first attempt at using formal grammars for modeling and grouping melodies. Later, Rüütel, at her own department, formed a new group for developing a similar chart-based automatic classification system for Estonian melodies, though based upon rather different principles of codification. Remmel and I continued for some years in our efforts to develop means of grammatical modeling, in which melodies were treated as sequences of symbols in a simplified alphabetic notation. We experimented with subjecting larger and smaller sets of melodies to computerized analysis, inferring from these sets a formal grammar and evaluating the typological distances between different groups of melodies (Lippus & Remmel 1977; Remmel 1977a; Rüütel 1977).

During the early 1980s, the Department of Computational Linguistics organized a number of annual international symposiums. Several included presentations about music. In 1982 a symposium organized by Remmel and Jaan Ross was dedicated to commonalities between the processing of linguistic and musical data, and about half of the papers presented considered music (Ross 1982). At that meeting, very different approaches to music were represented; several papers discussed problems of music perception, tasks of formal segmentation and pattern recognition, statistical analysis and semiotics. It may be incidental, but the papers presented at this symposium considered either abstract elements of music or art music; only one paper was devoted to folk music specifically (Arnolds Kloṭiņš and Vilnis Detlovs described interval patterns in Latvian folksongs). While formal analysis of folk music could be explained with recourse to the practical needs of processing and analyzing very large numbers of melodies collected in archives, when applied to individual musical compositions, these same procedures really did constitute a 'formalist' approach of the sort condemned by mainstream Soviet musicologists. This small conference, however, did not attract any critical attention. To present this sort of research under the rubric of 'processing data' and to draw parallels between linguistic and musical analysis was, apparently, sufficient to align it with the officially acceptable 'positive sciences' – with emerging technologies and with studies in artificial intelligence. The papers presented at the symposium varied widely in their quality, but the meeting was important for the international contacts it enabled; in particular, Adrian Houtsma (from the Institute for Perception Research in Eindhoven) and Eero Tarasti (of the University of Jyväskylä) both gave lectures introducing their research.

In many respects, the heyday of the Department of Computational Linguistics – and the scholarly activities of Mart Remmel – culminated with the organization of the International Congress of Phonetic Sciences in Tallinn in 1987, which included a session on music perception. After that, changes in the musicological scene, which had already begun to make themselves felt a few years earlier, gradually overtook the department's work. First, the political changes set in motion by Gorbachev's *perestroika* took more and more radical turns, fundamentally transforming academic life throughout the USSR. Second, the enthusiasm for positivistic approaches to musicological research (as in other areas of artistic and humanistic inquiry) began to abate. Some aspects of the department's work were rendered obsolete by new technologies (the explosive distribution of personal computers and other technological developments in both hardware and software thoroughly transformed the nature of the problems investigated as well as the research methods employed). And musical cognition and perception came to constitute a new and independent field of study with its own societies and meetings. Finally, postmodernist trends in musicological and ethnomusicological discourses were strengthening, moving the interest of scholars away from the scientifically oriented description of musical texts and towards new methodologies of music research more closely allied with sociology and cultural criticism.

Conclusion

In this brief survey of Estonian musicology, starting from its very beginnings in the first Republic and ending with the first signs of the disintegration of Soviet power in the mid-1980s, I have concentrated primarily upon the institutional establishment of the discipline, and less strongly upon specific research projects, publications and the work of individual scholars. Moreover, I have paid special attention to those persons who contributed to the organization of musicological life during this period. I must stress, however, that this does not reflect any critical evaluation of individual contributions to Estonian musicology; that would – of necessity – be the subject of a slightly different story, peopled, in part, by the same cast of characters. Likewise, I have not considered the work of the heads of the musicology section of the Estonian Composers' Union. My reason for this is that the main line of my examination was to be the rise of professional academic music research in Estonia. Hence, only those institutions providing full-time positions for research, or teaching combined with research, were considered in detail. To be sure, the Composers' Union did support many related activities, providing resources for conferences, fieldwork, publications, and so forth. But it was neither a professional organization of musicologists nor an academic research institution. Most of the members of its musicological section were journalists, and its main function was to support the promotion of new Estonian music.

Recounting the development of Estonian musicology over the course of the twentieth century, one cannot assert – literally, at least – that its 'normal' growth was restricted during the period of Soviet rule, for it is very difficult to specify what such 'normal' growth would be. However, we can indeed observe several turns in its development that were brought about by the intervention of political authorities, and *that* is certainly not 'normal' in any academic discipline. To be sure, only a small part of those interventions were made directly and publicly, like the Stalinist campaign against 'bourgeois nationalism and formalism', the censoring of certain views or the names of suspect persons in published texts, and so forth. A more subtle way of suppressing undesirable themes than prohibiting them outright was to exercise strict control over financing for research and the themes approved for dissertations. The widespread claim that Soviet authorities prohibited research in this or that area outright (for example, studies of religious music, of Baltic German musical culture, or of the musical activities of Estonian refugees in Western countries) is not exactly true. But it would have been possible to study such topics only as an amateur historian, delving into the archives after working another job and with no hope of publishing one's findings.

For professional musicologists, studying folk musics (in contrast to Estonian art music, which had been subjected to ideological interpretation since the beginning of the Soviet period) provided a relatively safe haven and an opportunity to engage in one's research without the danger of unexpected ideological attacks. Indeed, to apply a wide variety of new scientific research methods to the study of folk repertoires was to associate one's work with the technological progress so highly prized by Soviet authorities. Such projects found broad institutional support, and those of us who engaged in them were able to defend our degrees successfully. The choice of such research projects was certainly conditioned, to some extent, by practical and professional considerations. But in the 1970s there was also a great deal of enthusiasm for transforming the study of music into a science as an end in itself. And that goal provided ample opportunities and adrenaline for young scholars seeking to transcend the limits and hermetic nature of the local musicological scene.

Notes

1   On musicology in Finland and Sweden in the early twentieth century, see Bengtsson (1976), Haapanen (1939) and Lappalainen (1990).

2   Leichter's article originally appeared in *Kunst ja Kirjandus*, a supplement to the daily newspaper *Päevaleht*, 31 March 1940.

3   It should be noted, however, that the faculty of the Tallinn Conservatory also had to conduct research as part of their workload; this was a requirement at all university-level institutions. Practicing musicians were permitted to substitute composing or performing for written research, but many chose instead to study the history of their field or any number of pedagogical problems. A handful of musicologists (mostly folklorists) were also employed within the system of the Academy of Sciences.

4   Leichter's copy of this letter is preserved in the archives of the Estonian Museum of Theatre and Music: TMM, f. M 159, n. 1, s.ü. 553, l. 28. Leichter's plans for

the department (TMM, M159, s.ü. 553, l. 34–5) read: A. Estonian music history: (1) Riho Päts (part-time), 'The Life and Works of Rudolf Tobias', (2) Aurora Semper (part-time), 'Miina Härma and Her Musical Life-Work', (3) Karl Leichter (part-time), 'The Development of Estonian Music (General Survey)', (4) Hillar Saha (senior researcher), 'Music in Estonia in the Middle Ages', (5) Paul Sarv (junior researcher), 'The Life and Works of Aleksander Läte'; B. Collecting and studying Estonian folk music: (a) continuation of collecting folk music in cooperation with the students of folklore at the University of Tartu and the Tallinn Conservatory, (b) systematization of folk melodies, (c) publication of folk melodies, (d) investigation of Estonian instrumental folk music and folk instruments; researchers: (1) the best leader for the field is Herbert Tampere, (2) Elman Pass (senior researcher), (3) and (4) technical assistants; equipment: (1) library, (2) four phonographs, (3) two transportable tape-recorders.

5   Some drafts of the content list for this study include a chapter on folk music. However, the published study opens instead with a brief survey of early art music in Estonia and continues by concentrating upon the rise of Estonian musical life and music composed by Estonians in the nineteenth century.

6   For example, Ofelia Tuisk wrote in the introduction of her article 'Muusika sümfooniaorkestrile' [Music for the Symphony Orchestra] (Tuisk 1975, p. 181): 'A new generation of symphonists became active only in the beginning of the 1930s, and only a few of them could compete, in terms of their professional level, with earlier graduates of the St. Petersburg Conservatory. (We must remember that *Don Carlos* by Arthur Kapp, *Dawn* by [Heino] Eller, *Julius Caesar* by [Rudolf] Tobias, and the First Symphony of [Arthur] Lemba were all student works!) Nevertheless, the natural potential of the new generation of symphonists was not less than the talents of their teachers. It is also important to note that the professional profile of these [Estonian] composers was narrower. While graduates of the St. Petersburg Conservatory had a wide profile and became prominent as composers and performers, organizers of musical life, theoreticians, and critics, graduates of Estonian music schools, as a rule, were trained narrowly, only as composers.' We must note, however, that this declaration does not prevent Tuisk from evaluating the student compositions of Eduard Tubin very highly, and his later works as the greatest of all symphonic music composed during these years. Though criticizing impersonally the narrow profile of local graduates, Tuisk nonetheless praised a number of young Estonian composers (Tubin, Karl Leichter, Riho Päts, Voldemar Leemets, Eduard Oja) for their competent criticism, especially when compared to a more conservative older generation of reviewers.

7   I provide additional discussion of this situation in Lippus (1999).

8   Tampere's five-volume collection of Estonian folksongs, published during this period, was of seminal importance for Estonian music and musicology (Tampere 1956–1965). Tampere's basic systematic grouping of songs into genres according to their function is still used, although his own description of melodic types based upon this system (Tampere 1965) has been largely superseded by more recent descriptive schema.

9   In the 1970s, an ethnographer, Igor Tõnurist, and a musicologist, Ofelia Tuisk, served as researchers at the Institute of History. A handful of other musicologists were affiliated with the Institute as *aspirants* (postgraduate students writing their dissertations).

10   Rüütel defended her dissertation, 'Eesti uuema rahvalaulu kujunemine' (The Formation of the More Recent Style of Estonian Folk Song), at the University of Tartu in 1969, and published several articles based upon this research in the 1960s (e.g. Rüütel 1969). Her later work includes the two-volume folksong collection *Eesti uuemad laulumängud* (Rüütel 1980–1983). Her more recent research focuses upon ancient folksongs of the Estonians and other Baltic-Finnish peoples. Olli Kõiva's work has touched less strongly upon music, but her dissertation on the wedding tradition and songs of Kihnu Island ('Regivärsilise rahvalaulu traditsioon Kihnu saarel', University of Tartu, 1965), along with numerous publications (e.g. Kõiva 1961) based upon that research, constitute important contributions to our understanding of that singing tradition.

11   The last conference, held in 1989 after Estonia had become a member of the International Council of Folklore Festivals (Conseil International des Organisations de Festivals de Folklore et d'Arts Traditionnels), was part of the first international Baltica festival. It was open to all scholars and had two working languages, English and Russian.

12   See, for instance, Lippus (1981). The problem discussed in this article was abstract and could be applied to diverse sets of melodies.

13   Gasparov visited the seminar twice. On 24 and 25 November 1975, he delivered the lectures 'The Structure of the Syntactic Component of Musical Language' and 'The Role of Acoustical Principle and Cultural Environment in the Formation of Musical Structure'. On 4 and 5 March 1976, he delivered two lectures on monographic analysis: 'Johann Sebastian Bach: St. John Passion and St. Matthew Passion' and 'Modest Mussorgsky: *Khovanshchina*'. The term 'monographic analysis' was used by Lotman's group to refer to a detailed analysis of a single artwork approached from a variety of methodological directions.

14   In the spring of 1976, the seminar's participants, including myself, analyzed three songs, based upon folk melodies, by Veljo Tormis, describing their sources, text, form, texture and acoustics; see Sarv *et al.* (1976). In this study, an attempt was made to avoid using traditional approaches to music analysis (classifying formal schemes, describing the tonal plan, etc.), and to examine instead means of segmentation and the appearance of groupings based upon different structural characteristics. At the time, our attempt at discussing these various methodological aspects of analyzing music proved more valuable than the published text that was finally produced. In the late 1980s, together with Jaan Ross (and without Mart Remmel), we revived the seminar for the purpose of discussing recent works and organizing lectures of visiting scholars (e.g. Raymond Monelle and Johan Sundberg in 1989, Eugene Narmour and Charles Rosen in 1990).

15   With the rapid development of personal computers and commercial hardware for speech analysis, this area of research grew considerably in popularity during the 1980s. See, for instance, Lippus (1980); Remmel and Rüütel (1980); Rüütel and Ross (1985).

References

Bengtsson, I. (1976) 'Musicology' in *Acta Universitatis Upsaliensis 5, Uppsala University 500 Years: Faculty of Arts at Uppsala University: History, Art and Philosophy* (Uppsala, Uppsala University).

Bibliographia Studiorum Uralicorum 1917–1987, Vol. 2, *Ethnology and Folkloristics*, Part 2, *Folkloristics* (1990) (Moscow, Akademiya nauk SSSR).

Gasparov, B. M. (1975) *K probleme izomorfizma urovnei muzykal'nogo yazyka na materiale garmonii venskogo klassicizma* (Tartu, Tartu Riikliku Ülikooli Toimetised).

Gasparov, B. M. (1979) *Poslednyaya Sonata Mozarta* (Tartu, Tartu Riikliku Ülikooli Toimetised).

Goshovskii, V. L. (ed.) (1977) *MAAFAT 75. First All-Union Seminar on Machine Aspects of Algorithmic Formalized Analysis of Musical Texts. Materials* (Yerevan, Armenian Academy of Sciences).

Haapanen, T. (1939) 'Die musikwissenschaftliche Forschung in Finnland', *Archiv für Musikforschung*, 4, 2, pp. 230–43.

Kõiva, O. (1961) 'Kihnu regivärsilise rahvalaulu funktsiooni ja esitamisviisi küsimustest', in *Paar sammukest eesti kirjanduse ja rahvaluule uurimise teed. Uurimusi ja materjale*, 2 (Tartu, Fr. R. Kreutzwaldi nim. Kirjandusmuuseum).

Lappalainen, S. (1990) 'Musiikki on viihtynyt Helsingin Yliopistossa', *Musiikkitiede*, 1, pp. 159–89.

Lehtonen, J. U. E. (1981) 'Uuno Taavi Sirelius, Student of Finno-Ugric Ethnology', *Ethnologia Scandinavica*, 11, pp. 13–21.

Leichter, K. (1932) 'Rahvaviiside korjamisest Eestis' in *Õpetatud Eesti Seltsi Kirjad 1, Vanavara vallast* (Tartu, Õpetatud Eesti Selts).

Leichter, K. (1982), *Valik arikleid* in jürisson, J. (ed.) (Tallinn, Eesti Raamat).

Lippus, U. (1980) 'K voprosu o vzaimodeistvii rechevoi i muzykal'noi intonatsii v rodnoi narodno-pesennoi traditsii', in Rüütel, I. (ed.) (1980). pp. 159–67.

Lippus, U. (1981) 'On the Formal Description of Monodic Melodies' in *Congressus Quintus Internationalis Fenno-Ugristarum. Turku 20.–27. VIII 1980*, Part 8, *Dissertationes sectionum: Ethnologica, folkloristica et mythologica, archaeologica et anthropologica* (Turku, SKS).

Lippus, U. (1999) 'Baltic Music History Writing: Problems and Perspectives', *Acta Musicologica*, 71, 1, pp. 50–60.

Lippus, U. & Remmel, M. 'Opyt grammaticheskogo vyvoda na materiale estonskikh runicheskikh pesen', in Remmel, M. (ed.) (1977b). pp. 56–74.

Remmel, M. (1977a) 'Nekotorye polozheniya taksonomii v primenenii k melodiyam', in Remmel, M. (ed.) (1977b). pp. 75–9.

Remmel, M. (ed.) (1977b) *Problemy taksonomii estonskikh runicheskikh melodii* (Tallinn, AN ESSR).

Remmel, M. & Rüütel, I. (1976) 'Automaatse noodistuse vahendid ja taust', *Keel ja Kirjandus*, 19, 12, pp. 731–3.

Remmel, M. & Rüütel, I. (1980) 'Opyt notatsii i issledovaniya vepsskikh prichitanii', in Rüütel, I. (ed.) (1980). pp. 169–95.

Remmel, M. *et al.* (1975) *Automatic Notation of One-Voiced Song* (preprint KKI-4) (Tallinn, Eesti NSV Teaduste Akadeemia).

Ross, J. (ed.) (1982) *Symposium on Common Aspects of Processing Linguistic and Musical Data* (Tallinn, Academy of Sciences of the ESSR).

Rüütel, I. (1969) 'Muistne "Loomislaul" eesti uuemas rahvatraditsioonis', in *Paar sammukest eesti kirjanduse uurimise teed. Uurimusi ja materjale*, 6 (Tallinn, Eesti Raamat).

Rüütel, I. (1977) 'Opornaya sistema i zakonomernosti var'irovaniya mobil'nykh elementov kak strukturnye priznaki tipologii narodnykh napevov', in Remmel, M. (ed.) (1977b). pp. 80–117.

Rüütel, I. (ed.) (1980) *Finno-ugorskii muzykal'nyi fol'klor i vzaimosvyazi s sosebnimi kul'turami* (Tallinn, Eesti Raamat).

Rüütel, I. (1980–83) Eesti uuemad laulumängud, Vols 2 (Tallinn, Eesti Raamat).

Rüütel, I. & Ross, J. (1985) *A Study of Pitch Contours and the Scale Structure in Votic Folk Music* (preprint KKI-37) (Tallinn, Academy of Sciences of the ESSR).

Sarv, J. *et al.* (1976) *Towards a Monographical Analysis of Some Folk-Song Arrangements* (preprint KKI-6) (Tallinn, Academy of Sciences of the ESSR).

Tampere, H. (1932) 'Tähelepanekuid rahvaviisidest ja rahvalaulude ettekandmisest lõunapoolses Lääne-Eestis' in *Kultuuri ja teaduse teilt* (Tartu, Loodus).

Tampere, H. (1934) 'Mõningaid mõtteid eesti rahvaviisidest ja selle uurimismeetodist', in *Eesti Muusika Almanak*, 1 (Tallinn, Eesti Lauljate Liit).

Tampere, H. (1935) *Eesti rahvaiiside antoloogia* (Tartu, Eesti Rahvaluule Arhiivi Toimetused), Vol. 1.

Tampere, H. (1937) 'Eesti vana rahvalaulu rütmiprobleemist', *Looming*, 2, pp. 190–8.

Tampere, H. (1956–65) *Eesti rahvalaule viisidega*, Vols 1–3 (Tallinn, Eesti Riiklik Kirjastus), Vol. 4 (Tallinn, Eesti Raamat), Vol. 5 (Tallinn, Valgus).

Tampere, H. (1965) 'Eesti regivärsilise rahvalaulu meloodika stiilitüübid', *Etnofraafiamuuseumi aastaraamat*, 20, pp. 50–66.

Topman, M. (1999) *Mõnda möödunust. Eesti Muusikaakadeemia 80* (Tallinn, EMA).

Tuisk, O. (1975) 'Muusika sümfooniaorkestrile', in Vahter, A. (ed.) (1968–75). pp. 181–271.

Vahter, A. (ed.) (1968–75) Eesti muusika, Vols 2 (Tallinn, Eesti Raamat).

Viires, A. (1986) 'Folklorismi sünd Eestis', *Keel ja Kirjandus*, 10, pp. 595–602.

MUZIKOLOĢIJA/MŪZIKAS ZINĀTNE: A CRITICAL HISTORY OF LATVIAN MUSICOLOGY

Martin Boiko

Beginnings of a Discourse

In Latvia, writing about music, in its published form, extends well back into the eighteenth century. As both *muzikoloģija* (musicology, encompassing scholarship and criticism) and *mūzikas zinātne* (the 'science of music', referring explicitly to academic research), its history constitutes an integral part of the nation's cultural heritage.[1] At the beginning of the nineteenth century, essays on music, primarily in the form of critical reviews, appeared in such Baltic German periodicals as the *Nordisches Archiv* and the *Rigisches Theaterblatt*. In the second half of the century, they assumed an important place in the widely read *Zeitung für Stadt und Land* and the *Rigaer Tageblatt*. It was during this latter period that they also appeared, for the first time, in the Latvian-language press: in *Mājas Viesis* (*The Home-Visitor*), *Latviešu Avīzes* (*Latvian Newspaper*, whose music critics included the composers Jānis Cimze and Juris Caunītis), *Baltijas Vēstnesis* (*Baltic Messenger*) and *Dienas Lapa* (*The Daily Page*, whose critics included Ādolfs Alunāns and Jānis Straume).

The final decades of the nineteenth century also saw the establishment of Riga's first schools of music. The Schule der Tonkunst (Music School) was founded in 1877, Rīgas Mūzikas Skola was established in 1885 and Das Erste Musikinstitut in Riga (The First Music Institute of Riga) opened its doors in 1864 on the model of the Dresden Conservatory. At these institutions, music theory was taught alongside instrumental performance and singing. The most thorough training in music theory seems to have been provided by Das Erste Musikinstitut in Riga, in whose classroom a number of distinguished Latvian musicians, among them the brothers Jāzeps and

Jēkabs Mediņš, received their training. During this period, elementary instruction in music theory was also provided at the teacher-training seminary schools in the towns of Valka and Irlava. Among the teachers of theory and composition at the Schule der Tonkunst was the historian and critic Moritz Rudolph (1843–1992), who also wrote for the *Zeitung für Stadt und Land* and produced a number of works of lasting value for the study of Latvian music history, including *Die Rigaer Oper von 1782 bis 1886* (1887) and the *Rigaer Theater- und Tonkünstlerlexikon* (1890).

Throughout this period, most of the music-related essays that appeared in the Latvian-language press focused upon a handful of closely related themes: the emergence of professional Latvian music-making, Latvian song festivals and questions regarding the nature and substance of Latvian national identity. This was, of course, a period of intense interest in the latter topic, when evidence of Latvian national character was widely sought in folklore and, above all else, folk song. For this reason, it comes as no surprise to find that the first significant achievements in music study were accomplished in the field of folk music research. In the 1880s, the composer, music theorist and publicist Andrejs Jurjāns (also Jurjānu Andrejs; 1856–1922) began substantial work collecting, studying and writing about folk music. As we would say today, his was truly a long-term project. His efforts gave rise to the first scholarly publication of Latvian folk melodies and texts, *Latvju tautas mūzikas materiāli* (*The Materials of Latvian Folk Music*), which appeared in six volumes between 1894 and 1926. This publication left a lasting mark upon the subsequent development of both professional music-making and folk music research. Indeed, more than 60 years later, Jurjāns' study would figure prominently in the 'new folklore movement' of the final quarter of the twentieth century. While intensely engaged in ethnographic work, Jurjāns was also active as a music critic, and he also completed the first comprehensive historical surveys of Latvian music and its development.[2] Jurjāns' musicological endeavors touched upon the whole of Latvia's musical culture. His approach to his material was systematic and comprehensive, and his work exhibits real affinities to that of his contemporaries working in Central Europe. Characterized by methodological rigor, breadth of vision and a high level of professionalism, his scholarship has proven to be of lasting value. Jurjāns was the first Latvian musicologist in the true sense of the word.

Another figure who left an important mark on the history of Latvian musicology was the author, publicist, journalist and composer Jānis Straume (also Straumes Jānis; 1861–1929). Between 1890 and 1892, Straume published the *Baltijas Mūzikas Kalendārs* (*Baltic Musical Calendar*), the first periodical devoted exclusively to music to appear in the Latvian language. This publication lay the foundation for later writing about Latvia's professional musical culture. Straume's *Calendar* featured extensive essays on the composers Jānis Cimze, Jānis Bētiņš, Kārlis Baumanis and Ernests Vīgners, as well as news about the activities of regional choral societies and music schools. With his *Calendar*, Straume truly became the father of writing about Latvian professional music, and he would continue to produce important studies through the 1920s. Among his later publications was the first substantial study of Latvian folk instruments. Another important early publication, *Mūzikas Druva* (*The Musical Cornfield*), appeared only briefly, in 1906, 1908 and 1909. It was edited by Atis Kauliņš (1867–1944), a graduate of the St. Petersburg Conservatory. The short run of this journal, like that of Straume's *Calendar*, seems to suggest that Latvian society was not yet ready, at the turn of the century, to support the regular publication of a periodical devoted exclusively to music. There was not yet sufficient demand.

Social and Institutional Changes: The Republican Period

By around 1900, the development of Latvian cultural life had given rise to a broad and rapidly expanding circle of professional composers and performers. These figures constituted a new musical elite, who enjoyed the support of an audience that was musically literate and numerically substantial. This situation both signaled and fostered an increasingly refined sensitivity to music and musical thought within Latvian society. Under such conditions, it was only natural that a kind of professional musicology would coalesce, and this indeed took place. But as we have seen, Latvia's first attempts at musicological work were tentative and fragmentary, characterized by diverse intellectual currents and inspired by numerous initiatives and impulses. Moreover, those engaged in musicological work never attempted to unite their efforts into a single, comprehensive movement or endeavor. At the end of the nineteenth century and during the early decades of the twentieth, the field still remained in its infancy. With the exception of Jurjāns' *Materials*, no large-scale projects were attempted. The central question of musicological inquiry – what can one conclude, objectively speaking, from the materials at hand – hardly figured in the intellectual discourse of the period. Perhaps not surprisingly, no attempt was undertaken to find an institutional home for the discipline. The Latvian Conservatory, founded in 1919, did not recognize musicology as an autonomous field of research or instruction. This was also the case at the University of Latvia, also founded in 1919. It cannot be said that the republic lacked individuals who conducted research on historical and theoretical topics and were capable of teaching in those areas. Indeed, Latvia had a vibrant community of figures specializing in traditional music. Yet the *idea* of musicology as an academic discipline simply did not exist during this period. Unlike many other parts of Europe, Latvia had no professional musicological societies dedicated to the development and advancement of the discipline. This situation seems especially perplexing when we consider the fact that, during this same period, numerous models for musicology's academic institutionalization could be found even in places both geographically and culturally nearby. Academic chairs in musicology were founded as early as the 1890s at both the University of Vienna and Prague's Czech University, for instance. And the universities of Helsinki, Krakow, Turku and Königsberg, among others, saw the founding of chairs and the establishment of musicological institutes during the first three decades of the twentieth century.

Such examples were not followed in Latvia. The case was the same in Estonia and Lithuania, which leads one to suspect that causes might be found in historical circumstances and attitudes common to all three Baltic republics, which prevented them from following Western and Central European models with regard to the foundation and structure of their systems of higher education. But whatever the causes might have been, the fact remains that, in contrast to the situation in many European countries, musicology lacked an institutional base in Latvia as late as the 1920s and 1930s.[3] As we will see, this situation would have profound implications for the fate that the discipline would soon meet.

Given its lack of an institutional home and the *ad hoc* manner in which it had developed, it is perhaps not surprising that the discipline as a whole produced little of note during the Republican period of the 1920s and 1930s. This did not mean, however, that no musicological work was undertaken at all. Indeed, there are a number of names, works and achievements that deserve our attention. As mentioned previously, the work of Jānis Straume continued in the 1920s. In 1921, a number of his essays appeared in the journal *Latvju Mūzika* under the rubric *Materiāli latviešu mūzikas vēsturei* (*Materials for a History of Latvian Music*). These included articles on the composers Ernests Vīgners, Andrejs Jurjāns, Jāzeps Vītols and Alfrēds Kalniņš. The following year, Straume published a series of essays in brochure form, collectively entitled *Mūsu mūzikas mākslinieki* (*Our Musicians*).

The central figure in Latvian musicology in the 1930s was Jēkabs Vītoliņš (1898–1977), a historian, prolific essayist and great popularizer of music. Vītoliņš graduated from the Latvian Conservatory's faculty of Composition and Music Theory in 1924 and later studied at the University of Vienna (1929 and 1931) and at the Sorbonne in Paris (1936–1937). In 1938, he began teaching at the Latvian Conservatory. In 1930, he and Roberts Kroders edited an important volume, *Latvju skaņu mākslinieku portrejas* (*Portraits of Latvian Musicians* 1930). Four years later, Vītoliņš completed his *Mūzikas vēsture* (*History of Music* n.d.), the first comprehensive history of the art to be published in the Latvian language. This volume included a significant treatment of Latvian music – both its history and leading figures – and musical life. Although it is marked by a number of methodological problems that limit its utility today, Vītoliņš's *History* undeniably ranks among the greatest achievements of Latvian musicology of the Republican period. As it happened, the volume's treatment of Russian music would bring its author his first round of troubles with Soviet authorities in later years.

The breadth of topics addressed by Latvian musicologists expanded significantly during the inter-war years. Those themes that had been treated most widely during the preceding period – song festivals, questions relating to national identity and works by contemporary Latvian composers – retained their central place in the literature. But the breadth of Latvia's musical life was now reflected much more vividly. Performances of operas and ballets, musical events taking place in far-flung locales (in Latgale, for instance), the day-to-day activities of such institutions as the National Opera and the music schools, and even the use of music in cinema were addressed. Questions regarding Latvia's musical history also received much broader treatment. This was largely the result of a greater level of interest in historical subjects shown by the popular press, and also of the founding of several new specialist music periodicals. To be sure, the specialist music press was still quite unstable as a whole, with several periodicals launched only to cease publication within a handful of years. Collectively, however, such journals spanned nearly the whole of the period of the first Latvian Republic: *Latvju Mūzika* (1921–1922), *Mūzikas Nedēļa* (*The Week in Music* 1923–1929), *Mūzika* (1925–1927) and *Mūzikas Apskats* (*Musical Review* 1932–1939).

Throughout these decades, significant research was undertaken in the area of folk music as well. One year after its founding in 1925, the Archives of Latvian Folklore (Latvijas folkloras krātuve) recorded 155 phonograph cylinders and pressed numerous records. By 1941, the Archives had acquired transcriptions of 16,271 unique works. The most prolific collector of folk music during this period was Emilis Melngailis (1874–1954), one of most brilliant, influential and paradoxical personalities in the history of Latvian music. By 1941, Melngailis had transcribed nearly 4,500 melodies. Of these, approximately 4,350 were Latvian; the rest were Lithuanian, Russian, Hebrew, Belorussian, Roma, Estonian and Liv.[4] Melngailis wrote extensively about his collecting efforts in the 1920s and 1930s, and those writings are themselves of significant musicological interest.

Another notable figure in the area of folk music research was the composer Jēkabs Graubiņš (1886–1961). In the mid-1930s, Graubiņš published widely on general characteristics of Latvian folk music, and in particular on the metrical properties of Latvian folk song. His contributions are characterized by precision and attention to detail, breadth of focus, and a clear and direct manner of exposition. From 1938 onwards, he lectured on folk music at the Latvian Conservatory. The third major figure in the sphere of folk music research was the composer Jūlijs Sproģis (1887–1972). In his intellectual development, Sproģis was influenced by the Finnish school of folkloristics. This influence is evident in his *Jāņu dziesmu melodijas* (*St. John's Festival Melodies* 1941), the first monograph devoted exclusively to a single genre of Latvian folk music.[5]

Transformations of the Discipline under Soviet Rule

The consequences of the Soviet invasion and the events of World War II were dramatic for the whole of Latvian society. In addition to the loss of independence and an untold number of lives, one of the greatest blows that the nation experienced was the division of its members into two distinct communities: those who remained in Latvia and those who emigrated to the West. This cleavage divided every social class and group. In the early post-war years, members of that community of Latvians residing in the free world applied themselves with great vigor to the task of carrying on the cultural work begun during the Republican period. Their efforts bore significant results in many areas. However, as decades passed and hopes of returning to Latvia dwindled, the cultural activities and academic work undertaken by members of the émigré community declined. In contrast, the community of intellectuals who remained in Latvia suffered great losses during the first years of Soviet rule through the deportation and marginalization of many formerly leading figures in academic and cultural life. Moreover, this latter community experienced the full effects of the Sovietization of culture, which continued even after the cessation of wide-scale physical repressions in the mid-1950s.

All of these events and processes left deep marks upon Latvia's musical life. A great many musicians and scholars of music fled the country.[6] Admittedly, one cannot speak literally of a cleavage within the ranks of professional musicologists, since, as we have seen, musicology as an institutionalized discipline – and therefore as a cohesive professional group – did not exist in the independent Republic. But after World War II, two distinct and parallel traditions of studying and writing about music took shape. Those musicologists who remained in Latvia would ultimately prove more productive, but significant work was also undertaken by émigré scholars. In the West, the 1960s and 1970s saw the publication of important studies of folk music and Latvian musical culture more generally. Among these one must note especially Valentīns Bērzkalns' *Latviešu dziesmu svētku vēsture, 1864–1949* (*History of the Latvian Song Festival* 1965) and *Latviešu dziesmu svētki trimdā, 1946–1965* (*The Latvian Song Festival in Exile* 1968). One must also mention Longīns Apkalns' *Lettische Musik* (1977), which, despite its frequently unbalanced and politically biased treatment of its material, is distinguished as one of only a handful of major studies of its subject to appear in a language other than Latvian. Members of the émigré community also made important contributions to music journalism. But let us return to the momentous changes that took place within Latvia itself in the aftermath of the Second World War.

As a barometer of the political climate, it is illuminating to compare the fates experienced by our three leading inter-war scholars of folk music: Melngailis, Graubiņš and Sproģis. Melngailis was chosen as the favorite son of the Soviet regime. His folklore collecting expeditions of the 1940s and 1950s and the subsequent publication of his findings received substantial support from Soviet authorities. In 1945 Melngailis was awarded the title of People's Artist of the Latvian SSR. In return, the authorities received from Melngailis effusive proclamations of loyalty.[7] The most academically promising of the three scholars, Jēkabs Graubiņš, experienced a very different fate. He became one of over 200,000 Latvian residents subjected to repression. In the spring of 1949, Graubiņš was dismissed from the Conservatory; in the spring of 1950 he was arrested and sentenced by a *troika* to exile in Siberia. Five years later, during the period of the Khrushchev 'Thaw', Graubiņš returned to Latvia and was rehabilitated. In spite of his rehabilitation, however, all doors to teaching at the Conservatory remained closed to him. Sproģis, the third of our scholars, was not deported. But he was considered ideologically suspect and was consequently barred from teaching, research and membership in the Composers' Union.

It was amidst these oppressive conditions that the institutionalization of musicology finally took place. A faculty of Music History (Mūzikas vēstures nodaļa) was established at the Latvian Conservatory in 1946, and the circumstances in which this took place tell their own story. That year, there arrived in Riga a figure who described himself as 'one of many soldiers in the battle for the renewal of musical life'. This was Vladimir Muzalevskiy (1894–1964), who was sent to Latvia by the Soviet State Bureau for Educational Institutions (Gosudarstvennoye Upravleniye Uchebnymi Zavedeniyami). Muzalevskiy was charged with organizing a music history faculty at the Conservatory. He received a chilly reception, but he carried out his work as assigned. Appointed Conservatory Professor by the Soviet Bureau, Muzalevskiy set to work. In one of his first public appearances at the institution, he lectured on 'The Role of Russian Music in World History'. He delivered this talk, as he recalled in his memoirs, 'in order to establish contact'.[8]

At the beginning, the Faculty of Music History had three members: Muzalevskiy, Lija Krasinska and Jēkabs Vītoliņš. A few years later they were joined by Nilss Grīnfelds. All of these figures played leading roles in the process of establishing the discipline's institutionalized credentials. Together, they would determine the character of musicological study during this decisive phase in its development. They were profoundly influential throughout the Soviet period, and their influence is still felt today.

Muzalevskiy's mandate was clear. He was to lay the institutional foundations for the discipline, to assure its ideological correctness, to appoint trustworthy individuals to its faculty, to make sure that the traditions and cultural values of the independent Republic were not carried over into the post-war era, and to orient Latvian musicology around the study of Russian music and culture. He was the founding chair of the fledgling faculty. In 1948 he was named vice-rector and, if his memoirs are to be trusted, he fulfilled, for a time, the rector's duties as well. He returned to Russia in 1956.

Lija Krasinska (b. 1911) graduated from the Latvian Conservatory in 1933, having studied composition and theory with Jāzeps Vītols and piano with Annija Sokolovska. Between 1934 and 1945, she taught in a number of cities within the USSR. She returned to Latvia after the war and was appointed to the Conservatory's faculty in 1945; ultimately, she was named Conservatory Professor. Krasinska was known for her erudition in the area of Russian music and her talents as a lecturer. She remained an active member of the Conservatory's faculty through the mid-1990s. Almost every prominent Latvian musicologist, and many composers as well, studied with her or attended her lectures. Even today, she remains, for many, a figure of utmost authority, widely remembered with gratitude and warm feelings. Her contributions to research on the history of Latvian music were substantial.

The composer, pianist and historian Nilss Grīnfelds (1907–1986) graduated from the Moscow Conservatory in 1931 after studying with the pianist Aleksandr Gedike. After that, he found work in Moscow as a concertmaster and director at All-Union Radio. During World War II, Grīnfelds was a member of the Latvian SSR State Art Ensemble in the city of Ivanov. In 1945, he was named Distinguished Artist of the Latvian SSR. After the war, he became an active member of the Composers' Union and a member of the Latvian SSR Philharmonic. He taught at the Conservatory from 1949 until 1986, and served for many years as professor and head of the faculty of music history. He also served as vice-rector. I myself never had close contact with Grīnfelds, but I did engage in some communications with him that I recall as generally pleasant. He was erudite and personable, yet he left little in the way of books or essays that can be considered of lasting value. As a whole, Grīnfelds' work was characterized by a strongly ideological bent.

Jēkabs Vītoliņš, as we have already seen, began work at the Conservatory in 1938 – that is, before the Soviet invasion and the outbreak of the Second World War. In 1946, he was appointed to the Conservatory's newly founded historical faculty. He was named head of the faculty in 1957 and retained that position until 1962, when he was demoted amidst a scandal that erupted in 1960 in connection with a volume, edited by Vītoliņš, of writings by the composer and critic Jānis Zālītis (1884–1943). In that volume there appeared a 'grave ideological error': some sort of rhetorical cliche about 'the new order' in Europe that appeared in one of Zālītis' essays written during the years of German occupation (1941–1945).

As soon as the offensive text was discovered, the volume was removed from circulation. This mishap determined Vītoliņš' subsequent fate as chair of the faculty and as Conservatory Professor. He was summarily dismissed, and he never returned to the institution. With Vītoliņš' departure, the Conservatory's faculty lost the only remaining historical musicologist who had been active during the Republican period and whose thinking had been shaped by the academic traditions of Western Europe. It also lost the period's foremost authority on Latvian folk music and music history. After 1962, Vītoliņš would never again exert an influence upon the development of Latvian musicology through the training of younger scholars. He would never again be able to instill within them his attitudes and values, to introduce them to his approach to research, to lecture on his work, or to direct dissertations. Thereafter, his educational influence was limited to directing folklore research during the summers and to contributing, in an informal capacity, to the work of the Composers' Union.[9]

In summary, one can identify three essential features of the discipline's institutionalization. (1) The institutionalization of musicology as an academic discipline occurred quite late in Latvia. (2) The latter occurred according to an Eastern European, indeed Soviet, model. Unlike in Western and Central Europe (including Finland), where musicological faculties were established within research universities, the Latvian discipline found its institutional home at the Conservatory – an arrangement common throughout the USSR and in many of its satellite states. (3) During the process of its institutionalization and the laying of its methodological and ideological foundations, Latvian musicology was understood as a local branch of Soviet musicology. This situation must not be regarded as merely another example of the broad-based process of Sovietization experienced by all inhabitants of the republic. It also testifies to the general weakness of Latvian musicology during Latvia's first period of independence. If musicology had found institutional security during the Republican period and if Latvian musicologists had established a pattern of steady and productive work, it is doubtful that the Sovietization of the discipline would have been so comprehensive and absolute. By the time of the Soviet invasion, the discipline would have already produced well-qualified scholars and established a solid tradition of scholarship and training that could not have been so easily dismantled. When the Soviets arrived, they would not have found this niche in Latvia's academic life almost entirely unfilled. (Of course, one might counter this assertion by arguing that the regime was certainly capable of emptying out any previously filled niche that they encountered.) With regard to the question of establishing an academic home for the discipline at the Conservatory rather than at the University, it is clear that, under the conditions that prevailed following the Second World War, any possibility that might have once existed to found a musicological faculty at the University were dashed. The Soviet regime powerfully projected its own schemas upon the educational system of the 'new republic'. After 1946, Latvian musicology evolved in complete isolation from musicological scholarship as it was practiced outside the USSR. The difficulties that the discipline has experienced in the wake of the transformations of the 1980s and 1990s are a direct consequence of this situation. Indeed, the discipline is still a long way from overcoming those difficulties.

Musicological Scholarship in the Soviet Period

What, then, *was* official thinking about musicology's disciplinary identity and mission during the 1950s and 1960s? We find these pithy lines in a book entitled *Jāzepa Vītola Latvijas Valsts Konservatorija 1940–1965* (*The Jāzeps Vītols Latvian State Conservatory* 1965):

> Academic music study [*mūzikas zinātne*] addresses problems of a theoretical nature. Musicology [*muzikoloģija*], which encompasses an array of specialized historical and theoretical disciplines, considers music's historical development, the evolution of musical styles, and the musical characteristics of individual works, and it elucidates these in light of the philosophical and aesthetic principles of Marxism–Leninism. During the period of building Communism, the role of art and culture in society and daily life accelerates rapidly, and musicology must assume responsibility for the aesthetic education of the nation and for propagandistic work in the musical sphere. In Riga and Liepaja, in Ludza and Valmiera, in Cēsis and Tukums – everywhere, listeners want to hear not only music itself but also inspiring lectures about music, which elucidate the content of individual compositions, shed light upon composers' lives, and help the listener to understand music's beauty and its role in our lives. To satisfy these demands, we need musicians and musicologists of broad purview and well-grounded education, who understand well the literature of music and its history, and who are armed with substantial theoretical knowledge. Such musicians are trained by the Faculties of Music History and Music Theory. (p. 26)

Two features of this passage merit our attention: (1) musicology's necessary foundation in Marxist–Leninist ideology; and (2) the identification of the musicologist's mission as the 'aesthetic education of the nation', which requires the scholar to direct his or her work toward a lay audience. Indeed, when viewed through the prism of Soviet ideology, these features were two sides of the same coin.

During the years of Soviet rule, musicology was granted a license to be tendentious, to sacrifice facts on the altar of ideology, to select its objects of study – themes, personalities, genres, and repertoires – based upon ideological and political criteria, to slander those deemed ideologically untrustworthy, and to pass over important facts in silence. Indeed, such things were not only permitted but demanded, especially in the 1940s, 1950s and 1960s. Examples are abundant in Latvian musicological writings published during those decades. This does not mean, however, that one cannot also find examples of healthy empiricism and honest scholarship, of promising initiative and brilliant revelations. But far more frequently one encounters rational arguments and fact-based, logical judgments intermixed, in a grotesque muddle, with ideological interpretation.

In some cases, it is easy enough to separate this layer of ideology – demanded as the political cost of doing business – from the scholarly content of a book or essay. And in the 1970s and 1980s, a distinct tendency toward liberalization is notable in much Soviet scholarship. During those decades, the demand for ideological interpretation became something of a formality – a situation felt especially in major academic centers such as Moscow and Leningrad. So long as they focused their attention upon ideologically acceptable themes, scholars felt relatively free to carry out their work as they saw fit. This sort of separation of historical scholarship from ideological interpretation is evident in Vītoliņš and Krasinska's *Latviešu mūzikas vēsture* (*History of Latvian Music* 1972). Of course, one must note that such separation was, in the latter case, enabled to some extent by the content of the book, which addressed only the relatively distant past, the seventeenth century through 1917. The closer one came to the present day, the more difficult it was to separate these elements.

In any case, in the 1970s and 1980s a certain amount of space did indeed open up in which Soviet musicologists were able to bypass official ideology. Often, it was possible to confine the obligatory citations from Marxist–Leninist literature to one's introduction, or even to dispense with them altogether. In their better works, Latvian musicologists took full advantage of this situation. One would search in vain for ideological interpretation within the essential content of such studies as Ludvigs Kārkliņš' *Garmoniya Myaskovskogo* (*Myaskovsky's Harmonic Language* 1971) or Arnolds Klotiņš' *Alfrēds Kalniņš. Komponista dzīve un darbs* (*Alfrēds Kalniņš: The Composer's Life and Work* 1979). The same holds true for the more distinguished works of the 1980s. These include Vizbulīte Bērziņa's *Tautas muzikālā atmoda latviešu publicistu skatījumā* (*Musical Awakening of the Nation: A View from the Latvian Press* 1983); Jānis Torgāns' pedagogical volume, *Mūzika šodien. Apraksti par XX gadsimta mūziku* (*Music Today: Essays on Twentieth-Century Music* 1983); Ilma Graudziņa's *Tūkstoš mēlēm ērģeles spēlē* (*A Thousand Languages of Organ Playing* 1987); and Ingrīda Zemzare's *Paula Dambja spēles* (*The Plays of Pauls Dambis* 1989), a study residing at the crossroads of musicology and literary criticism.

During the 1980s, Latvian musicology gradually came unbound from Soviet ideology. Yet there remained significant problems of other sorts, many of which remain unacknowledged or ignored in Latvia, even in the present day. As early as 1982, the émigré scholar Joachim Braun called attention to some of these problems in a seminal essay entitled 'Some Preliminary Considerations on the Present State of Baltic Musicology' (Braun 1982; reprinted in Braun 2002). Braun's assertions were hardly flattering to Latvian musicology. He observed that there still existed significant aspects of Latvia's musical history and culture that remained wholly untouched by scholars, and he asserted that the level of scholarship produced by Latvian musicologists, when compared to that of their Western counterparts, was, for the most part, mediocre. Braun's critique focused upon the following points. First, no attempt had been made, by 1982, to employ computational analysis in the study of traditional music. Second, no attempt had been made to bridge the gap between ethnographical and historical approaches to music study. Third, no scholar had yet attempted to bring interdisciplinary perspectives to bear upon the study of music history. Fourth, a significant body of primary source materials, housed in Latvian libraries and archives, remained unacknowledged and unstudied by historians. More generally, Braun observed that no significant attempts had been made to study music-making from a sociological perspective, or to evaluate critically essential aspects of Latvia's post-war musical culture.

A quarter-century has now passed since Braun published these observations. Yet his critique has lost none of its urgency. Indeed, his observations might apply just as well to the present-day musicological discourse as they did to the academic scene of the 1980s. But before looking more closely at the contemporary situation and enumerating its discontents, it is important that we acknowledge those scholars who indeed held themselves to high standards in the 1970s and 1980s. These include, in the area of Latvian music history, Oļģerts Grāvītis, Vizbulīte Bērziņa, Arnolds Klotiņš, Ingrīda Zemzare; in the field of music analysis, Jeļena Ļebedeva; in analysis, pedagogy and history, Ilma Graudziņa; in the area of Western European music history, Jānis Torgāns and Vita Lindenberga; in counterpoint, Georgs Pelēcis; and in harmony and pedagogy, Ludvigs Kārkliņš.[10] Each of these scholars – and many others as well – have made important contributions to Latvian musicology, without which the discipline as a whole would have been far poorer. Joachim Braun also occupies an important place in this history.

Concluding Thoughts

In the years that have followed the restoration of Latvia's independence, the problems facing the discipline of musicology have only become more acute. First among them has been the dramatic worsening of the financial situation, which has compelled many musicologists to seek work in other fields. With this, the number of students pursuing musicological studies has dwindled. The discipline has lost its only periodical, *Latviešu mūzika*, whose final, 19th volume appeared in 1990. By the middle of the 1990s, the annual conferences of Baltic musicologists had become intellectually insipid and attendance had plummeted. Indeed, well-founded questions have been raised about the value of continuing to hold those conferences at all. Looking ahead to the future of our discipline, it is difficult to envision anything other than a continuation of the situation that prevails today: a field populated by a small number of scholars working in isolation and estrangement from each other and from the broader European academic community. The present state of musicology in Latvia can be summarized as follows:[11]

1. Despite some significant attempts to develop contacts with scholars in other countries during the 1980s and early 1990s, Latvian musicologists' interactions with their international colleagues have now shriveled to a minimum. No significant attempts have been made to engage in cooperative projects or research with Western scholars. At the same time, ties to the historical 'mother' discipline of Russian musicology have eroded.
2. Interdisciplinary approaches to scholarship have hardly been broached. The interchange of ideas and approaches with such disciplines as sociology and anthropology, which is indispensable for musicological research today, has not occurred in Latvia. Such approaches are neither taught nor adopted by musicologists. The fact that music-making is a phenomenon of significant sociological interest is rarely acknowledged. One of only a handful of studies to consider a musical topic from a sociological perspective, *Dziesmu svētki mainīgā sociālā vidē* (*The Song Festival in a Changing Social Milieu* 2003), can be read online at http://www.km.gov.lv/UI/Main.asp?id=13655. It is telling, however, that none of its authors is a musicologist; the study is a cooperative effort of sociologists and social anthropologists.

3. The country's sole program of musicological study, at the Jāzeps Vītols Latvian Academy of Music (formerly the Latvian Conservatory), treats neither popular music nor jazz in a serious manner, and it provides no consideration of anthropological or sociological approaches to music research. Moreover, ethnomusicology still lacks institutional status as an independent discipline and a formal program of study. As a consequence, traditional and popular musics are marginalized as subjects of study and research. Thus Latvian musicology, as an institutionalized discipline, cannot be said to encompass the entire field of music as it exists in our culture and society. Rather, it remains focused upon only one of music's many branches: professional music in the Western classical tradition.

4. Today, the discipline remains isolated academically within a single institution of higher learning: the Academy of Music. This has significant implications not only for musicology but also for Latvia's system of higher education as a whole. Music study and the acquisition of musicological knowledge are indispensable not only for musicologists but also for students in many disciplines represented in Latvia's universities, including sociology, anthropology and various fields of pedagogy. Yet the institutional divide between the Academy of Music and Latvia's universities can be bridged only with difficulty. (This situation is a direct result of the narrow conception of music-making that still prevails in Latvian scholarship.)

Surely, the situation the discipline faces will hardly improve without a systematic attempt to address these problems. Only if this is undertaken can we hope to see Latvian musicology develop into a discipline in tune with the intellectual currents of present-day Europe and Latvia's contemporary cultural life.

Acknowledgements

The author wishes to thank Jānis Torgāns, Oļģerts Grāvītis, and Arnolds Klotiņš for their invaluable advice and suggestions throughout the process of writing and editing this essay, and Ilze Liepiņa for inspiring his work on this project. Thanks also to Kevin C. Karnes for translating the article from Latvian.

Notes

1   The word *musicology* is an English translation of the German term *Musikwissenschaft*, which was first widely used during the period of the discipline's founding and academic institutionalization in the final third of the nineteenth century. In contrast to English, modern Latvian has two distinct terms to connote what is widely understood by the German *Musikwissenschaft*: *muzikoloģija* and *mūzikas zinātne*. According to oral testimony from the musicologist Arnolds Klotiņš, the term *muzikoloģija* was introduced into the lexicon in the late 1950s by the historian Nilss Grīnfelds, who hoped to replace the older term *mūzikas zinātne* (literally the 'science of music') with one derived from the English *musicology* and the French

musicologie. Today, the word *muzikoloǵija* is generally preferred, though *mūzikas zinātne* is still encountered. In general, *muzikoloǵija* tends to denote a broader field of discourse than *mūzikas zinātne*. While the latter refers to academic research specifically, the former includes scholarship as well as criticism and other forms of writing about music.

2   For a selection of Jūrjans' critical writings, see Jūrjans (1980, pp. 51–91, 126–35). For Jurjāns' surveys of Latvian musical life, see the unpublished manuscripts 'Latviešu tautas mūzikas literatūra no viņas sākuma līdz 1891. gadam' ('The Literature on Latvian Folk Music from Its Beginnings through 1891' 1891) and 'Kritisks pārskats par latvju jaunāko mūzikas literatūru' ('A Critical Survey of the Latest Latvian Musical Literature' 1895); both are preserved in the archives of Latvijas folkloras krātuve (Riga), file Bb 43.

3   It should be noted that historical and theoretical subjects were indeed taught at the Latvian Conservatory in the 1920s and 1930s, but they were taught by composers rather than musicologists. The Conservatory did have a faculty of composition and music theory. But although graduates of this faculty were called *theorists*, the label did not mean the same thing in Latvia as it did in Central and Western Europe. In Latvia, 'theorists' were individuals who exhibited competence in music analysis and theory, but who lacked the aptitude for composition. They attended courses in composition and acquired their theoretical training in that environment rather than in courses and seminars dedicated specifically to analytical and theoretical inquiry. Music theory was, in itself, not regarded as an independent field of research or instruction.

4   Melngailis began his work as a collector of folk songs in 1899, when he transcribed 120 Hebrew melodies in the Lithuanian village of Ķēdaine. He worked most actively in this field in the 1920s and 1930s, and was able to expand his collection further in 1941, under the Soviet regime. A relatively small collection of Turkmen and Uzbek music, transcribed by Melngailis between 1906 and 1920, was lost upon his return to Latvia after a period of residence in Tashkent. Though lost, this collection constituted the first significant work undertaken by a Latvian scholar on non-European musics.

5   Sproǵis' second book, *Senie mūzikas instrumenti un darba un godu dziesmu melodijas Latvijā* (*Ancient Musical Instruments and Work- and Honor-Song Melodies in Latvia* 1943) only made it to galley-proofs. Its planned publication was canceled by the regime.

6   Joachim Braun has estimated that between 1945 and 1982 approximately 70% of scholarship on Baltic music was undertaken by Baltic residents, with the rest undertaken by émigré scholars residing in Western Europe, North America and Australia (Braun 1982, pp. 41–2; reprinted in Braun 2002, p. 240).

7   It is difficult to assess the degree to which Melngailis assumed the position he did as a strategy of self-preservation, to what extent his actions reflected his bitterness regarding the professional setbacks he had experienced in the independent Republic, and to what extent he truly sympathized with the new regime which repressed some of Melngailis' relatives. It is also important to understand that if Melngailis had resisted the regime's overtures, he too would have been

repressed, his work would have remained unpublished, and his collections would most likely have been ignored or even destroyed.

8 See Muzalevskiy (1969, pp. 171–200).

9 Until his death in 1977, Vītoliņš remained a central figure in Latvian folk music research. Beginning in 1946, he worked as a researcher at the Archives of Latvian Folklore (called, during the Soviet period, the Folklore Section of the Institute of Language and Literature at the Academy of Sciences) alongside his Conservatory appointment. After his dismissal from the Conservatory in 1962, the Archives became his primary place of employment. Vītoliņš' work touched upon many facets of Latvian folk music, including aspects of rhythmic, melodic and polyphonic structures; formal and genre characteristics; and the relationship between texts and melodies (see Vītoliņš 1959, 1960; Vītoliņš & Krasinska 1972). Another important facet of Vītoliņš' work is the published corpus of folk musics collected by him over the course of his life. The latter was published in the series *Latviešu tautas mūzika* (*Latvian Folk Music* 1958–1986), which remains the most significant body of traditional Latvian music published to date. After Vītoliņš was fired from the Conservatory, a substantial tradition of folk music study withered at the institution. With his death, an important line of scholarly work came to a halt.

10 Kārkliņš also contributed in important ways to the development of Latvian music terminology. As the leading scholar of twentieth-century Latvian symphonic music, Kārkliņš' books include *Jāņa Ivanova simfonisms* (*Jānis Ivanovs' Symphonic Language* 1978) and *Simfoniskā mūzika Latvijā. Simfoniskie orķestri, diriģenti, mūzika, kalusītāji laikabiedru skatījumā* (*Symphonic Music in Latvia: Symphony Orchestras, Conductors, Music, and Listeners from the Perspective of Contemporaries* 1990).

11 Alongside this enumeration of problems, one must note that valuable works of scholarship have indeed been published in recent years. A partial list of books treating themes and subjects that were either marginally addressed or not considered at all by Latvian musicologists in earlier decades would include Zemzare (1994), Lindenberga *et al.* (1997), and Gailīte (2003).

References

Apkalns, L. (1977) *Lettische Musik* (Wiesbaden, Breitkopf und Härtel).

Bērzkalns, V. (1965) *Latviešu dziesmu svētku vēsture 1864–1949* (New York, Grāmatu draugs).

Bērzkalns, V. (1968) *Latviešu dziesmu svētki trimdā 1946–1965* (New York, Grāmatu draugs).

Bērziņa, V. (1983) *Tautas mūzikalā atmoda latviešu publicistu skatījumā* (Riga, Zinātne).

Bielenstein, A. (1918) *Die Holzbauten und Holzgeräte der Letten*, Vol. 2, *Die Holzgeräte der Letten* (Petrograd, n. p).

Braun, J. (1982) 'Some Preliminary Considerations on the Present State of Baltic Musicology', *Journal of Baltic Studies*, 13, 1, pp. 40–52.

Braun, J. (2002) *Raksti. Mūzika Latvijā*, Boiko, M. (ed.) (Riga, Musica Baltica).

Gailīte, Z. (2003) *Par Rīgas mūziku und kumēdiņu spēli* (Riga, Pētergailis).

Graudziņa, I. (1987) *Tūkstoš mēlēm ērģeles spēlē jeb grāmata par Latvijas ērģeļu būvētājiem, spēlētājiem, instrumentiem un mūziku* (Riga, Liesma).

Jāzepa Vītola Latvijas Valsts Konservatorija 1940–1965 (1965) (Riga, Liesma).

Jurjāns, A. (1894–1926) *Latvju tautas mūzikas materiāli*, Vols 1–4 (Riga, Rīgas Latviešu Biedrība), Vol. 5 (Riga, Latvijas Kultūras fonds), Vol. 6 (Riga, Latvju komponistu biedrība).

Jurjāns, A. (1980) *Raksti*, Mūrniece, L. (ed.) (Riga, Liesma).

Kārkliņš, L. (1971) *Garmoniya Myaskovskogo* (Moscow, Muzyka).

Kārkliņš, L. (1978) *Jāņa Ivanova simfonisms* (Riga, Liesma).

Kārkliņš, L. (1990) *Simfoniskā mūzika Latvijā. Simfoniskie orķestri, diriģenti, mūzika, klausītāji laikabiedru skatījumā. Dokumentāla versija* (Riga, Liesma).

Klotiņš, A. (1979) *Alfrēds Kalniņš. Komponista dzīve un darbs* (Riga, Zinātne).

Lindenberga, V., Torgāns, J. & Fūrmane, L. (1997) *Gadsimtu skaņulokā* (Riga, Zinātne).

Muzalevskiy, V. I. (1969) *Zapiski muzïkanta* (Leningrad, Muzïka).

Rudolph, M. (1887) *Die Rigaer Opera von 1782 bis 1886. Eine statistische Zusammenstellung* (Riga, Rigaer Tagblatt).

Rudolph, M. (1890) *Rigaer Theater- und Tonkünstlerlexikon* (Riga, N. Kymmel).

Sproģis, J. (1941) *Jāņu dziesmu melodijas* (Riga, Latviešu folkloras krātuve).

Sproģis, J. (1943) *Senie mūzikas instrumenti un darba un godu dziesmu melodijas Latvijā* (Riga, Latvju grāmata).

Straume, J. (1904) 'Par latviešu tautas mūziku un seniem mūzikas instrumentiem', *Vērotājs*, 5, pp. 648–60.

Tisenkopfs, T., Pisarenko, O., Daugavietis, J., Putniņa, A. & Locika, K. (2003) *Dziesmu svētki mainīgā sociālā vidē* (Riga, Baltijas studiju centrs), available at: http://www.km.gov.lv/UI/Main.asp?id=13655, accessed 20 May 2005.

Torgāns, J. (1983) *Mūzika šodien. Apraksti par XX gadsimta mūziku* (Riga, Zvaigzne).

Vītoliņš, J. (n.d.) *Mūzikas vēsture* (Riga, Grāmatu draugs).

Vītoliņš, J. (1958–1986) *Latviešu tautas mūzika*, Vol. 1 (Riga, Latvijas Valsts izdevniecība), Vols 2–5 (Riga, Zinātne).

Vītoliņš, J. (1959) 'Latviešu tautas dziesmu melodika', in *Latviešu literatūras vēsture* (Riga, Latvijas Valsts izdevniecība).

Vītoliņš, J. (1960) *Issledovaniya v oblasti latïshskoy narodnoy muzyki* (habilitation diss., Leningrad Conservatory).

Vītoliņš, J. & Krasinska, L. (1972) *Latviešu mūzikas vēsture* (Riga, Liesma).

Vītoliņš, J. & Kroders, R. (eds) (1930) *Latvju skaņu mākslinieku portrejas* (Riga, Ozoliņš).

Zemzare, I. (1989) *Paula Dambja spēles* (Riga, Liesma).

Zemzare, I. (1994) *Tālivaldis Ķeniņš. Starp divām pasaulēm* (Riga, Garā pupa).

EXILED MODERNISM: LITHUANIAN MUSIC THROUGH THE SECOND WORLD WAR

Gražina Daunoravičienė

Introduction

The panorama of twentieth-century professional music is varied and dense, with an intensive interaction of musical trends, compositional techniques and aesthetic philosophies. If the map of nineteenth-century European music inspired by romantic idealism consisted of separate national schools, the merging of modernist European and large continental musical cultures (North American, Latin American, Asian and North African) gave rise, in the twentieth century, to panoramic trajectories of artistic experimentation. At the end of the nineteenth century, the developmental processes of Lithuanian professional music accelerated rapidly. The intelligentsia of this provincial territory, annexed by Russia, discovered its own historical and cultural memory and began, with great effort and enthusiasm, to engage in creative work that laid the foundations of its national cultural identity. The coalescence of Scandinavian (Finnish and Norwegian) and Lithuanian, Latvian and Estonian musical cultures began at roughly the same time. These movements were accompanied by complex political events, including wars, annexations, occupations and struggles for freedom and independence. Within this context, the creative sphere became a means of consolidation, of assuring the self-representation and survival of nations. Separating from Sweden, Norway became independent in 1905; in 1917, Finland declared its independence; and in 1918, Poland, Lithuania, Latvia and Estonia gained their independence from Russia.

In Lithuania, the coalescence of the foundations for a professional musical culture and its later dissemination took place under exceedingly difficult historical and cultural circumstances. This process was strongly influenced by the prohibition of Lithuanian publishing using the Latin alphabet in 1864–1904, which gave rise to

40 years of Russification and cultural resistance on the part of the Lithuanian nation (Merkys 1994). Several waves of Lithuanian emigration also had a negative impact (Truska 1961, pp. 78–9).[1] At the end of World War II, approximately 60,000 Lithuanian inhabitants left the country ahead of the Soviet annexation of the republic (Mockūnas 1989, p. 7). A large part of the Lithuanian intelligentsia, after living for a while in camps for displaced persons in Germany, moved to the United States, Canada, South America and Australia, and among them were the most radical of inter-war Lithuanian composers: Vytautas Bacevičius (1905–1970), Jeronimas Kačinskas (1907–2005), Julius Gaidelis (1909–1983), Kazimieras Viktoras Banaitis (1896–1963) and Vladas Jakubėnas (1904–1976), who collectively represented an early and subsequently exiled modernism in twentieth-century Lithuanian music. This essay takes a close look at the work of these artists, while at the same time analyzing the development of Lithuanian professional music and the interplay of the latter with the broader developmental processes of pan-European musical modernism.

On the Question of the Lithuanian National School

In discussing the foundations of Lithuanian professional music at the beginning of the twentieth century, we cannot omit consideration of such terms as 'national school' and 'school of composers'. Undoubtedly, these terms have not only ideological connotations but also diverse historical configurations, particularly when we attempt to define the self-consciousness of national music and the affinity of artistic forms influenced by ethnic conscience and aspirations. The function of the national school of composers is carried out by the conscious aspirations of its representatives to emphasize the national uniqueness of their work and to create a national style as a complete system of separate national elements (Ambrazas 2007, pp. 71–8). However, already from the time of Schoenberg, the devaluation of the binary opposition of 'national' and 'international' and the proliferation of attempts to interpret common compositional techniques in original and individual ways made the idea of a 'national school' completely 'outdated', in Octavian Lazǎr Cosma's words, 'due to the lack of technical terms to sustain it' and the loss of a precise meaning of concept of 'school' (Cosma 2004, p. 71).

Today, identification on the basis of national identity has been largely replaced by a more complex sense of multiple identifications within contemporary society. For instance, Ivan Florjanc describes identifications based on assimilation, race, language, geopolitical belonging, etc. (Florjanc 2004, p. 77). Nonetheless, at the end of the nineteenth century and the beginning of the twentieth, the notion of a 'national school' was indeed highly influential; factors contributing to its creation included not only the matrices of ethnic culture but also the patriotic intention to identify the difference and individuality of a given culture. In Lithuania, possibilities and strategies for constructing a modern national Lithuanian musical culture were widely discussed during this period. As the Lithuanian composer and critic V. Jakubėnas wrote in 1935, 'We must know how to remain Lithuanians, inhabitants of colorful dwellings, forests and swamps, creators of folksongs, threnodies and glees, but we also have to present our provincialism in a way that is interesting for a wider world'

(Jakubėnas 1935, p. 262). Moreover, the notion of a 'school', meaning precisely the unbroken transmission of knowledge from a teacher to his pupils, points to the model of a 'pedagogic school of composers', a set of attitudes regarding compositional techniques and skills and even the beginnings of a creative position (com-position). The analysis of this dimension of contemporary discourse can help us to answer the following questions. How do a teacher's works, aspirations, technological attitudes or ideals influence the development of national music through his pupils? How are national and pedagogical schools formed? And, on what principles do they function and interact?

During the first decades of the twentieth century, Mikalojus Konstantinas Čiurlionis (1875–1911), Juozas Naujalis (1869–1934), Česlovas Sasnauskas (1867–1916), Teodoras Brazys (1870–1930), Mikas Petrauskas (1873–1937), Stasys Šimkus (1887–1943) and other Lithuanian composers unambiguously and self-consciously laid the foundations for a national school of Lithuanian composers. However, the works of all of these figures except for Čiurlionis belonged to the so-called romantic-academic trend and, as such, did not eschew a variety of borrowed creative influences. Nonetheless, these composers took rather traditional approaches to composition and did not attempt to follow those modernist trends that characterized much of music-making at the beginning of the twentieth century. Essentially, they contributed to the foundations of Lithuanian musical professionalism.

Because of the lack of a system of musical education, Lithuanian composers received their education abroad throughout this period. One of the most important nineteenth-century centers was the Warsaw Institute of Music, founded in 1861 on the basis of the long political coexistence of the Polish and Lithuanian states. At this institution, many students from Lithuania, including Juozas Kalvaitis, Juozapas Gudavičius, Juozas Neimontas, Antanas Vaičiūnas, Vaitiekus Gavronskis (Wojciech Gawroński), and Alfredas Konradas Gužauskis (Gużewski), attended classes in piano, organ and conducting. All of these figures would later work as composers as well (see Palionytė-Banevičienė 2002, pp. 262–301). The most important Lithuanian composers to emerge from the Warsaw Institute, however, were Juozas Naujalis and M. K. Čiurlionis. Other Lithuanians studied at the St. Petersburg Conservatory in Russia: Juozas Dryja-Visockis, Petras Juozas Pranaitis, A. K. Guževskis-Gužauskis, Česlovas Sasnauskas, Mikas Petrauskas and Jurgis Karnavičius. Many composers of Lithuanian church music studied at the Regensburg Kirchenmusikschule. Naujalis too studied at the latter institution in 1894, before beginning his studies in Warsaw.

After completing his studies at the Warsaw Institute, Čiurlionis received further training at the Leipzig Conservatory in 1901–1902. His experiences at the latter school shed interesting light upon the broader experiences of his generation of Lithuanian composers studying at foreign institutions. In his music (Čiurlionis was also a prolific painter), the spiritualism of late Polish and German Romanticism interacted with manifestations of modernist constructivism. All of Čiurlionis' musical works were naturally imbued with the tonal structures of old Lithuanian folklore and a certain rhythmic monotony. In them one can hear 'a certain strange complaint, lamentation, longing and heartache' – all things that originated in the oldest Lithuanian songs (Čiurlionis 1960, pp. 299–300). Čiurlionis' letters to his family and to E. Morawski, professor of composition, demonstrate that he was attracted neither by German pedagogy nor by the creative mood prominent at the Leipzig Conservatory.[2]

Čiurlionis described his conversation with his professor of composition and instrumentation, Carl Reinecke (1824–1910), in a letter of 26 June 1902, written to his former teacher, Eugeniusz Morawski. In this letter, he wrote of Reinecke's dissatisfaction with his work, and of Reinecke's difficulty in grasping the Lithuanian spirit of his compositions – Čiurlionis' 'Lithuanian longing', 'deep mystical manner' and 'seeming religious yearning and quiet unworldly sadness' (Čiurlionis 1960, pp. 299, 303). These features were reflected most strongly in Čiurlionis' melodic structures, which, according to his sister Jadvyga Čiurlionytė, were based, perhaps unconsciously, upon the natural minor characteristic of Lithuanian folksong and the tricordic and quarto-quintic intonations of *Dzūkai* (southeastern Lithuanian) melodies (Čiurlionytė 1957, p. 219). After examining the beginning of an overture that Čiurlionis had planned to dedicate to him, Reinecke remarked: 'Yes, it is very musical, but why is it so gloomy and sad? Please write something somewhat different' (Landsbergis 1986, p. 65). According to Landsbergis, Reinecke did not change his opinion even in later years; indeed, he even recorded it on Čiurlionis' transcript (Landsbergis 1979, p. 67).

What Čiurlionis called a 'folk note' becomes clear in his article 'On Music' (1910), in which he wrote about a 'strange, old and elusive chord' that was the most significant for Lithuanian music (Čiurlionis 1960, p. 287). In his opinion, this chord could not be understood by 'Reinecke (of course) who is German' (Čiurlionis 1960, p. 154). To his students of various national backgrounds, including Edvard Grieg, Christian Sinding, Johan Svendsen, Leoš Janáček, Isaac Albéniz, Emil Nikolaus von Reznicek, Sir Arthur Seymour Sullivan and others, Professor Reinecke would recommend works by Felix Mendelssohn and Carl Maria von Weber as the examples most worthy of following (see Čiurlionis' letter to E. Morawski of 26 June 1902, in Čiurlionis 1960, p. 167). Reinecke's orientation reflects not only the narrowness of the German pedagogical school in general but also the conservative academic direction of the Leipzig Conservatory in particular. The influence of foreign schools of composers (in Leipzig and elsewhere) and their own intentions to create a national music inspired, in many Lithuanian composers, an acute awareness of questions of national identity.

At the beginning of the twentieth century, the conditions for a pedagogical tradition of professional music-making in Lithuania finally emerged. In 1905, the first Lithuanian bookstore selling published musical works was opened; in 1909, the first Lithuanian music magazine, *The Organist* (edited by J. Naujalis), was founded; in 1911, St. Gregorian the Great's Association of Organists was established. The classes for organists that had earlier been founded by Naujalis evolved, in 1919, into the Kaunas School of Music. After Juozas Gruodis (1884–1948) assumed the post of director of the school in 1927, a division of composition ('free creativity') was opened. In 1933, the Kaunas School of Music was reorganized into the Kaunas Conservatory, which offered classes in composition, organ, piano, string instruments, singing, wind instruments and, from 1945, conducting.

We can safely assert that Gruodis' pedagogical and creative activities at the Kaunas School of Music and Kaunas Conservatory produced the first national pedagogical school of composers in Lithuania with all of its components (program, methods, tradition, teachers, tutors and students). Many important composers of the next generation studied with Gruodis, including Julius Juzeliūnas (1916–2001) and Antanas Račiūnas (1905–84, a student of both Gruodis and Nadia Boulanger) (Daunoravičienė 2007, pp. 25–35). Relating his aspirations to both the structural principles of European modernist composition and the expressive, coloristic harmony of Lithuanian folklore, Gruodis defined the purpose of his creative work as a search for national modernism: 'Using modernist devices I am trying to become a national composer' (Gruodis 1932, p. 1232).

Nonetheless, Gruodis' notion of the so-called 'national principle', to say nothing of his conception of a 'national composer', was not developed comprehensively during the pre-war years. The problem itself was often simplified and reduced to a discussion of the necessity of using the 'material' (*daiktiškąji*) element of national music: folksong melodies (Gabšys 1991, p. 11). It was this issue that became the most important axis in the discussion between Bacevičiaus and Kačinskas, on the one hand, and Jakubėnas and Gruodis on the other. In this discussion, different attitudes toward the mechanisms of the development of national music and different understandings of its maturity clashed; their opinions about the forms and ways of using folk songs in modern composition also differed. Although neither side identified explicitly folkloric structures with representations of nationality in music, they did not agree about the creative premises of pre-war Lithuanian music. Delivering a paper entitled 'Matters of Contemporary Music' at the Kaunas School of Music in 1928, on the decennial anniversary of the founding of independent Lithuania, Gruodis acknowledged that 'It is possible to create a national work without using any folksong. Conversely, it is possible to make a work foreign by using a different folksong for each theme.'[3] Bacevičius, like Kačinskas, also argued openly that a number of folk songs used in a work did not prove its 'Lithuanianness', 'because even a work without any folk themes can be Lithuanian' (Bacevičius 1938, p. 216). However, Gruodis thought that this principle could not be applied to the music of the present, of the time of 'building true foundations'. He felt that it would apply only in the future.[4] The radical modernists Bacevičius and Kačinskas, in contrast, were not troubled by such issues; they felt that such a time had already arrived.

Lithuanian Professional Music at the Beginning of the Twentieth Century

Many composers who had earlier studied abroad and had embraced the German academic tradition lived and worked in Lithuania during the first decades of the twentieth century. Their intentions to create and disseminate a national musical culture focused, for the most part, on the melodies of Lithuanian folk songs rather than on the more profound aspects of world-view and aesthetic consciousness addressed in Lithuanian folklore (Čiurlionis). The first three decades of the twentieth century constituted, essentially, a time for the cultivation of large musical genres. The first Lithuanian symphonic poems, operas, operettas, symphonies, piano concertos, string quartets, masses and Requiems, piano music, solo and choral songs, and folksong arrangements were created during this period. At the same time, the intensity of contacts with the processes of European modernism varied widely, and attitudes regarding strategies for the creation of national musics clashed. On the whole, Classical compositional norms in their romantic guise were still dominant. However, already during the second half of the 1920s and the beginning of the 1930s, oppositional creative positions and orientations began to emerge both in music and in the press with the return of a number of radically inclined composers educated abroad (Gruodis, Bacevičius, Jeronimas Kačinskas and Jakubėnas). With respect to differences among the views of the period's musicians, it is possible to distinguish – tentatively, at least – five trends in Lithuanian professional music with regard to their aesthetic and technical orientations and their relationship to the modernist innovations in European music more broadly:

- The romantic–academic trend (Naujalis, Sasnaukas, Petrauskas and Šimkus)
- The romantic–constructivist trend with some manifestations of modernism (Čiurlionis)
- The traditionalist or academic–classical trend (Brazys, Tallat-Kelpša and Kačanauskas)
- The trend of moderate modernism (Gruodis, Banaitis, Jakubėnas, Nabažas, Gaidelis and Pakalnis)
- The trend of radical modernism, which might be called the first Lithuanian avant-garde (Bacevičius and Kačinskas)

To gain a sense of the diversity of ways in which the works of Lithuanian composers of this period resonated with pre-war aesthetic paradigms, we may single out three among them for closer examination: Čiurlionis, Bacevičius and Kačinskas, the latter two coming to represent the 'exiled modernism' of Lithuanian music after they emigrated to the United States after World War II. Through an examination of their music, we will consider the following questions. What is the modernist paradigm of the first half of the twentieth century, and how is it reflected in the compositional practices of a concrete nation? And, what can those national cultures that found themselves at the margins of twentieth-century compositional innovation and did not directly influence the central experiences of European modernism and the avant-garde tell us about European modernism more generally?

At the intersection of the three problematic discourses of this article – the development of Lithuanian professional music, Lithuanian modernism, and exiled modernism – we are confronted with all of those compositional practices of the first half of the twentieth century commonly identified with the general notion of 'modernism'. Emphasizing the contraposition of romanticism dominant in Lithuanian music and broader aesthetic attitudes relating to the idea of European modernism, we will mention here only some of the main controversies concerning the idioms of romanticism and modernism. According to Richard Taruskin, the 'spirituality, sincerity, naturalness, spontaneity, naiveté, authenticity, pastoralism and transcendence of the worldly', inherent in romanticism, were contrasted with modernist 'enthusiasm, an enthusiasm requiring audacity, high self-regard and self-consciousness ... and urbanity of every meaning of the word from "citified" to "sophisticated" to "artificial" to "mannered"' (Taruskin 2005, iv, p. 2). Under the rubric of modernism, we find Anton Webern's anti-romantic slogan of *Neue Musik*, the denial of tradition, intellectualism, a teleological conception of musical progress, the fetishism of originality and individuality (Schoenberg, Varèse, Ives, Cowell, Vyshnegradskii and Hába), and the constructivist and structuralist interpretation of ethnic and folkloric models (Bartók and Stravinsky).

In Čiurlionis' later works, composed 1904–1909, other traits of modernism emerged that were later called, by Carl Dahlhaus, 'thinking in matter' (*Materialdenken*; Dahlhaus 1984, pp. 45–55) and that reflected formulations of musical material suggested by Theodor Adorno in his *Philosophie der Neuen Musik* (1949). Those formulations resonated with both Arnold Schoenberg's enthusiasm for revealing the creative possibilities posed by primary material (what he referred to as *Modell*) within various levels of compositional structure and also the modernist position that the structuring possibilities of provided by one's compositional material determined the concrete form of a work's realization. In other words, modernism interpreted compositional material as pre-formed matter (*vorgeformtes Material*), waiting to be given further structure by the composer (Adorno 1970, p. 222).

Constructions of Modernism in Čiurlionis' Music

In discussions of European musical modernism, several key dates are often mentioned. Dahlhaus calls the years 1890–1910 a transitional period, in which the critical opposition between ideological-stylistic traditionalism (e.g. the works of the 'anti-modernist' Pfitzner) and the more radical music of Mahler, Strauss and Debussy ushered in deep transformations (Dahlhaus 1989, p. 334). Daniel Albright dates the origins of musical modernism to 1894–1995 (focusing on Debussy and Strauss), regarding comprehensiveness, density, extensions and destructions of tonality, semantic specificity and depth as its main identifying characteristics (Albright 2004, pp. 6–7). In Lithuanian music, the beginnings of musical modernism can be located in the first decade of the twentieth century, in the late creative period of Čiurlionis. Though he worked more as a painter than as a composer during this time, Čiurlionis distanced himself in his musical works of this period (often left unfinished) from romantic paradigms. In turn, traits of expressionism, constructivism and neoclassicism appeared. Čiurlionis' piano works of 1904–1909 were characterized by their intended purpose (they were not intended for public performance) and their unpublished, often unfinished state.[5] Indeed, they were mere sketches made in a search for constructive structural-compositional ideas, a 'diary of his works and perhaps his whole life or his creative laboratory' (Landsbergis 1986, p. 133).[6]

In these works, linear polymelodic tendencies gradually emerge: the compositional texture eschews a homophonic harmonic conception and verges on the coexistence of distinct melodic lines, layers, tonic keys or extended tonalities (as, for instance, in his Preludes for Piano, VL303, VL335, VL338 and VL339). It seems that Čiurlionis filled the staves of his sketches as a painter would, structurally modeling and multiplying, in an ornamental way, the details of a compositional text. Often, Čiurlionis constructed a textural layer by repeating, through means of transposition, structural elements of various kinds at the intervals of a sixth, a second and a seventh – or, for example, in his Prelude, VL 303 (1906), by transposing the ostinato, based on the tricordic structure E-F-G$_{sharp}$, through all 12 degrees of the chromatic scale (such a principle was also adapted in his Prelude, VL 272; see Jurkėnaitė 2001, p. 51).

While speaking of some specific aspects of Čiurlionis' compositional technique, we must, first of all, pay attention to his predilection for cryptography. His construction of musical ciphers, his transformation of alphabetical symbols into musical ones, and the signification of a compositional text by using the system of correlations (a cryptographic key) between the alphabet and musical tones are hallmarks of Čiurlionis' creative thinking. Indeed, his late piano preludes enabled the composer to form the rudiments of an original serial technique, as thematic structures encoded cryptographically were made to function as series. Alphabetical and musical ciphers have survived in several of Čiurlionis' notebooks.[7] By inserting musical equivalents of the letters of his musical alphabet into Čiurlionis' fragmentary notes for his *Composition* (*Kompozicija*), for example, Darius Kučinskas has reconstructed the composer's musical signature as shown in Figure 1 (taken from Kučinskas 2004, p. 84).

According to Landsbergis (Landsbergis 1980, p. 177), the decoded monogramic musical version of Čiurlionis' signature – Mi(koł)a(j) (Kon)s(t)a(nty) C(zurł)a(ni)s: E [=mi] A eS [=E$_{flat}$] A C A eS [=E$_{flat}$] – was used by Čiurlionis himself in his two undeveloped (eleven measures in each) and discarded variation-sketches on the theme *Eaesacaes*, written in 1906.[8] We should also note the fact that a partial symmetry characterizes the composer's musical 'signature': E A | eS A ← ||C|| → A eS |. This might have prompted his creation of an original system of transpositions, which we will discuss later. The permutation of the first tones of Čiurlionis' musical signature (E ↔ A) makes this theme close to another cryptographic series used by the composer (B-E-eS-A-C-A-eS), as V. Landsbergis thought, inspired by the musical representation of the letters of the painter Bolesław Czarkowski's first and last names.[9] This latter seven-note series, treated as a row, functions both in structural (ostinato) and thematic capacities in Čiurlionis' cycle of five variations on *Besacas* (VL, 265, 1904–1905). While its characteristic motives are sometimes spread throughout a number of voices, it functions primarily in a linear manner, taking full advantage of the compositional manipulations characteristic of serial music. One form of the row is used as the basic set, which constitutes the center of compositional gravity. Indeed, Čiurlionis seems to have found, in this work, a sophisticated intellectual solution to the main problem of composition that, in Karlheinz Stokhausen's view, every composer must resolve: how to spread one's pre-compositionally prepared material throughout the compositional structure (Stockhausen 1963, p. 60). We see his solution in the *basso ostinato* of the work (Figure 2).

In the fourth variation on *Besacas*, Čiurlionis created, a transpositional scheme for the row, treated as a *basso ostinato*, that was unique for his time and first discovered by Landsbergis (Landsbergis 1980, p. 177). Here the row or *basso ostinato* is transposed six times (Figure 3), extrapolated each time from its own next successive pitch (i.e. the level of each successive transposition is determined by each successive pich of the original row).

Mikoł aj Kon s t ant y Czurł ani s

FIGURE 1   Reconstruction of Čiurlionis's notes for *Kompozicija*.

Moreover, Čiurlionis apparently attempted to spread the effect of the principles of symmetry and retrogradicity to all pitches of *Besacas* row by returning to the retrograde of its opening tritone (B$_{flat}$-E) at its end: B$_{flat}$-E-E$_{flat}$-A$\leftarrow$C$\rightarrow$A-E$_{flat}$-(E-B$_{flat}$) (see Jurkėnaitė 2001, pp. 55, 58). In this way, this addition to the end of the row, E-B$_{flat}$ elides the original row with the first cycle of its transposition shown above.

It is indeed possible that it was this hint of symmetry in the *Besacas* row that prompted Čiurlionis to create such transpositional system in the first place. We should also note that similar analogies between various elements, including symmetry and proportional equivalence, are characteristic of Čiurlionis' paintings as well, particularly of his multilayered 'Sonata' cycles of 1907–1908 (*Sonata of the Sun*, *Sonata of Spring*, *Sonata of a Grass-Snake*, *Sonata of the Sea*, *Sonata of Summer*, *Sonata of Pyramids*, *Sonata of Stars*) and cycles *Prelude and Fugue* of 1908 (Figure 4).[10]

The above-mentioned function of the row in Čiurlionis' *Besacas* reminds one of the technique of transpositions of series used in many post-war avant-garde compositions, all parameters of which were, in some cases, serially controlled

IV

FIGURE 2 Čiurlionis, *Besacas*, VL 265 (1904–1905), fourth variation.

(multiple serialism and total serialism). Of course, in contrast to composers of multiply serialist works, Čiurlionis did not use all 12 chromatic pitches in the *Besacas* row, and he did not employ them in the non-repeating manner characteristic of classical serialism. Nevertheless, Čiurlionis' experiments with four-, six-, seven- and nine-tone rows in his late piano music correspond perfectly to the broader processes of musical modernism widely observable at the beginning of the twentieth century. To be sure, we must answer in the negative the question of whether the compositional procedures used by Čiurlionis exerted any concrete influence upon the work of Schoenberg, Heinrich Klein, or other pioneers of mainstream European serialism. Yet his constructist experiments clearly participated in the broad trend of early

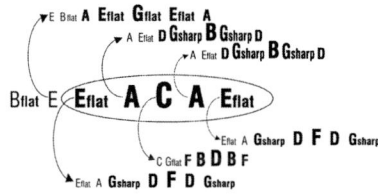

FIGURE 3   Transpositional scheme in *Besacas*, fourth variation.

FIGURE 4   Čiurlionis, *Fugue*, from *Prelude and Fugue* (1908). Paper, tempera; 62.2 × 72.6 cm.

modernism that Taruskin describes as 'a radical intensification of means toward accepted or traditional ends' (Taruskin 2005, Vol. IV, p. 46). Nonetheless, the process of modernization of Lithuanian music that we have sketched thus far, which occurred within the still-prevailing atmosphere of romantic aspirations, academic compositional conventions and traditionalist composition, largely ceased from the time of Čiurlionis' death in 1911 until the end of the 1920s.

The Short-Lived Flowering of Lithuanian Modernism: Bacevičius and Kačinskas

At the end of the 1920s and the beginning of the 1930s, many active manifestations of European musical modernism began to emerge in Lithuania. The most radical manifestations appeared in the works of those composers who had studied not in Polish, German or Russian pedagogical schools but at the centers of new music in Paris or Prague. The modernist inspirations of Lithuanian music prompted Lithuanian composers to revisit and renew many aspects of composition: transformations of tonality took place, microtonal systems were introduced, and new strategies of formal organization appeared. And the conception of national music also changed: the earlier opposition of 'national' versus 'universal' or 'cosmopolitan' composers was felt less strongly, and the character of the national 'material' used in musical works changed as well. Active modernization followed along the lines of Čiurlionis' attitude towards the national specificity of music (as being psychologically elaborated and marked by individualism). And the declarative and descriptive use of folk melodies on the 'linguistic' level diminished considerably; as Jakubėnas observed in 1938, 'the use of folk melodies is the cheapest and easiest way to acquire nationality' (Jakubėnas 1938b, p. 346). 'Deriving the basis of nationality only from ancient folk songs', wrote Jeronimas Kačinskas in 1933, 'we usurp the freedom of a contemporary creator of Lithuanian music' (Kačinskas 1933, p. 22). In short, the search for a more organic and profound representation of Lithuanian nationality intensified.

In 1928, Vytautas Bacevičius returned from Paris, where he had spent a year studying piano and composition in Nikolai Tcherepnin's class at the Russian Conservatory. Coming back from a metropolis full of pluralist modernist ideas – in which the French *Les Six* opposed not only 'foreign' German romanticism but also 'their own' French impressionism, and in which several neoclassical trends proliferated alongside other musical styles – Bacevičius brought to Lithuania a modernist, urbanized spirit of musical creativity. Bacevičius himself called his first creative period (1925–1930) 'expressionism transformed into atonal expressionism' (Narbutienė 2005, p. 310; see also Palionytė 2005, p. 337). His works of these years were influenced by 'heavy German romanticism' – that is, Wagner and Strauss – and also by Skryabin's colorism and harmonic constructivism.

It is possible to describe Bacevičius' Poem No. 4 for piano, op. 10 (1929), as an example of *extended tonality*. In the context of contemporary Lithuanian music, Bacevičius' works were distinguished by their manner of expressive musical language and expanded harmonic vocabulary. In his early works, the forms of tonal indeterminacy described by Schoenberg in the last chapters of his *Harmonielehre*

(1911) appeared in various guises: as oscillatory tonality (*Schwebende Tonalität*), the instability of a tonal center, 'oscillation' between several tonalities without fixating on any of them, and the elimination of tonality altogether (*Aufgehobene Tonalität*) (Schoenberg 1911, p. 460). In his music, one may also speak of 'dissonant tonality' (*dissonantnaya tonal'nost'*) as described by Juri Kholopov, which emphasizes the phenomenon of a dissonant tonal center (Kholopov 1988, pp. 387–8).

Figure 5 shows the introduction (mm. 1–5) and main thematic idea (mm. 6–13) from Bacevičius' Poem No. 4. The introductory motif of a perfect fifth (F_{sharp}-C_{sharp}), repeated in several of the composer's Poems for piano, reminds one of the the lyrical sixth of Wagner's famous prelude to *Tristan und Isolde*. Even more 'swampy' than Wagner's, Bacevičius' harmonic atmosphere evinces further development of the harmonic processes of late romanticism, where the role played by vertical harmonies moves away from traditional functionalism and is transformed into a technique of sequences or rows of individualized, coloristically treated chords.

Characteristic in this work is a spacious interplay of levels and their polyharmonic coexistence with variations in the quality of basic vertical structures (tritone + fifth; tritone + fourth, tritone + tritone, combinations of thirds). Although rather complicated functional relations give rise to a functional polysemy of the harmonic language, the sense of a tonal center does not disappear entirely. Indeed, Bacevičius' Poem No. 4 was written *in C*, and a sense of a tonal center is indeed attained with the dissonant hexachord based upon C that appears in m. 11 (an analogous harmonic structure concludes the composition). The deformations of tonality characteristic of late romanticism are reflected not only in the dissonant quality of this 'tonality' but also in the harmonic field of the Poem as a whole, as colored by numerous densely dissonant sonorities. In this way, the notion of functionality is essentially transformed, and the boundary between dissonant 'tension chords' and consonant 'resolution chords' (to use Ernst Kurth's categories) disappears (Kurth 1973, pp. 63, 69). Moreover, the supporting bassline (E_{flat}-G-E_{flat}-D-E_{flat}-C) suggests, in a subtle

FIGURE 5 Bacevičius, Poem No. 4, op. 10 (1929), mm. 1–13.

manner, hints at a functional strategy. Bacevičius further complicates our sense of a central tonality by introducing a second potential tonal center, E_{flat}. Both of these centers, C and E_{flat}, function in 'dense' septaccordic and nonaccordic forms, and a competing sonority based upon E_{flat} is constantly reharmonized towards more intensive harmonic colorations. We should also note the exceptionally chromatic flow of the melody, permeated by 'melodic dissonances' and the polysemy of structural caesuras.

After returning to Kaunas from Paris and assuming an active role in Kaunas' musical concert life (prior to his emigration, he gave around 300 piano recitals), Bacevičius encountered the dilemma in his attempts to create a national music. In his opera *The Priestess* (1929), his ballet *In the Vortex of Dance* (1933), and his two Piano Concertos (1929 and 1933), the composer still used themes drawn from Lithuanian folksong repertoires.[11] However, Bacevičius later moved decisively away from this sort of 'descriptive' national music.[12] Furthermore, a verbal, declarative, citational level of folklore usage was not, for Bacevičius, an inner necessity inspired by creative intuition. Rather, such citation was an action provoked by 'common rules of behavior' and prevalent conventions. Bacevičius later described his changing position in an article entitled 'On National Music' (1938):

> A number of folk songs put into a work do not make it Lithuanian, because a work can be national without containing any folk themes. The time has come to become interested in new achievements in the sphere of art; it is time to create such artistic values that would correspond to the spirit of the twentieth century . . . instead of eternally 'playing' with [folk] songs. Let's create a modern Lithuania. (Bacevičius 1938, p. 216)

The most radical of Bacevičius' pre-war offerings was his *Poème electrique* for symphony orchestra (1932). With this work, the urban sounds of the 'machine age' crashed down like an avalanche upon the moderate soundscape of Lithuanian music. Incorporating the sounds of twentieth-century industrialization, machinery, technology and the 'victorious kingdom of Electricity' (Luigi Russolo), *Poème electrique* seemed to sever, in one instant, all links with the romantic past of Lithuanian music. The futuristic rhetoric of the manifestos of the Italian Futurists Russolo, Marinetti and Pratella permeated Bacevičius' explanations of this work in his writings: 'It is necessary to understand machinism not only as an external phenomenon of our lives, but also as an inner element. . . . [my] work is a direct denial of so-called "sentimentalism"' (cited in 'Naujas V. Bacevičiaus kūrinys' 1932, p. 114). Rejecting all national aspirations and romantic sentimentalism, Bacevičius constructed an impression of technological progress and mechanization with an aggressively dissonant style. In his *Poème*, he destroyed the artistic conventions prevalent in Lithuania at the time and surprised his contemporaries with his radical symphonic sound and impulsive rhythmic vitality. The impression made by the work was close to those made by other 'mechanistically' inspired compositions of the 1920s and early 1930s (i.e. Honegger's *Pacific 231*, Mosolov's *The Iron Foundry*, Antheil's *Ballet méchanique*, S. Prokofiev's ballet *La Pas d' acier*, Varèse's *Ionisation*). As Kačinskas observed, during the premiere of *Poème electrique* on 9 January 1934, the Kaunas Philharmonic was overwhelmed by the work's spontaneous 'aleatory; the orchestra members played it with scorn, displaying the score upside down' (Narbutienė 2005, p. 103). Some even played the score in reverse. The audience in attendance seemed divided into three irreconcilable groups. A minority responded enthusiastically (e.g. Kačinskas), the majority responded with only reserved enthusiasm (e.g. Jakubėnas and Gruodis), and some responded with open hostility (e.g. Naujalis and T. Brazys) (Gapšys 1991, p. 11).

Speaking of beliefs widespread among twentieth-century composers, we may note that Webern's elegantly provocative *Neue Musik* was accompanied by other slogans and calls to action. We may mention here the uproarious futurist slogan *Freie Musik* (Nikolai Kulbin), and also the unabashedly radical proposal of Feruccio Busoni to revise the overexploited system of 12-tone temperament by introducing intervals smaller than a semitone (Busoni 1907). Quarter-tones, employed by Charles Ives in his Symphony No. 4 (1909–1916), similarly resounded in the ear as a response to the poetic-philosophical utopias of American transcendentalism. These 'notes between the cracks' of the piano, as Ives called them, by which music might be written using more subtle gradations than a semitone, became yet another important feature of musical modernism during the first half of the twentieth century. The first Lithuanian quarter-tone composition was created in the spring of 1931 by a student of the Czech composer Alois Hába, Jeronimas Kačinskas, who later emigrated from Lithuania: Kačinskas' Second String Quartet.

After successfully passing his exams at the Prague Conservatory in 1930 and studying at Hába's Department of Quarter-Tone and Sixth-Tone Music in 1930–1931, Kačinskas absorbed his teacher's modernist attitudes and his ideas about microtonal and athematic composition. Indeed, he and Hába had many things in common. The sources reveal that, for instance, both Hába and Kačinskas had perfect pitch. In his *Neue Harmonielehre* (1927), discussing the psychological underpinnings of the quarter-tone system, Hába told of his reminiscences of childhood, and about how his father and brother used to sing, play and whistle sounds distant to well-tempered tuning. Hába was required by his father to sing, play the violin or whistle the closest 'correct' tone in the tempered, 12-semitone tuning and then to repeat the microtonal sounds produced by his father and brother on the spot. This 'game' ended by stating whether the pitch played was higher or lower than the nearest tempered pitch (Hába 1927, p. 135). Hába's perfect pitch enabled him to recognize microintervals perfectly. Similar 'games', as Kačinskas recalled, constituted part of his work at Hába's Department. In 1931, upon Kačinska's receipt of a certificate from the department, Hába wrote: 'Mr. Jeronimas Kačinskas, having perfect pitch, easily mastered the system of quarter-tones and the sound of its new harmony. He perfectly mastered the compositional devices of this system, in both its thematic and non-thematic aspects' (Petrauskaitė 1997, p. 36).[13]

In his work, Kačinskas took a highly individualistic path, to move 'individually on the path of progress', as he wrote in a letter to Hába in 1935 (cited in Petrauskaitė 1997, p. 48). He also followed closely Ivan Vyshnegradskii's metaphysical notion of 'pansonority' (*pansonorité, vsezuchie*). By this I mean Vyshnegradskii's individualistic substantiation of the microtonal system ('Hearing the space between pitches leads to hearing space *per se*'; Vyshnegradskii 2001, p. 6) and his concept of 'ultra-chromaticism'. Unfortunately, almost all the scores for his microtonal works disappeared during the Second World War. The only works to survive are those that were published in the supplement of the magazine *Fields of Music* (*Muzikos barai*), or left in performers' collections.

Like Hába, who commissioned the construction of quarter-tone instruments, wrote theoretical essays on microtonal composition, and established courses on the subject, Kačinskas undertook an array of similar tasks after returning to Lithuania in 1931. He had both a quarter-tone harmonium and a quarter-tone trumpet shipped to Lithuania. Attempting to establish a class of microtonal composition at the Kaunas Conservatory, Kačinskas introduced students to microinterval music by playing the quarter-tone harmonium. Thanks to his efforts, a course on quarter-tone music was briefly established at the Klaipėda School of Music in 1933. In 1932, Kačinskas, along with Bacevičius and V. Žadeika, founded the Association of Musician-Progressivists (*Muzikininkų progresistų asociacija*), a group of young artists dedicated to advancing new music, organizing lectures and concerts, publishing new musical works, and establishing orchestras and choirs. Although the activities of this association did not last for long, its example helped modernist composers establish, in 1936, a Lithuanian section of the International Association of Contemporary Music.

Another radical innovation that Kačinskas borrowed from Hába was the idea of athematic composition, which fundamentally challenged core assumptions about both compositional process and musical structure. Significantly, Arnold Schoenberg's attitude towards the forms of dodecaphonic music, well known at the time, were, in spite of his own provocative serialist innovations, deeply traditionalist. In his study *Die alten Formen in der neuen Musik* (1927), he wrote: 'In new music, tones (*Klangs*), melodic intervals and their sequences are difficult to grasp. Therefore, it is advisable to choose a form that will guarantee clarity from a different side because it offers something already known' (Blumröder 1981, p. 153). Hába, who had attended Schoenberg's concerts in Vienna and had studied Schoenberg's compositions, was influenced not by the latter's traditionalist attitudes of the 1920s but by Schoenberg's early monodrama *Erwartung* (1909), with its 'free athematic style'. In his own theory of 'athematic composition', Hába rejected classical forms and the traditional modes of their realization. In their place, he advocated the idea of an abstract, athematic kind of musical structuring and called for the creation of a stream of melodies, rushing forward continuously and eschewing audible thematic relations (Hába 1925, 1934). Both of Hába's passions – for microtonal music and for athematic music – he viewed as characteristic of a new musical style, a *Musikstil der Freiheit* (a 'musical style of freedom') or *vollständige Freiheit von allem Traditionellen* ('complete freedom from all traditions') (Henzel 1995, p. 220). This idea was first mentioned in Hába's 1929 article '*Casellas Scarlattiana* – Vierteltonmusik und Musikstil der Freiheit' (Hába 1929, pp. 331–4). One should note, however, that Hába's theoretical statements were more radical than his own creations. Already in 1943, he began searching for a compromise between thematic and athematic methods of composing, and he attempted to combine the two in his works. And although Hába produced athematic and microtonal compositions until the end of his life, tonal centers in his music are always audible.

We may acquire a sense of Kačinskas' athematic style by looking at his *Nonet* (1931–1932), composed during his Kaunas period, for nine strings and winds. Kačinskas constructed this work as a linear polymelodic stream of individual melodic lines. The individual instrumental parts of *Nonet* consist of expressive, instrumentally powerful and transformable melodic fragments; they vary by alternating between the general forms and shapes of the individualized intonational structures. Kačinskas constantly reforms these instrumental lines with regard to vertical layers; the resulting dissonant verticals of the *Nonet* emerge from the melodic lines and heterophonic layers themselves. The passage from the fourth part of this work shown in Figure 6 demonstrates the principle characteristics of Kačinskas' athematic compositional style: irregular melodic lines, the constant variation of small melodic formations, the coexistence of different rhythmic principles and the natural development of a non-narrative polymelodic texture.

The music of *Nonet* is non-programmatic, non-illustrative and somewhat abstract and rationalistic. Nonetheless, already during its premiere, Jakubėnas saw in it a certain temperamental quality, arguing that this 'whole work is enveloped in a certain darkly mystical, visionary reverie' (Jakubėnas 1938a, p. 1). Kačinskas, however, considered the work to demonstrate his opposition to music as an art expressing feelings and to musical elements as 'figures' of emotional states typically conveyed through words. H. H. Eggebrecht's statements about the essential *objectivity* of music itself and the essential *subjectivity* of musical content (*Gehalt*) as interpreted by the listener (Eggebrecht 1995, p. 49) would be close to Kačinskas' position. In *Nonet*, Kačinskas exploited the natural energy of musical structures organized in untraditional ways. He composed a work by following literally Hába's fundamental principle: '[by] not repeating and by thinking ahead, [by] always looking forward' (Spurný 2005, p. 6).

The documents pertaining to the performance and reception of Kačinskas' *Nonet* vividly reveal the musical climate in early twentieth-century Lithuania. After the premiere of the work in Prague in 1932, it was performed in in Lithuania, Latvia and Estonia. In a single Lithuanian program, it was performed alongside Hába's own *Nonet*, op. 40 (Reiner 1932, p. 197). In a review published in a local newspaper in the provincial town of Panevėžys, we find a series of derisive remarks. It is compared to 'cat music' and 'the delirium of a madman', and it is said to exemplify the 'misery of the spirit of modern music' as a whole (K. V. B. 1932, p. 4). Actually, these impressions resonate very nicely with Taruskin's comment, cited above, about the fundamentally 'urbane' qualities of modernism. For indeed, contemporary critics in the larger city of Kaunas called attention to a number of interesting moments in the *Nonet*, as well as to its impressive technique. However, many of these same, urban critics also acknowledged that Kačinskas' creative method, not yet firmly established in Western Europe, would be all but inaccessible to most Lithuanians (Jakubėnas 1932, p. 6).

Epilogue: The Exiled Modernism of Lithuanian Music

Thanks to the efforts of the inter-war modernists and Kačinskas' appeal to the International Society for Contemporary Music (ISCM), Lithuania became an official member of that association in 1936. The Lithuanian group that participated, for the first time, in the 1937 forum of the ISCM consisted of modernists of the so-called

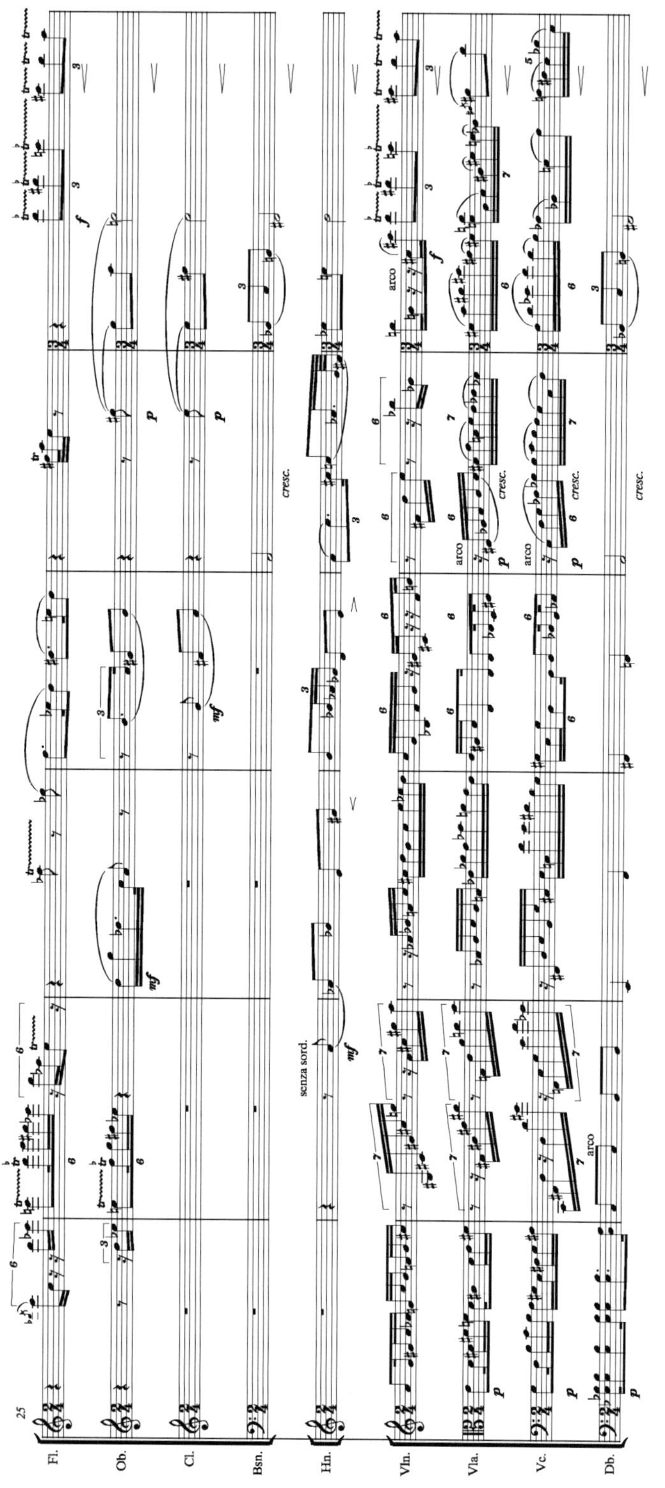

FIGURE 6 Kačinskas, *Nonet* (1932), Part 4, mm. 25–30.

'radical new wing' (*Lietuvos aidas*), including Bacevičius, Kačinskas and Jakubėnas. The obligatory recommendation submitted in support of Lithuania's application to the society was supplied, with the help of Hába, by Czechoslovakia. In many respects, this event can be regarded as marking the culmination of Lithuanian professional music. In the mid-1930s, the work of Lithuanian composers reflected many European modernist innovations and was widely performed abroad: Bacevičius' in Poland, France, Latvia, Czechoslovakia; Kačinskas' in Czechoslovakia, England, Latvia and Estonia; and Jakubėnas' in Germany and the United States. From an obscure geographic-cultural territory at the beginning of the twentieth century, Lithuania had become, by the mid-1930s, a distinct national musical culture with its own map of musical representations and manifestations.

Soon, however, the natural development of Lithuanian professional music would be destroyed and deformed by political events: World War II, the Soviet occupation, deportations of the republic's inhabitants and, most importantly, the emigration of all of the most prominent modernist composers and leaders of the Lithuanian avant-garde of the inter-war period: Bacevičius, Kačinskas, Jakubėnas and others. All of this resulted in the subsequent marginalization of Lithuanian musical culture on the European scene. Moreover, once resettled abroad, the social status of the émigré and the psychological discomfort of living within a foreign cultural context contributed to the fact that the most radical of Lithuania's modernist composers eventually took up different professions. After moving to the United States, Kačinskas found work as a conductor, and Bacevičius as a teacher of piano.[14] Eventually, Kačinskas renounced microtonal music and moved towards a more conventional musical language. Bacevičius, in turn, converted to theosophism, and experimented with a new, mystical, 'cosmic music'.

Of those more moderately modernist composers who remained remained in Lithuania after the War, all were traumatized by Soviet politics and ideology. The institutionalized ideology of occupation required that one create art that was 'national in form and socialist in content' (Stalin 1934). In his tireless struggle against 'formalism', the state ideologist Andrei Zhdanov hewed close to this ideological formulation. Most manifestations of musical modernism were regarded as remnants of 'bourgeois ideology'. Gruodis, who had regarded the formal aspects of composition as signs of professionalism, was accused of formalism after the Communist Party's 1948 decree concerning Vano Muradeli's opera *The Great Friendship*, and he died during that same year.[15] The composer Juozas Pakalnis, a graduate of the Leipzig Conservatory, was severely criticized by the Union of Soviet Lithuanian Composers and likewise passed away in 1948. Nabažas stopped writing music altogether. Under Soviet rule, the first 12-tone composition, Julius Gaidelis' *Trio for Violin, Clarinet, and Bassoon*, did not appear until 1961. It was only during the latter decade that the processes of modernization in Lithuanian music, which ceased at the end of the 1930s, were renewed.

In conclusion, responding to the question of how pre-war Lithuanian modernism has become a part of the pluralist Lithuanian postmodernism of the present day, we may mention briefly two examples. First, we should call attention to the dodecaphonic theory and musical language of Osvaldas Balakauskas (b. 1937), which explores intensively the harmonic possibilities of the 12-tone system and the axiom of 'quintic' harmony (Balakauskas 2000). And, if we wish to speak of the further development of pre-war Lithuanian microtonal music, we should mention Rytis Mažulis (b. 1961), who has created an original compositional system that explores interactions between microtonality (dividing the semitone into as many as 30 parts), canon, and minimalist techniques (Daunoravičienė 2004, pp. 82–108). As the work of these and other artists makes clear, our present attempt to rethink widely held views of twentieth-century Lithuanian musical culture must entail, among other things, a critical examination of the relationship between two historically distinct manifestations of musical modernism: between the exiled modernism of Kačinskas, Bacevičius, and their contemporaries on the one hand, and the more recent, post-war trends on the other.

Notes

1   Between 1899 and 1910, one in every 212 Lithuanians emigrated from the country, most frequently to the United States. According to L. Truska, 55,000 Lithuanians left for the US in 1868–1998. In 1899–1914, 252,594 more followed. Prior to 1914, 9,000 Lithuanians emigrated to Great Britain, and between 1899 and 1914, approximately 74,000 Lithuanians moved to Riga, Liepaja, St. Petersburg, Odessa, Moscow and other Russian cities (Truska 1961, pp. 78–9).

2   In many respects, Čiurlionis' experiences at the Leipzig conservatory remind one of Edvard Grieg's at the same institution, as recorded in his discussions with Niels Gade and Julius Röntgen. See Andersson (2004, p. 370); Schwab (1992, p. 197); and Seidel (1998, p. 137).

3   Juozas Gruodis, 'Matters of Contemporary Music', unpublished lecture preserved in the Archive of Lithuanian Literature and Art (hereafter LLMA), fond 46, inventory 1, file 106.

4   'Later on, folk songs will, of course, disappear from our music altogether. However, the rays of the soul that created them will always shine upon us, and if we lay a genuine foundation, our music, whatever its development, will always remain Lithuanian forever' (Gruodis, 'Matters of Contemporary Art', LLMA, fond 46, inventory 1, file 106).

5   Čiurlionis dated most of his manuscripts himself. In some of these, we also find references to other works. Much of this manuscript material consists of scrapbooks and sketches that were later organized and supplemented by various editors. Significantly, previously unknown manuscripts by Čiurlionis are still being uncovered. For instance, Darius Kučinskas found 11 previously unknown pages of the composer's notes at the Vilnius University Library in 2006.

6   These sketches were later edited and published by S. Šimkus, J. Čiurlionytė, V. Landbergis and others.

7   See, for instance, National Art Museum of M. K. Čiurlionis (hereafter ČDM), Čiurlionis fond, Čiurlionis' Music (hereafter Čm) 21, Mg 776, p. 260; and ČDM, Čiurlionis fond, Čm 6, p. 00411. These documents are described in Kučinskas (2004, p. 84).

8   See ČDM, Čiurlionis fond, Čm 21, Mg 776, pp. 210–11.

9   It should be noted that similar cryptographic schemes were used for the construction of melodic fragments by members of the Second Viennese School:

Arnold Schoenberg, Alban Berg and Anton Webern. See, for instance, the use of the monogram B-A-C-H ($=$B$_{flat}$-A-C-B) in Schoenberg's *Variataions for Orchestra*, op. 31, and in Webern's *Bagatelle No. 1*; and Berg's use of monograms representing all three members of the school in his *Chamber Concerto* (1923–1925).

10   The reproduction is taken from Verkelytė-Fedaravičienė (1997, p. 150).

11   The subtitle given by Bacevičius to both of his piano concertos – *sur les thèmes lithuanien* – indicates that he still sought for 'material' Lithuanian-ness to use G. Gabšys' term) at this time. In the score of his *Concerto No. 1*, the composer even underlined and marked the Lithuanian folk motives with an asterisk. At the conclusion of the work, the folk song *Oh, You Eve, Little Eve* was also provided with a text underlay. Quotations from four Lithuanian folk songs appear in Bacevičius' *Concerto No. 2*.

12   Here I invoke Stevan Hristič's distinction between 'psychological nationalism' and 'descriptive nationalism'; see Hristič (1912, pp. 316–17).

13   Jiří Vysloužil has suggested that Hába's eagerness to compose microtonal music might have been inspired by the traditional microtonal singing and playing of his native Wallachian (Eastern Moravian) folk songs and ensembles (Vysloužil 1970). However, neither Hába nor Kačinskas mentioned ethnographic motivations for their microtonal experiments.

14   Kačinskas arrived in Boston in 1949, where he worked, until 1995, at the Lithuanian St. Peter's Church. He was active as a conductor from 1952 onwards and taught at the Berklee College of Music from 1967 through 1986. After traveling in South America in 1939, Becevičius settled in New York in 1940. He taught at the Brooklyn Conservatory and the Long Island Institute of Music, publishing articles and performing regularly. His solo performances included seven recitals in Carnegie Hall.

15   On the day of Gruodis' death, 16 April 1948, an article signed with his name and entitled 'Music Has to Come from the People and Must Be Addressed to the People' was published in the Soviet Lithuanian daily *Tiesa* (*Truth*). Before his death, Gruodis had confessed to his student, J. Juzeliūnas, that he had been forced to write this article, which denounced his own creative work as 'formalist' (Ambrazas 1981, p. 211).

References

Adorno, T. (1970) *Ästhetische Theorie (Gesammelte Schriften, 7)* (Frankfurt am Main, Suhrkamp).

Adorno, T. W. (1949) *Philosophie der neuen Musik* (Tubingen, Mohr Verlag). New edition: Adorno, T. W. (1978) *Philosophie der neuen Musik* (Frankfurt am Main, Suhrkamp).

Albright, D. (2004) *Modernism and Music: An Anthology of Sources* (Chicago, University of Chicago Press).

Ambrazas, A. (1981) *Juozo Gruodžio gyvenimas ir kūryba* (Vilnius, Vaga).

Ambrazas, A. (1991) *Juozas Gruodis ir lietuvių kompozitorių mokyklos formavimasis* (PhD diss., Institute of Art Studies, Moscow).

Ambrazas, A. (2001) 'Die Harmonielehre Sigfrid Karg-Elerts in ihrer Bedeutung für litauische Komponisten', in Žiūraitytė, A. & Koch, K. P. (eds) (2001).

Ambrazas, A. (2007) *Ambrazas, Algirdas Jonas. Muzikos tradicijos ir dabartis: Studijos. Straipsniai. Atsiminimai*, Daunoravičienė, G. (ed.) (Vilnius, Lietuvos kompozitorių sąjunga).

Andersson, G. (2004) 'Die Musik in Schweden im Spannungsfeld zwischen Nationalem und Internationalem im 20. Jahrhundert', in Loos, H. & Keym, S. (eds) (2004) *Nationale Musik im 20. Jahrhundert* (Leipzig, Gudrun Schröder Verlag).

Ashby, A. (1995) 'Of "Modell-Typen" and "Reihenformen": Berg, Schoenberg, F. H. Klein, and the Concept of Row Derivation', *Journal of the American Musicological Society*, 48, 1, pp. 67–105.

Bacevičius, V. (1938) 'Apie tautišką muziką', *Naujoji Romuva*, 671, pp. 216–17.

Balakauskas, O. (2000) *Osvaldas Balakauskas: muzika ir mintys*, Gaidamavičiūtė, R. (ed.) (Vilnius, Baltos lankos).

Blumröder, C. (1981) *Der Begriff 'neue Musik' im 20. Jahrhundert* (Freiburger Schriften zur Musikwissenschaft, 12) (Munich und Salzburg, Musikverlag Emil Katzbichler).

Bohn, R. & Engelbrecht, M. (eds) (1992) *Weltgeltung und Regionalität. Nordeuropa um 1900* (Frankfurt am Main and New York, Peter Lang).

Busoni, F. (1907) *Entwurf einer neuen Ästhetik der Tonkunst*, reference is to the 1973 edition (Hamburg, Verlag der Musikalienhandlung Wagner).

Buveris, J. (2004) 'M.K. Čiurlionis: tautiškumo problema', *Lietuvos muzikologija*, 5, pp. 6–28.

Čiurlionis, M. K. (1960) *Apie muziką ir dailę. Laiškai, užrašai ir straipsniai*, Čiurlionytė-Karužienė, J. (ed.) (Vilnius, Valstybinė grožinė leidykla).

Čiurlionytė, J. (ed.) (1957) *M.K. Čiurlionis. Kūriniai fortepijonui* (Vilnius, Valstybinė grožinės literatūros leidykla).

Cosma, O. L. (2004) 'Romanian Music', in Loos, H. & Keym, S. (eds) (2004) *Nationale Musik im 20. Jahrhundert Kompositorische und soziokulturelle Aspekte der Musikgeschichte zwischen Ost- und Westeuropa* (Leipzig, Gudrun Schröder Velag).

Dahlhaus, C. (1984) 'Abkehr vom Materialdenken', in Hommel, E. (ed.) (1984).

Dahlhaus, C. (1989) *Nineteenth-Century Music*, Robinson, J. B. (trans.) (Berkeley and Los Angeles, University of California Press).

Daunoravičienė, G. (2004) 'Microdimensional Compositions by Rytis Mažulis: From Mensurations to Fractals', in Stanevičiūtė-Goštautienė, R. & Žiūraitytė, A. (eds) (2004).

Daunoravičienė, G. (2007) 'Algirdo Jono Ambrazo *Opus magnum*: Juozo Gruodžio kompozitorių mokyklos genealogijos medis', in Ambrazas, A. (2007).

Eggebrecht, H. H. (1995) *Musik Verstehen* (Munich, Piper).

Florjanc, I. (2004) 'Übernationales und nationales in der Musik', *Musikalische Identität Mitteleuropas*, 40, 1–2, pp. 73–84.

Gapšys, G. (1991) '"Elektrinė poema" ir modernizmas Lietuvoje', *Literatūra ir menas*, 5 January, p. 11.

Grues, H., Kruttge, E. & Thalheimer E. (eds) (1925) *Von neuer Musik. Beiträge zur Erkenntnis der neuzeitlichen Tonkunst* (Köln am Rhein, F. J. Marcan).

Gruodis, J. (1932) 'Mūsų menininkai namie', *Banga*, 48, pp. 1231–2.

Hába, A. (1924) 'Die Beziehungen zwischen der alten und der modernen Musik', *Neue Musikzeitung*, 45, pp. 200–5.

Hába, A. (1925) 'Grundlagen der Tondifferenzierung und der neuen Stilmöglichkeiten in der Musik', in Grues, H., Kruttge, E. & Thalheimer E. (eds) (1925).

Hába, A. (1927) *Neue Harmonielehre des diatonischen, chromatischen, Viertel-, Drittel-, Sechstel-und Zwölftel-Tonsystems* (Leipzig, Fr. Kistner & C. F. W. Siegel).

Hába, A. (1929) 'Casellas Scarlattiana — Vierteltonmusik und Musikstil der Freiheit', *Anbruch*, 11, pp. 331–4.

Hába, A. (1934) 'Schoenberg and the Further Possibilities of Music-Development', Monzo, J. (trans.), available at: http://sonic-arts.org/monzo/haba/schoenbergbook.htm, accessed 14 July 2007.

Henzel, C. (1995) 'Alois Hába und der "athematische Musikstil". Theorie und kompositorische Praxis', *Musiktheorie*, 10, 3, pp. 219–34.

Hommel, E. (ed.) (1984) *Algorithmus, Klang, Natur: Abkehr vom Materialdenken?* (Darmstädten Beiträgen zur neuen Musik, 19) (Mainz, Schott).

Hristič, S. (1912) 'O nacionalnoi muzici', *Zvezda*, 5, pp. 316–17.

Jakubėnas, V. (1932) 'Čekų noneto koncertas', *Lietuvos aidas*, 7 November, p. 6.

Jakubėnas, V. (1935) 'Lietuvių muzikos plėtros perspektyvos', *Naujoji Romuva*, 218–19, pp. 259–64.

Jakubėnas, V. (1938a) 'J. Kačinsko kūrinys skamba Londone', *Lietuvos aidas/Kultūros priedas*, 25 June, p. 1.

Jakubėnas, V. (1938b) 'Tautinės muzikos klausimais', *Naujoji Romuva*, 376, pp. 346–8.

Jurkėnaitė, A. (2001) 'Sisteminio konstruktyvizmo apraiškos vėlyvojoje M.K. Čiurlionio fortepijoninėje kūryboje', *Menotyra*, 3, pp. 50–8.

Kačinskas, J. (1933) 'Tautiškos liefuvių muzikos kūrybos klausimai', *Muzikos basai*, 2, pp. 22–3.

K. V. B. (1932) 'Česky Nonet', *Panevėžio balsas*, 13 November, p. 4.

Kholopov, Yu. (1988) *Garmoniya: teoreticheskii kurs* (Moscow, Muzyka).

Kučinskas, D. (2004) *M. K. Čiurlionio fortepijoninės muzikos tekstas: Genezės aspektas* (Kaunas, Technologija).

Kurth, E. (1973) *Die Voraussetzungen der theoretischen Harmonik und der tonalen Darstellungssysteme*, 2d ed. (Munich, E. Katzbichler).

Landsbergis, V. (1979) 'Das Königliche Konservatorium zum Leipzig mit den Augen eines Studenten. Briefe von M. K. Čiurlionis', *Beiträge zur Musikwissenschaft*, 21, 1, pp. 42–69.

Landsbergis, V. (1980) *Vainikas Čiurlioniui: menininko gyvenimo ir kūrybos apybraižos* (Vilnius, Mintis).

Landsbergis, V. (1986) *Čiurlionio muzika* (Vilnius, Vaga).

Merkys, V. (1994) *Knygnešių laikai 1864–1904* (Vilnius, Valstybinis leidybos centras).

Mockūnas, L. (ed.) (1989) *Egzodo literatūros atšvaitai: Išeivių literatūros kritika, 1946–1987* (Vilnius, Vaga).

Narbutienė, O. (1996) *Kazimieras Viktoras Banaitis* (Vilnius, Baltos lankos).

Narbutienė, O. (ed.) (2005) *Vytautas Bacevičius: Gyvenim partitūra* (Vilnius, Petro ofsetas).

'Naujas V. Bacevičiaus Kūrinys' (1932), *Muzikos barai*, 7–8, p. 114.

Palionytė, D. (2005) 'Vytauto Bacevičiaus simfoninės muzikos vizija', in Narbutienė, O. (ed.) (2005) *Vytautas Bacevičius: Gyvenim partitūra* (Vilnius, Petro ofsetas), i, pp. 312–53.

Palionytė-Banevičienė, D. (ed.) (2002) *Lietuvos muzikos istorija*, Vol. 1, *Tautinio atgimimo metai1883–1918* (Vilnius, Kultūros, filosofijos ir meno institutas, Lietuvos muzikos akademija).

Petrauskaitė, D. (1997) *Jeronimas Kačinskas. Gyvenimas ir muzikinė veikla. Straipsniai, laiškai, atsiminimai* (Vilnius, Baltos lankos).

Reiner, K. (1932) 'Kūryba Vakaruose', *Muzikos barai*, 12, p. 197.

Schoenberg, A. (1911) *Harmonielehre*, 7th ed. (Vienna, Universal Edition).

Schwab, H. W. (1992) 'Zur kontroverse um "Weltmusik und Nordischen Ton"', in Bohn, R. & Engelbrecht, M. (eds) (1992).

Seidel, K. (1998) *Carl Reinecke und das Leipziger Gewandhaus* (Hamburg, Bockel Verlag).

Spurný, L., (2005) 'Hábova "Musik der Freiheit" pohledem německy píšící muzikologie', *Acta musicologica* [Brno], 2, 2, pp. 1–10.

Stalin, I. V. (1934) *Marksizm i natsional'no-kolonial'nii vopros*, Sbornik izbrannych statei I retsej, Tovstucha, I. (ed.) (Moscow, Partizdat CK VKPb).

Stanevičiūtė-Goštautienė, R. & Žiūraitytė, A. (eds) (2004) *Constructing Modernity and Reconstructing Nationality: Lithuanian Music in the 20th Century* (Vilnius, Kultūros barai).

Stockhausen, K. (1963) 'Texte zur elektronischen und instrumentalen Musik', in Schnebel, D. (ed.) (1963) *Texte zur elektronischen und instrumentalen Musik* (Cologne, DuMont Buchverlag).

Taruskin, R. (2005) *The Oxford History of Western Music*, Vol. 4, *The Early Twentieth Century* (New York and Oxford, Oxford University Press).

Truska, L. (1961) 'Emigracija iš Lietuvos 1868–1914 metais', *Lietuvos TSR MA darbai*, ser A, 10, pp. 71–85.

Verkelytė-Fedaravičienė, B. (ed.) (1997) *Mikalojus Konstantinas Čiurlionis: Paintings. Sketches. Thoughts.* (Vilnius, Fodio).

Vyshnegradskii, I. (2001) *Piramida zhizni: dnevniki, stat'i, pis'ma, vospominaniya*, Bretanitskaya, A. L. (ed.) (Moscow, Kompozitor).

Vysloužil, J. (1970) *Alois Hába – Profile, Work, Bibliography, Documents* (Brno, House of Further Education and Culture).

Žiūraitytė, A. & Koch, K. P. (eds) (2001) *Deutsch-baltische Musikalische Beziehungen: Geschichte – Gegenwart – Zukunft. Bericht über die 35. Konferenz der Musikwissenschaftler des Baltikums in Vilnius, 18–20. Oktober, 2001* (Sinzig, Studio Verlag/Edition IME).

INDEX

Page numbers in **bold** and 'n.' or 'nn.' plus note number indicate figures/tables and notes respectively.